Space Battle

ALSO BY JAMIE LENDINO

Adventure: The Atari 2600 at the Dawn of Console Gaming

Attract Mode: The Rise and Fall of Coin-Op Arcade Games

Breakout: How Atari 8-Bit Computers Defined a Generation

Faster Than Light: The Atari ST and the 16-Bit Revolution

Starflight: How the PC and DOS Exploded Computer Gaming 1987-1994

Space Battle

The Mattel Intellivision and the First Console War

by Jamie Lendino

Steel Gear Press
Audubon, NJ

© 2024 Jamie Lendino. All rights reserved. No part of this book may be reproduced in any form by any electronic or mechanical means (including photocopying, recording, or information storage and retrieval) without permission in writing from Jamie Lendino or the publisher.

Steel Gear Press
PO Box 459
Audubon, NJ 08106

Printed and bound in the United States of America.
Edited by Matthew Murray.

Although every precaution has been taken in the preparation of this book, the publisher and author assume no responsibility for errors or omissions, or for damages resulting from the use of the information contained herein.

ISBN: 978-1-957932-11-8
Library of Congress Control Number: 2023924342

To my dad, who taught me math on the Intellivision

| Introduction

Many video game enthusiasts already know the late 1970s marked a golden age of video games. Early popular coin-ops such as *Pong*, *Breakout*, and *Sprint 2* gave way to blockbusters like *Space Invaders*, *Asteroids*, and *Galaxian*. Atari, already credited with launching the industry, released the Video Computer System, the first popular game console that brought the arcade home.

But as compelling as many video games were, they weren't yet considered family friendly. They offered plenty of action but were simplistic. They lasted just a few minutes, unless you were good. And the arcade's smoky-bar reputation—a leftover from the early days of pinball—prevented families from embracing them.

If anyone could change that, it was Mattel. The world-famous toy company behind the Barbie doll and Hot Wheels toy cars advanced the state of the art with its groundbreaking Intellivision console. The Intellivision—its name a portmanteau of "intelligent television"—promised more cerebral and sophisticated games than Atari's console (later known as the 2600). Most Intellivision games had better sound and music, with animated characters. The cartridges emphasized strategy over action and took longer to play through. And although some players disliked the distinctive controller design, with its gold direction disc and abundance of buttons, it enabled realistic sports games for the first time.

A Revolution in Video Games

Magnavox signed up Hank Aaron to endorse its Odyssey console in 1974, although his name didn't appear on the console packaging or games.[1] Atari licensed its *Superman* and *Pele's Soccer* 2600 cartridges from its parent company Warner. But Mattel was the first to license professional organizations such as the NFL, MLB, and NBA for its many sports games. The practice continues to this day with Xbox, PlayStation, and PC titles.

Mattel broadened the "family friendly" concept as the Intellivision grew in popularity. The company made licensed games for Disney's *Tron*, The Electric Company, Hanna-Barbera cartoons such as *The Jetsons* and *The Flintstones*, and Mattel's own *Masters of the Universe* toys. It also released the first two licensed *Dungeons & Dragons* titles.

The Intellivision was responsible for plenty of technical "firsts" as well. It was the first 16-bit game console, arriving almost a decade before the Sega Genesis. It was the first with a directional gamepad, tile-based playfields, a complete character set, downloadable games, and music keyboard support. It was the first popular console that "talked," thanks to the Intellivoice module. It had the first real-time construction and management sim. It even had the first "baseball sim," with multiple 3D camera views, player stats, manager player substitutions, play-by-play speech, and saved games in progress. For more than 4 million households in the 1980s, if somewhat fuzzy estimates are correct, the Intellivision defined video games.[2] Although other consoles were available, the Intellivision was the first to challenge Atari for real in what became known as the first "console war."

If the Intellivision were only about "firsts," it would remain a historical curiosity. But contained within its original 125-cartridge lineup were some of the best video games ever released—nearly all of which were family friendly. These games are still inviting and fun to play today.

Why I Wrote This Book

I wanted to highlight the Intellivision games that made the most difference or were the most significant, and what it was like to play them when they were new. This book covers the highs, the lows, and the in-betweens—everything that mattered to us about experiencing this wonderful game console.

I was extremely fortunate and had both systems as a child. My parents bought the 2600 in 1979 and the Intellivision in 1980, when I was seven. It meant I had a front-row seat to the early cartridge lineups of both systems before each's first hit games. Even so, I also wanted to remove the last vestiges of competition as I discuss where each platform excelled next to its peers. An inherent pitfall in how I've approached my platform-centric books is the potential for reigniting turf wars. All platforms have their pros and cons. Some were significant enough to change the trajectory of each's history. Every system from the dawn of computing and console gaming has its fans. But in the end, it's about the people, the friendships, and the joy the games bring us. With decades of distance, we can, and should, enjoy them all now.

Whether the Intellivision was your favorite, one of many favorites, or just something you're curious to learn more about, I promise you'll find plenty to like in this book.

Structure and Conventions

I wrote this book in chronological order. It includes full write-ups of 60 of the best games from the original lineup, intertwined with the history, the development, and the many fun things that embodied what the Intellivision was about. I step through all the most significant Intellivision-exclusive games.

I also touch on some important ports, especially those where the Intellivision version brought something new, as we'll see with several key Imagic releases. The focus always remains on what's special about the Intellivision. I cover one bad cartridge in depth, as it was a top seller despite itself and key to understanding why the Intellivision became one of the era's casualties.

Finally, I detail the exciting hobbyist efforts and community developments since the Intellivision exited production in 1990. From homebrew games to mods and collections of printed materials from the console's heyday, there's a fantastic amount to cover—and celebrate.

A few other notes: Tense, as in the written word, is a complex subject. For this book, I keep the narrative in the past tense for what happened back then but switch to the present tense for the games, as we can and still play them today.

Release dates are also tricky. Not everything was well documented. Months could lapse between when a game was announced, when magazines or stores ran ads, and when it became available on store shelves to purchase. Enthusiasts make educated guesses, which others copy from website to website. A given date could reflect any of those times. I cross-checked dates from as many sources as possible and pinned game releases down to the month. For our purposes, it doesn't matter if one game came out a few weeks before or after another.

With that, come along—let's step into a distant decade, full of custom vans, lava lamps, light-up floors, and terrific video games from a bygone era.

1 | Mattel

In its day, the Intellivision had a reputation as the "other" console. By the early 1980s, most people playing video games at home had an Atari 2600. But no such moniker would apply to the company that made it.

In 1945, Ruth and Elliot Handler founded Mattel Creations in a garage in El Segundo, California, right by Los Angeles International Airport, along with Harold "Matt" Matson. The Handlers sold picture frames and decided to try making dollhouse furniture using some surplus wooden slats. They made $30,000 in profit on sales of $100,000 in their first year.[1] In 1947, Mattel began selling its first toy: the Uke-A-Doodle, a child-sized ukulele. After relocating to Hawthorne about a mile away and newly incorporated as Mattel, the company continued to expand its offerings of toy trucks, burp guns, cars, dolls, and jack-in-the-boxes—many of which are now worth quite a bit on the vintage market. In 1955, Mattel became the first sponsor of Disney's *Mickey Mouse Club* television show; its wild success revolutionized the way companies advertised toys on television. One big Mattel innovation was a music box that went into various toys, from guitars to lullaby cribs. Another was a voice recording box that let dolls say different phrases, leading to Chatty Cathy (1960), which launched a massive market for pull-string toys during the next several decades.[2]

Soon, Mattel became one of the world's largest toy manufacturers. Two big franchises stood out: Barbie (1959), which became the best-selling toy in the company's history, and Hot Wheels (1968), the wildly popular lineup of toy metal cars that I adored—well, me and 100 million other kids. Mattel also made some mistakes as it grew. In 1971, it purchased the Ringling Bros. and Barnum & Bailey Circus for $40 million, only to sell it two years later after Mattel lost nearly $30 million in a downturn. In 1974, the Securities and Exchange Commission ruled that Mattel had falsified its financial records, leading to the ouster of the Handlers.[3] The following year, Mattel settled five class-action shareholder suits for $30 million,[4] and a federal grand jury indicted Ruth Handler and three former executives.[5] Mattel was still a leading toy company, but by the mid 1970s, it had begun to fray at the edges.

Video Games

I won't spend too much time on the history of video games, but a brief refresher is relevant because playing them at home was a tricky problem to crack. The important thing to know is that video games were no longer new by the mid 1970s—just not mainstream yet. Researchers began developing computer games on mainframe systems in the 1960s, most notably *Spacewar!* at MIT in 1962. The same decade saw the rise of solid-state, skill-based pinball games, an evolution of the old electromechanical games that were more akin to gambling and had a seedier reputation. Around the same time, video games broke free from their academic and military research roots. Nolan Bushnell and Ted Dabney focused on making a less expensive, coin-op version of *Spacewar!*. They enjoyed moderate success with their creation, 1971's *Computer Space*, the world's first commercial video game.

Video games took a different path in the home. In 1967, Ralph Baer designed a game console hooked to a television. It had two controllers, and you and a friend could use them to play simple games together. After numerous iterations of a "brown box prototype" and many failed efforts to secure distribution, Baer signed a deal with Magnavox in 1972 to manufacture, distribute, and sell his new product, the sleek white plastic Odyssey game console. You connected the system to your television with a metal switch box that toggled between "TV" (whatever showed on the weaker of two channels, 3 and 4, in your area), and "GAME" (the Odyssey). The Odyssey played 12 built-in

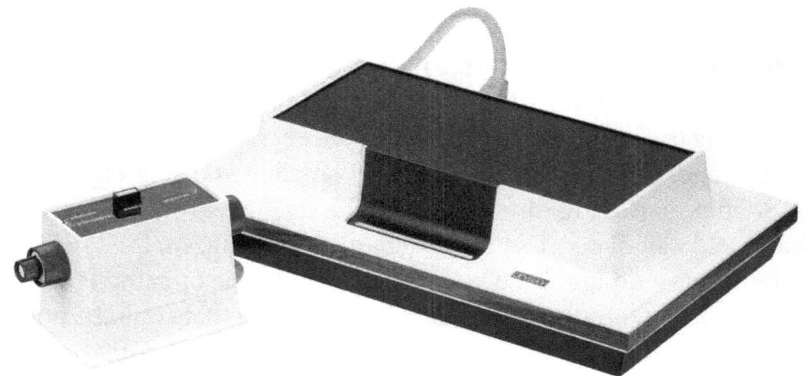

Figure 1.1: Ralph Baer's Odyssey, sold through Magnavox, ignited the home video game industry. (Credit: Evan Amos)

games but only became a modest hit. Magnavox sold about 100,000 consoles, but most people thought (incorrectly) the Odyssey required a Magnavox television. It did require cumbersome translucent overlays you applied to your television to depict each game's board.

Bushnell saw a prototype Odyssey at a fair in 1971 and thought he could do better with an arcade coin-op. Bushnell and Dabney hit the big time with *Pong*, a table tennis video game like the one in the Odyssey, designed by new Atari hire Al Alcorn. *Pong* drew crowds everywhere Atari delivered its machine—mostly bars at first, but soon, amusement parks, pinball arcades, restaurants, and more. A flood of competitors raced to clone *Pong*. Video arcades began to take off in earnest.

Things heated up during the 1975 holiday season when Atari developed a home version of *Pong* that connected to a television set like the Odyssey. Sears first sold it as Tele-Games Pong before Atari sold its version, *Home Pong*. The two companies sold several hundred thousand units. Atari followed up with many variations, such as *Super Pong 10*, *Super Pong Pro-Am*, *Stunt Cycle*, and *Video Pinball*. Sears released a console version of Taito's *Speedway IV*. Coleco introduced its own multigame console, the Telstar. These consoles did well for only so long because you couldn't change the built-in games. Once you got sick of playing them, that was it. Sales quickly peaked and started to decline.

Electronic Handhelds

Mattel was an unstoppable force in toys despite its financial and legal woes. But it needed something new. It found the answer in electronics.

"It was the mid-70s—a time when pocket calculators were a new product and were getting smaller and smaller and less expensive," said Mattel marketing director Michael Katz. "Everyone had to have a handheld calculator. I said to Richard Channing, Mattel's director of preliminary design: 'Can you design a new type of game that uses LED technology similar to that in a calculator but that could be portable, battery powered, and the size of a handheld calculator?' He went away and came back with the prototype of what was the first handheld game—an obstacle avoidance game where LEDs were coming down at you. You were at the bottom of the screen and had to try and avoid them and make your way to the top."[6]

In 1977, the company debuted the Mattel Electronics line of light-emitting diode (LED) handhelds. Channing's game became the first product in the lineup. *Auto Race* approximated Taito's coin-op *Speed Race* in handheld form. You had to drive your car to the top of the screen multiple times while avoiding other cars. Red LED lights and simple beep sounds represented the cars, track, and in-game action. *Auto Race* was small and portable, reasonably priced at $25, and it ran on batteries. Most importantly, *Auto Race* was addictive.

"You can't always have the computer win," said Mattel marketing executive Jeff Rochlis in a 1977 interview with *The Washington Post* about the company's new electronic handhelds. "It wouldn't be fun if you never beat it. You have to have a feeling of accomplishment at the end. So you program the chip so that you can beat it often enough."[7]

Retailers sold hundreds of thousands of *Auto Race* handhelds that holiday season.[8] To develop additional handhelds, Mattel contracted with a new company called APh Technological Consulting, formed by Caltech graduates John Denker and Glen Hightower in 1975.[9] APh developed Mattel's next game, *Football*. It featured an overhead view of the field and six buttons that let you play offense and defense. It became an even bigger hit. Mattel began selling more electronic games, such as *Baseball*, *Basketball*, and *Battlestar Galactica*, a licensed product based on the popular television series. Each sold for between $25 and $35. Soon, Mattel was manufacturing some 500,000 handhelds *per week*.[10]

Electronic handhelds became the hot new thing. The competition immediately caught on. Coleco introduced a line of handheld games dubbed *Head-to-Head*. These let two players compete against each other using opposite sides of the device, with a screen in the center. You positioned the unit on a table or on the floor and then sat opposite each other. Other toys also drew from the same technological developments. Texas Instruments released the Speak & Spell, which contained a built-in synthesizer that helped kids spell words using a keyboard. Milton Bradley unveiled *Simon*, another Ralph Baer design. It was a circular device with four pads in different colors that you had to press in the correct order after seeing the pads light up in patterns.

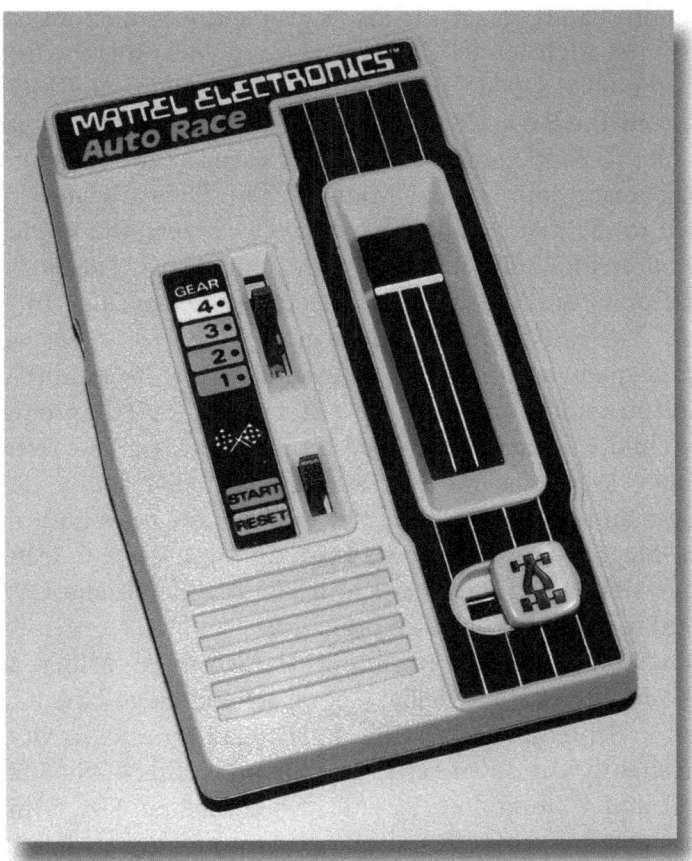

Figure 1.2: Mattel's line of handheld electronic games began with *Auto Race*. (Credit: Joe Haupt/CC BY-SA 2.0)

Mattel executives saw the rise of dedicated video game consoles such as Atari's *Home Pong* and the Coleco Telstar, which played arcade-style games on your living room television. Newer versions of these machines would soon pose a threat. Home video games could be the *next* hot new thing. But first, one more piece had to fall into place—and it was just about to.

Microprocessors

The arrival of low-cost microprocessors spurred the necessary technological development. The first commercially available microprocessor was the 4-bit Intel 4004, introduced in 1971. A single chip could control and process the data for an entire computer system for the first time. Eight-bit CPUs soon appeared, including the Intel 8008 (1972), the 8080 (1974), the Motorola 6800 (1974), the MOS 6502 (1975), and the Zilog Z80 (1976). These microprocessors gave rise to the first desktop computer kits such as the Altair 8800 and more complex arcade coin-ops like Midway's *Gun Fight*. The development soon led to the first so-called personal computers, the Apple II, the Commodore PET 2001, and the Tandy Radio Shack TRS-80.

Microprocessors also made for better game consoles. In January 1977, RCA released the Studio II, a more advanced system with two 10-key keypads as controllers, although you still couldn't change the built-in games and they weren't much fun. The programmable Fairchild Channel F, designed by Jerry Lawson and released in November 1976, was more compelling, with its ability to accept cartridges and run additional titles, not just the ones built into the system. Magnavox was close to finishing the Odyssey[2], featuring a cartridge slot, color graphics, and a built-in membrane QWERTY keyboard for writing your own programs.

Atari's top engineers, including Al Alcorn, Jay Miner, and Joe Decuir, developed the 2600, a compact cartridge-based console released in September 1977. The Atari 2600 harnessed a MOS 6507 CPU, a slightly cut-down version of the powerful MOS 6502 in the Apple II and Commodore PET. It also contained TIA, Miner and Decuir's graphics chip that displayed fast-moving sprites and up to 128 colors. The 2600 came with two joysticks, two paddles, and the *Combat* pack-in cartridge, which offered 27 variations based on

Atari's popular *Tank* and *Jet Fighter* coin-ops. Atari also released eight more cartridges for retailers to sell alongside the 2600. After the 1977 holiday season—the same one where Mattel's handhelds first went gangbusters—Atari began to follow up with more 2600 games. The additional titles meant you couldn't get bored of the system; you just needed to buy more cartridges.

Meanwhile, the new Apple, Commodore, and Tandy personal computers proved surprisingly versatile for work, education, and play. Enterprising programmers began developing and selling games for all three. Atari engineers figured this out almost immediately and began work on new video game hardware that could double as a powerful computer. The Bally Professional Arcade and the Magnavox Odyssey² promised built-in features or add-on components that made them more like home computers.

The microprocessor-based video game *and* personal computer revolutions had begun. Mattel was angling for a way into these emerging product categories. The market seemed to be leaning in a new hybrid direction, where computers could play video games, and game consoles could act like computers.[11] Maybe the answer was for Mattel to make something that could become both.

A Programmable Console

Mattel Electronics head Ed Krakauer began looking into the prospect of a hybrid computer console in May 1977. He teamed up with David Chandler and Richard Chang, two toy design and development employees. Chandler, who would one day be known as "Papa Intellivision," said the initial goal was for Mattel's new system to have "rich graphics" and "long-lasting gameplay," two qualities the company correctly identified as not yet existing in the home market.[12]

First, Chandler needed a chipset. National Semiconductor had one, but it cost $45 per package. General Instrument (GI) and MOS Technology had similar chipsets Mattel could purchase in bulk at lower prices. APh specifically suggested GI's Gimini TV Games, a video game system concept in the company's 1977 catalog that could be built with off-the-shelf GI chips.[13] Chandler contacted the three companies and began writing up proposals. General Instrument was glad to work with Mattel and offered to make design changes to its

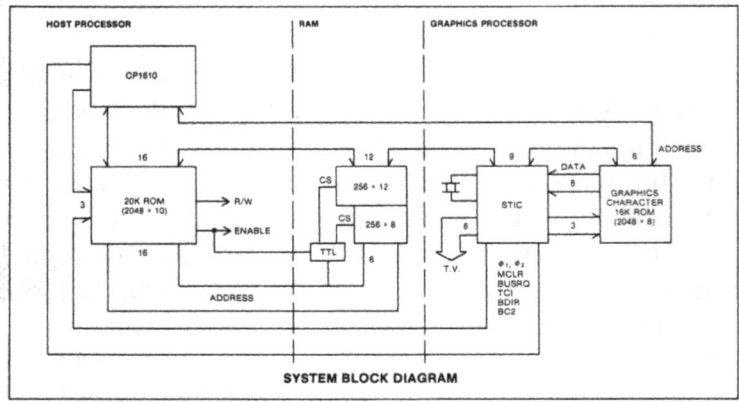

Figure 1.3: Several semiconductor manufacturers made prepackaged chipsets that could form the core of a video game system. Shown here is the block diagram for a Game System set from General Instrument's 1977 catalog.

chips, such as adding a way for programmers to define new graphics for each game instead of a built-in ROM library of graphics that every game shared. Chandler also worked with National to develop a lower-cost chipset from what they already had.

"By late August, we had talked National down [from $45] to a simpler chipset for $33," Chandler wrote, and had talked GI up from a $25 set that lacked graphics RAM to an "acceptable set for $30" with reprogrammable graphics. Chandler said they had decided to go with National, but a "handshake" meeting became a "scare Mattel into postponing project" meeting. The video game business had suddenly cooled, thanks to an oversaturation of discrete console systems and a mild recession on the coin-op side.[14]

Mattel's upper management hesitated to compete with Atari, so they focused on handheld games.[15] The Channel F had yet to take off, and the 2600 was only just being announced and released. It would take more work to develop a viable game console proposal. Rochlis felt Mattel needed more than electronic handhelds to compete in a changing market. He also thought that Mattel needed more than just a game console. "Basically these things [handhelds] are forerunners of the home computer," he said. "There's a logical transition involved. One way to get into the home-computer market is to sell games. Gameplay is one set of software. We'll see home systems in five years that not only play games but also store financial records, run the home security system, and turn the appliances on and off."[16] Chandler's team paused work until Mattel president Ray Wagner gave the go-ahead in October. GI's newly updated Gimini 8900 Programmable Game Set, which appeared in the company's new 1978 catalog, did the trick.[17] Mattel wanted to demo the console in some way at the 1978 Consumer Electronics Show in January.

Exec OS

Chandler outsourced the demo software to APh while he worked on the hardware. APh had some prototype emulation of the GI chipset and controllers and a veteran hardware engineer unfamiliar with writing machine code for microprocessors. The engineer was flailing, so in December APh head Glen Hightower called in Caltech student David Rolfe, who had experience programming larger systems like the DEC PDP-10 and the Z80-powered Exidy coin-op *Star Fire*.[18]

"[Mattel] wanted to show some sort of a demo at the Consumer Electronics Show," Rolfe said. "At the time, it was a really big deal. These days going to convention seems a lot less important. At the time you physically had to go places to see things, and it really was a place for announcements and the like. They wanted to have some sort of a prototype, some sort of a demonstration in their hospitality suite [where] they were going tell people about it."[19]

Rolfe knew from the outset that he wanted to do an operating system. The idea was that it would handle a core set of software features such as drawing and directing sprites, timing, and collision detection. This left more room in the cartridges for custom code. It meant there was less of a need to reinvent the wheel each time—and Mattel could pack more advanced games into smaller, less expensive ROMs.[20] In contrast, the Atari 2600 lacked an OS. Its earliest 2KB and 4KB games were exceedingly simple as a result.

"An Atari VCS cartridge contained the entire program for an Atari VCS game," Rolfe said. "With Intellivision, we wanted to get more mileage out of our cartridges, preferably without making them 8KB ROMs. An Intellivision operating system (the 'Exec') could help make this happen. The purpose of the operating system was to do the stuff that every cartridge would have to do, so that cartridges could spend their limited resources on game play rather than on mundane tasks. For example, the baseball cartridge can tell the Exec, 'Here's a pixel map of a baseball; turn sprite #3 into a baseball and move it from the pitcher to the catcher at a fast speed and let me know when it reaches the catcher,'" Rolfe continued. "So a lot of basic functionality (e.g., draw; rewrite; velocity; collide; time elapsed) ends up in the Exec, and the top-level direction ends up in the cartridge. And the Exec lives in a ROM in the main unit, so each cartridge can use it."[21]

Rolfe developed the OS and baseball game simultaneously. Within a month, he somehow managed to program enough of each in time for a behind-closed-doors demo at the January 1978 CES.[22] Programming under such tight time and space constraints was a "tricky business," as Rolfe put it in a grand understatement: "I was also strictly limited to 4KB for the size of each...My previous work on *Star Fire* helped me a lot, because I had developed techniques for controlling generic objects with specifiable attributes that I now adapted to the Intellivision environment. In a sense, I created a crude object-oriented programming model, only the 'objects' were real screen objects rather than software concepts...I was developing Baseball and the Exec at the same time, clarifying the details, and smoothing out this model into a workable form."[23]

Worse, Rolfe had to get it right the first time. The quirk in the console-with-an-OS approach was that once Exec was done, Mattel couldn't ever update it in future versions of the console because the game cartridges referred to specific ROM addresses in the Exec code.[24] "It's a chicken-and-egg system," Rolfe said later. "What do you need to put in the operating system? Well, you don't know until you write a game. You can't write a game without the operating system. You can't write the operating system without the game [and] knowing what goes in it. That was very confusing, so I had to basically become two people and have a lot of arguments with myself.[25]

OS and Hardware Features

One Exec benefit proved vital right from the start. Mattel's closed-door CES demo was the first known appearance of the famous "running man" the Intellivision would soon become known for. The running man had eight steps of animation. Rolfe coded it, while artist Dave James created the detailed graphics set that included eight frames running left to right and eight for running up and down on the screen. It was a massive leap over the usual "moving pixel block" seen on *Pong*-style games and early Atari 2600 cartridges.[26]

The Intellivision hardware had some other tricks. You could pause any game and black out the screen by pressing 1 and 9 or 3 and 7 together. Pressing them again restarted the action. Mattel wasn't the first to include a pause feature—that was the Fairchild Channel F and its Hold button—but the Intellivision was the first popular home console to have it. The feature dates to a May 18, 1978, memo from Chandler outlining the use of the two combined keypresses as an "Intermission Code," and that the octal code it generated (132) was a unique 8-bit code "which is not likely to occur in any of the normal uses of the controller."[27]

This innovation alone revolutionized playing video games at home. It was something you couldn't do in the arcade—how would any location make enough money off a machine you could pause indefinitely? The feature also headed off countless arguments about stopping playing before you had to eat or go to bed. You could just leave the console on, and someone else could move the switch box back to regular television channels in the interim, as long as no one

Figure 1.4: Mattel's closed-door 1978 CES demo showed off the Intellivision's famous 'running man' sprite. Each cartridge stored the running man graphics, which meant they could be customized for a particular game.

turned off the Intellivision—just the thing when pursuing a challenging high score record (personal or otherwise). Some later games, such as *Astrosmash* and various Activision titles, highlighted the feature on overlays. We all eventually figured out that it worked everywhere. I found out later it was in the Master Component manual (which I promptly lost as a kid) all along. Why Mattel buried it in there instead of trumpeting it from the heavens is a question for the ages.

Like the Atari 2600, the Intellivision came with a screen-saver-style "attract mode" to prevent screen burn-in. Retailers were concerned they would be liable for damage to customers' television sets, as this Feb. 27, 1978, memo from Osco Drug stores to Mattel demonstrated:

> As indicated in the Federal Trade Commission's release of December 19, 1977, reasonable use of electronic video games should not imprint the game pattern on TV screens. The Commission did report, however, that 'prolonged use of some games may imprint the game pattern on TV screens—in particular, those of black and white sets." Accordingly, the Commission is urging manufacturers and sellers to warn consumers prior to

Figure 1.5: Mattel had its work cut out for it in catching the Atari 2600, never mind holding off competing efforts from Bally, Magnavox, and Fairchild. It also wanted to get a jump on budget-priced home computers while it still could. (Credit: Jamie Lendino)

sales that prolonged display of a video game with a fixed pattern is likely to result in imprinting the game on the television screen.²⁸

The effect's extent depended on brightness, TV set model, and length of play. The letter said, "It is our opinion that video game manufacturers are in the best position to determine what imprinting effect, if any, their video games will have on TV sets. We are therefore requesting that you send us your plan for compliance..." To which point the memo has a handwritten note: "Timing circuit which shuts it off—send to J. Rochlis."

For all of Exec's benefits, it had a downside: Any cartridge that used it could only run at a 20Hz frame rate instead of 60Hz like the Atari 2600. Exec was so beneficial that nearly all Mattel games used it—that was the point. But using it wasn't required. And as we'll see later, bypassing it produced real dividends as ROM prices fell and developers had more cartridge memory to work with.

Run-Up to the Debut

Once Exec was complete, Rolfe headed up early Intellivision game development at APh. For this purpose, he hired a group of Caltech summer students.²⁹ Exec provided a baseline of reusable code that all games could harness, which saved memory and made it easier to program multiple games quickly. Dave James continued to draw the graphics for the new titles.

Mattel announced in May 1978 that it would unveil its new system at the Summer CES ahead of a limited release and would be priced at $160 to wholesalers.³⁰ But it became increasingly clear that the final hardware with General Instrument wouldn't be ready for the holidays that year.³¹ As a backup plan, Mattel engineers spoke with Texas Instruments, who also had a similar chipset to MOS and National Semiconductor. TI was developing its own computer, which would become the 99/4, and Milton Bradley was working on a video game system. Mattel didn't like TI's chipset as much as it did GI, and TI didn't want to modify its architecture to appease Mattel.³² The backup plan fell apart but proved unnecessary.

In the meantime, work had begun on the other half of the system, the part that would combine with the console to turn it into a personal computer. Mattel made Mattel Electronics a separate division with Ed Krakauer as general manager and Jeff Rochlis as president.[33] Rochlis announced in December that the console would be available by the second quarter of 1979 and that the two components together would cost $500. The company saw video games as the "base for home computers," in that they would be friendly, non-threatening, and that video game consoles were "really computers of a limited class."[34] With this in mind, Mattel planned a modular architecture permitting an upgrade to a family computer, stipulating that the modularity would not increase the cost of the base Master Component. Chandler believed the new system was for non-computer people. It "should not require knowledge or use of computer language," and "preprogrammed software will be used predominantly," with "convenient, fully computer controlled mass storage" and "mass audio storage [for a] friendly interface and many applications."[35]

The above principles drove the philosophy of the system, Chandler wrote. His team designed the hardware for the software, not the other way around, which is how it had usually worked with earlier consoles and coin-ops. The Intellivision was a home product, and—this is key to understanding where Mattel would soon try and head with the system—Mattel engineers believed "video games would always be the heart of home systems but are *dead-ended as a stand-alone product*" (emphasis added).[36]

As we now know with the benefit of hindsight, this belief helped decide the fate of the Intellivision—and Mattel Electronics.

The Grand Unveiling

By January 1979, Chandler said a small team of roughly 20 people was working on the console. The team included six electrical engineers, three each from Mattel and General Instrument. Mattel had one to two mechanical engineers and one software engineer on the project; APh Technological Consulting had three to four software engineers. One person oversaw purchasing, and six to eight people provided additional support for the project.[37]

Mattel unveiled the finished console at the Consumer Electronics Show in Las Vegas. The company introduced the system as modular, with the Master Component priced at $230 and a "soon-to-follow"

Figure 1.6: The Master Component looked like it wouldn't be out of place in a nice living room with a console television and stereo equipment. (Credit: Evan Amos)

Keyboard Component. When docked, the system became a 64KB computer with a QWERTY keyboard, a cassette drive for storing and retrieving programs, and a microphone for software that required audio input.

The system still didn't have a name. Mattel's booth contained a real console inserted into a mockup of the computer expansion system. The company announced a lineup of sports and strategy games, including *NFL Football* as the pack-in cartridge, plus financial planning and database software. It promised a release date of June 1, 1979, with 14 programs available at launch.[38] Mattel showed off some new LED-based handheld games, including *Football II*, *Hockey*, *Soccer*, *Armor Battle*, and *Sub Chase*, to complement its top-selling existing lineup of *Baseball*, *Football*, *Auto Race*, and *Battlestar Galactica*. You may recognize some of the titles in the list.

The main remaining hardware issue was that one of the GI chips and the RAM chips remained unfinished, which made the projected June 1 release impossible. A report in May suggested that Mattel's programmable game had "floated up to $250" from the $230 quoted at the January CES. Mattel showed off the system again at the June Summer CES in Chicago but revised its launch date to July. Mattel announced it had chosen Sylvania to manufacture the console, with an agreement that Sylvania could sell its own branded version in its GTE stores. Eventually, GI finished its part and Mattel finalized the architecture. Mattel also finally announced the system's name: Intellivision. But the company missed subsequent release dates in July, September, and October.

Final Architecture

The heart of the Intellivision was its chipset: the CPU, graphics chip, sound chip, and memory. Let's look at each in turn.

The General Instrument CP1610 CPU made the Intellivision the first game console with a 16-bit processor, nine years before Sega introduced the Mega Drive (the Genesis in the U.S.) and its "16-bit" moniker on the top panel. The CP1610 ran at 0.894MHz with a 10-bit bus. It included 1,024 opcodes, with an architecture resembling the much more expensive DEC PDP-11 minicomputer.[39] Each operation took between four and 12 microcycles to execute. Most 1610 instructions were 10-bit, and the system stored game programs in 10-bit ROMs.[40] Only the Intellivision marked wide use of the CP1600 family of processors; the word was that General Instrument preferred large orders for its chips, unlike Intel and MOS Technology.

For graphics, the Standard Television Interface Chip (STIC) was a repurposed General Instrument AY-3-8900-1 designed by Stephen Maine. STIC output at 159-by-96-pixel resolution and allowed for 20-by-12 tiled playfields, the first console to do so. Each 8-by-8-pixel tile could be one or two colors from a palette of 16. In Foreground/Background mode, the background could display all 16 colors, but the foreground could use colors one through eight for each tile. All 16 colors were available to foreground tiles in Color Stack mode, while the background could display four. And in Colored Squares mode, each tile could have four different colored 4x4 blocks.

STIC supported eight sprites, each of which was either 8-by-8 pixels and could all display on the same scan line, or 8-by-16 half-pixels high with up to 2x horizontal and 8x vertical stretching.[41] The best part was that programmers soon figured out ways to get around the eight-sprite limitation and display many more objects on screen using GRAM sequencing for more complex titles.[42] "The beauty of this system is that once the CPU has defined a background and a moving object shape, it can change the location of an object merely by writing a different address to the STIC," the IntellivisionLives entry for the Master Component said. "The moving objects can be located on a grid space wider and taller than the displayed background, allowing them to smoothly slide on or off the screen at the edges."[43]

For sound, the Intellivision had three channels and a noise generator to the 2600's two channels. This was thanks to the GI AY-3-8914 chip, a slight variant of General Instrument's ubiquitous AY-3-8910 found in coin-ops of the day, albeit with different control registers. Programmers could control each voice for frequency and volume.[44]

Moving on to memory, the system's 7KB ROM had an unusual split configuration. In those days, every byte counted. The Exec software took up 5KB of that—in this case, as 4,096 10-bit characters totaling 5,120 bytes. The graphics ROM took up the other 2KB (2,048 bytes). It included a full alphanumeric character set and some simple shapes. Programmers also had 1,352 bytes of RAM to work with: 240 bytes of 8-bit scratchpad memory for calculations, 352 bytes of 16-bit system memory (totaling 704 bytes), and 512 bytes of 8-bit graphics RAM.

Contrast the above with the Atari 2600, which had no internal ROM and 128 bytes of RAM. Instead, Atari cartridges contained all the necessary ROM, starting with 2KB and 4KB and eventually increasing. The Intellivision system had more memory in addition to the cartridge ROMs. But the still-tight constraints usually meant little room left for computer player AI code—a problem that soon surfaced in many of the platform's first titles.

Design and Controllers

The Intellivision Master Component had a distinguished and now-iconic rectangular design. It measured 2.6 by 14.9 by 9.1 inches (HWD) and weighed 5 pounds. For comparison, it was a bit larger and heavier than the Atari 2600, except that console had a panel in the back for the switches that rose about an extra inch over the Intellivision. The original Atari 2600 "Heavy Sixer" was almost the same weight as the Intellivision at 4.6 pounds, but the later varieties were just over 3 pounds.

Mattel's system was finished in dark brown plastic, with two striking metallic gold plates across the top and dark woodgrain paneling on the two long sides. A cartridge slot sat on the short right side of the unit. A small control section with a large, sliding power switch and a raised Reset button sat on the top panel near the bottom-right corner. The back of the console held the power jack, and a hardwired coaxial video cable connected to your television. The console looked simultaneously sleek, premium, and futuristic, with a design that would fit into any living room or den.

A big part of the console's sleekness was because of how it stored the controllers. In fact, the console's single most distinguishing characteristic was its controller design. Each controller was hardwired to the Master Component with a coiled cable you could fold and tuck underneath the small, grated housing in the console's center. Then the controller slid into two tracks that let you store them neatly. In theory, it was excellent. In practice, it was…a bit fiddlier than it looked, and "close enough" was the order of the day. The design meant you could never lose the controllers, but it also meant that if one failed, you'd have to bring the entire system in for service. It also meant all games for the Intellivision had to use the built-in controllers regardless of whether they were well suited for a particular cartridge. On the plus side, the lightweight controllers were easy to hold, although your hands would hurt after a while if you didn't grip

Figure 1.7: Equally loved and hated, the Intellivision's unique controller design is the most distinguishing feature of the system. (Credit: Evan Amos)

them loosely. Next to the Atari 2600, with its joysticks, paddle, driving, and keyboard controllers, the Intellivision at least had simplicity going for it in that fashion.

The simplicity didn't extend to the buttons, of which there were many. The controller's dominating feature was the 12-key membrane keypad in a shiny gold color, with keys numbered 0 to 9, plus Clear and Enter keys. These offered extra control in different games, as we'll soon see. But the most striking feature on each controller was the gold direction disc, located on the bottom of the front panel beneath the keypad. It was dubbed Object Control Disk in Mattel's first Intellivision dealer catalog and later rechristened as the Control Disc. Chandler filed patent #4,246,452 for its "Switch Apparatus" on Jan. 5, 1979. The patent described "first and second surfaces with conductive pattern segments thereon in proximate spaced overlying relation, each of the patterns being generally identical and having a circular array of alternating solid and interleaved conductive portion, one pattern being moveable toward the other by tilting of a disc for providing a plurality of discrete signals." The patent was granted on Jan. 20, 1981.[45]

The disc moved in an astounding 16 directions. It offered more precise control than four- and eight-way joysticks, and you could also swirl your finger around and gradually change the angle of a character running on screen—something that would soon prove ideal for sports games. Think of the disc as the world's first directional gamepad, years before the Nintendo Entertainment System made them commonplace. Four hard rubber buttons—two on either side of the controller—let you perform additional actions. The bottom two buttons were individual triggers, but the top two were wired together for a total of three actions. Pressing either top button would trigger the same action in game. Some players found these difficult to press, as you'd have to change up your grip on the controller to reach them and have enough leverage.

Overlays

All Intellivision games came with a pair of distinctive, thin plastic overlays that contained artwork or design cues from the game. A signature feature of the Intellivision, overlays made every game feel like it had a custom controller, much in the same way arcade coin-ops of the day all had distinctive hardware control layouts. Intellivision overlays included labels that let you know the button functions—something that I wish would make a comeback in today's era of 12-button gamepads with descriptive names such as "A," "X," and "Y."

The overlays slid into a tiny, thin space between the keypad and the rectangular plastic frame above it to hold it firmly during heated play sessions. If you weren't careful, you could bunch up the overlay against the edges of the frame and accidentally crease or bend it. They were also easy to lose. Insert a colorful overlay, and suddenly, it looked as though you'd bought a new game system, not just a new game. An overlay could depict an array of spaceship controls, inventory keys in an adventure game, a baseball diamond that matched the depiction of the field on-screen, or the different pieces on a chessboard. Overlays also made it easy to choose difficulty levels and the number of players in a game without getting up and walking over to the console.

The Intellivision hailed from an era where every video game manufacturer, whether for the arcade or home consoles, experimented with different control schemes. The Magnavox Odyssey came with paddles; the Atari 2600 had those and joysticks. The Fairchild Channel F had a thin grip design with a triangular joystick on top.

Next to all these, the Intellivision controllers were *still* weird, with their unique shape, gold discs, keypad, and ability to accept overlays for each game. But the key to the Intellivision's distinctiveness, at least for the first several years of game releases, was the use of overlays. Low-tech though they may be, overlays made gaming on the Intellivision feel special in a way that was unmatched at the time and still has no direct equivalent today.

Fresno

Word of test launches in select markets began to leak, only to not happen. An industry report in October 1979 said Mattel increased the retail price to $275 for each component[46] and $23 for each game but guaranteed it would honor JCPenney's prices. It listed test markets for Sylvania's branded unit in Philadelphia, Baltimore, and Washington, while Mattel would test-market the console in New York, Chicago,

Figure 1.8: Using the overlays was key to understanding and mastering each game, and they helped simplify control schemes that may ordinarily read as too complex. (Credit: Jamie Lendino)

Los Angeles, and San Francisco.[47] But four weeks later, the same publication said Sylvania's test had moved to mid November, and that Mattel wouldn't test-market the unit, thanks to a shortage of chips from General Instrument holding up production:

> While officials of Mattel couldn't be reached for comment, the company reportedly has put a hold on its planned pre-Christmas TV & print ad campaign for Intellivision and will hold up introduction drive until sometime next year. Games are being manufactured and delivered, and Sylvania is able to go ahead with the test "because our quantity requirements aren't very large at this stage," a spokesman said. Sylvania says it will list the game at $280, or $5 above Mattel's price, tag cartridges at $25, $2 above Mattel.[48]

Reports differ on whether any of the other test markets took place, but there's only one that every source confirms. On Dec. 3, 1979, Mattel's manufacturing partner Sylvania test-marketed the Intellivision in Gottschalk's department stores, a chain of seven locations based in

36 | Space Battle: The Mattel Intellivision and the First Console War

Fresno, California.[49] Krakauer said later that Mattel and Sylvania chose Gottschalk's because Mattel couldn't guarantee how many systems they could ship and "Gottschalk's proved an understanding partner."[50] The company delivered Intellivision consoles in a rented truck.[51] JCPenney included the Intellivision lineup in its nationally distributed Christmas 1979 catalog with seven cartridges listed.[52]

The Gottschalk's ad announced "the world premiere of the Mattel Intellivision," which was listed at $269.95. The picture showed *NFL Football*, but the text said *Las Vegas Poker & Blackjack* was the pack-in game. Additional cartridges were $29.95 each.[53] The Master Component cost $40 more than originally announced in January.

Thanks to its robust game lineup, the Intellivision made an excellent case for itself, with its more detailed graphics and gameplay than the Atari 2600. APh Technological Consulting readied 12 games in

Figure 1.9: Mattel test-marketed its console with a single, willing partner at retail some 3,000 miles away from where I grew up in Brooklyn.

1979. Although the JCPenney Christmas Book and some local retail ads that season listed up to eight games, and there's some disagreement about exact release dates, Mattel included four in the test launch for certain. Let's start with those.

Las Vegas Poker & Blackjack (APh/Mattel, December 1979)

Just as it says on the tin, *Poker & Blackjack* lets you play both card games—either by yourself against the computer "dealer" or with a human player. Programmed by David Rolfe, *Poker & Blackjack* cleverly depicts the dealer as a shifty-eyed character with various facial expressions and a large, white cartoon balloon that contains whatever he says. The game also features sharp graphics, with playing cards that look like they're from a real 52-card deck—something the Atari 2600 struggled with in its *Blackjack* and *Casino* cartridges.

The dealer sits across from you at a green felt card table. You start by entering in the amount in your wallet—say $200. The second human player does the same thing from the second controller; inputting $0 using that controller makes it a one-player session. The included variations are five-card stud, seven-card stud, five-card draw, and blackjack. Choose a game, and you'll hear the dealer shuffling the deck before he deals the cards to alternating players. The cards fly across the screen and land on the table in the right spot with a "thwip" sound effect. Pressing the disc reveals your hidden cards to you but not the dealer. If you're playing with another human, each of you must look away from the screen at this point, lest you see each other's cards.

The dealer bets in the three poker games, but only serves as a banker in blackjack. You can place a bet, raise, or call on each turn. The pot at the top-left corner of the screen tracks the total amount of money in play. Whoever wins that game collects the pot and it's added to the wallet. You can let the dealer choose the next game, play the same game again, or choose a different one. Empty your wallet and the dealer will call "bankrupt!" and end the session. Make a bet that's higher than what's in your wallet and he'll tell you to "get lost!"

All four games follow standard Vegas rules. For example, the dealer must stand if he has two cards totaling at least 17 in blackjack. Otherwise, he will continue to draw cards until he has at least 17 or until he goes over 21 and loses. The dealer is capable of bluffing, just

Figure 1.10: Beware the shifty dealer in the fun and addictive *Las Vegas Poker & Blackjack*.

like a human player. His eyes shifting to the side can be a clue, but not always. For example, during one seven-card stud hand I was playing recently, he suddenly flipped from "call" to "raise" $62. I dropped because I had nothing, but he had nothing, too. Sometimes he'll get frustrated, frown, and drop his cards if he thinks he's in trouble. After all these years, he still drives me crazy, which I imagine is the point.

The fact that the dealer is still engaging to play against today is a testament to the advance it was in 1979. I remember playing cards with my dad and grandmother quite a bit as a kid, and I'm pretty sure I first learned the rules for both games from this cartridge.

Mattel's decision to include *Las Vegas Poker & Blackjack* as the pack-in game seems odd from today's perspective. It made sense at the dawn of the video game era, when playing cards was a popular pastime. The real reason was fascinating and stemmed from a legal issue. Mattel knew when designing the Intellivision that a patent existed for interaction between moving objects on a video screen. To be safe, it didn't want to bundle a real video game with the console and later be forced to take the system off the market over a legal dispute.

"The [*Poker & Blackjack*] game had no interaction between moving objects, so that way, when Mattel was going to get sued, they couldn't get sued for the base of it, they could only get sued for the individual cartridges," Rolfe explained at the 2000 Classic Gaming Expo. "Mattel: always thinking ahead."[54] The following year, Mattel released the companion game *Las Vegas Roulette*, which features an on-screen roulette table that is clear and easy to read. Roulette requires zero skill, though, which makes it less compelling.

Armor Battle (APh/Mattel, December 1979)

Mattel released *Armor Battle* as a striking red electronic handheld, so it was only natural to commission APh for a video game version. You must destroy enemy tanks while defending your own on various battlefields. Players start the game with two tanks on each board. One side has black tanks, and the other has blue. You aim your tank by pressing the disc in the direction you want to face. As these are tanks, they turn very slowly. The bottom side action buttons move the tank; keep a button depressed, and you'll hear the engine growling away. Tanks can only move forward.

Unlike the 2600 game *Combat*, the tanks in *Armor Battle* look almost three-dimensional when they turn and even have treads, although they're not filled in with white the way they are on the box screenshot, which I always found strange. Different terrain types affect tank performance. Trees provide some cover from shots, although you move slowly through them. Roads let you move the fastest. Rivers and lakes slow you to a crawl and provide zero cover, making you a sitting duck for the opposition. You can hide behind buildings and other structures, emerging just to fire a shot before hiding again.

Pressing the top side action buttons fires your cannon. You can fire one shot at a time, and it travels roughly a half-screen length before disappearing. Each time you shoot, the tank recoils slightly, and the same goes for when a tank is hit; it will move somewhat from the blast. Hit an opposing tank three times, and you'll destroy it in a large explosion. A hulk of molten metal will be left behind. Another option is to lay an invisible mine. Your opponent won't know you did it until they drive over it and explode. Once laid down, the mine will explode in five seconds. Each player can lay one mine per battlefield map. Be careful not to drive back over your mine. If you do, get out of dodge quickly, or you'll be caught in the explosion.

Figure 1.11: *Armor Battle* **pits you against another player in a tense military conflict across 240 different battlefields.**

Pressing the big star button in the center of the overlay switches between your two tanks. Having two per side enables layered strategies. Cover is essential in keeping one tank out of danger while you use the other to attack the enemy—or if you've already been hit once or twice and need to bring your other tank into battle. You can time your shots to shoot one tank and immediately switch to the other to attack from the second position. There's potential for strategic combat instead of just twitch reflexes. Memorizing positions doesn't help, either. Each round takes place on a different battlefield; the cartridge contains some 240 different maps. The game ends when one player loses both tanks on a single board, or when they lose a total of 50 tanks.

Developed by Chris Kingsley, *Armor Battle* is the only test-market title to require two players, but it foreshadowed what was to come. The additional two-player cartridges that arrived in the following 15 to 18 months cemented the console's early reputation as a two-player machine during its crucial first year on the market.

ABPA Backgammon (APh/Mattel, December 1979)

The Intellivision cartridge that made me a lifelong fan of the board game, *ABPA Backgammon* brings the excitement and strategy of the real thing to your television screen. For the uninitiated, *Backgammon* is a mixture of strategy and luck. The game is played with dice on a board with 24 "points," or locations. Each player has 15 pieces, and the object is to move all the pieces around the board and then off of it before the other player can. Mattel said the cartridge had an official license from the American Backgammon Players Association, a little-known group of which I could only find some contemporary references in Backgammon publications published that same year. It sure sounded official, though!

In *Backgammon,* the full-color board takes up most of the screen. It's oriented horizontally and features a felt look with red and black points. The chips look real, with a rounded design and two or three lines inside to indicate stacks. The colorful overlays depict a vibrant backgammon table and six dice, with green action buttons below them.

You play as white, and the computer plays as black; two-player games are also available. You roll the two large dice by pressing the button on the controller; both turn blue and animate as they roll. Once they come to a stop, they change to the color of whichever side's turn it is. You select the piece you want to move with the disc and then select the die you want to use with the keypad. For example, if

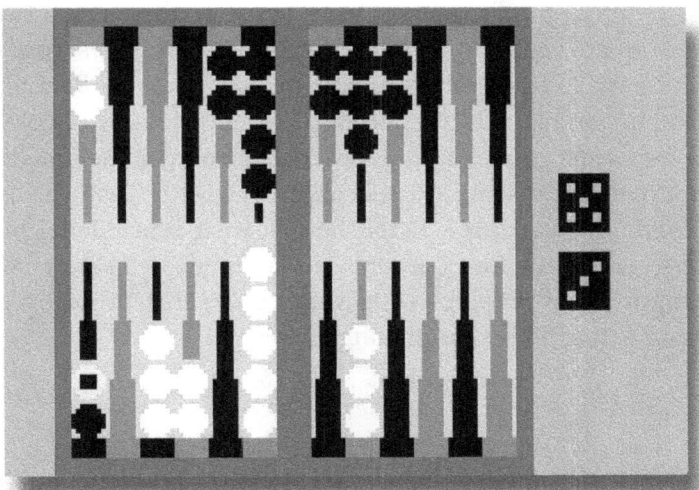

Figure 1.12: The Intellivision's *Backgammon* cartridge showed how addictive the game could be with a solid computer opponent.

you roll a three and a two, you position the cursor over a piece at the top of one of the columns, press the "3" key on the overlay to move it three spaces, and press the "2" key to move it two more spaces. The overlay also lets you select the difficulty level, whether you want a two-player game, and whether you want to use two dice for the move. APh programmer Kevin Miller did an excellent job with the interface.

I remember playing this game incessantly in our den, on the brown shag carpet in front of a wooden console television. I loved how I could play against the computer repeatedly. I used to imagine that, while it was making its computerized thinking noises, it was snickering at me. "Well, look at this, I rolled double-sixes, so I have four sixes to work with," the delighted computer said in my imagination, between the blips and bleeps. "Let's see, what should I do next..." I was also fascinated with the PIP score you display by pressing one of the side buttons. Every game starts with each player at 167. The pip score goes down the more moves you make, corresponding with the die rolls on each turn. It gives you a good idea of whether you're ahead or behind. If you have rotten luck, you could have an even higher number as the computer captured your pieces.

Although strategy plays a large part in every backgammon game, that core element of luck remains with each dice roll, unlike in chess or checkers. No matter how good you are and how you optimize your moves, if you keep rolling a two and a one, or a three and a two, and your opponent keeps rolling double fours, fives, and sixes, your opponent will have to be a terrible player to lose. Even so, *Backgammon* contains just enough strategy to become addictive. In 1979, it was rare to see a video game flawlessly execute a board game. Intellivision *Backgammon* did it—and it looks and plays better than the comparable Atari 2600 cartridge. Early the following year, Mattel released *Checkers*, which includes a one-player mode. *Checkers* features well-proportioned graphics with round chips that fit neatly on the board and text prompts for making moves.

Math Fun (APh/Mattel, December 1979)

In The Electric Company's *Math Fun*, named after the popular children's television series on PBS, you and another player each control gorillas walking in the jungle along a river. You must complete a series of math problems to get past different animals standing in the way. Each time you successfully solve one, you hear a short drumbeat, and the gorilla runs down the river to the next animal. Solve all the problems correctly and you'll do a brief victory dance before exiting to the left (or right if you're the right player). Get a problem wrong and the gorilla will jump into the river where dangerous crocodiles await. A new problem will appear while the gorilla is in the water. The game also adjusts the difficulty level if you have trouble exiting the river. Fortunately, at no point does a crocodile eat the gorilla. (I mean, you never know; it was the late 1970s. We played with rusty, sharp metal toy trucks and doll houses and ate packaged baloney containing who knows what.)

The game includes 18 difficulty levels, spread out among five color levels (black, blue, yellow, purple, and red) and four numbered skill levels (with just two for red). *Math Fun* is suitable for elementary school kids, with problems as simple as single-digit addition and as tricky as long division with four-digit numbers. It helps to play with pencils and paper alongside the game controller. The overlays are mostly unnecessary but fun; they depict colorful gorillas surrounding the 12 keypad keys. The first five are outlined and correspond with the five difficulty colors. At the start of each game, players choose the number of problems they want to solve (from 1 to 99) and the difficulty level. The game keeps a tally, showing the number of problems you've gotten correct against the total number of problems encountered. For more difficult problems, you enter the numbers from right to left. For example, if the answer is 428, you enter "8," "2," and "4" in that order. Some customers complained to Mattel that they preferred to answer in the final order, so the company ordered a running change—something I wasn't aware of at the time.[55] Of the four launch titles, only *Math Fun* plays a musical fanfare on the title screen.

I almost left *Math Fun* out of the book because it's an educational cartridge. I don't see many of us returning to relive our memories of pixelated zoo animals and doing simple math problems. But it's also behind some of my earliest memories with my dad. He sat with me next to the Intellivision and TV, showed me how to do the problems on paper, and then gradually let me do them myself. Soon, I was traveling down the riverside as fast as possible. The least I can do is discuss why the game is important and also fun for young children.

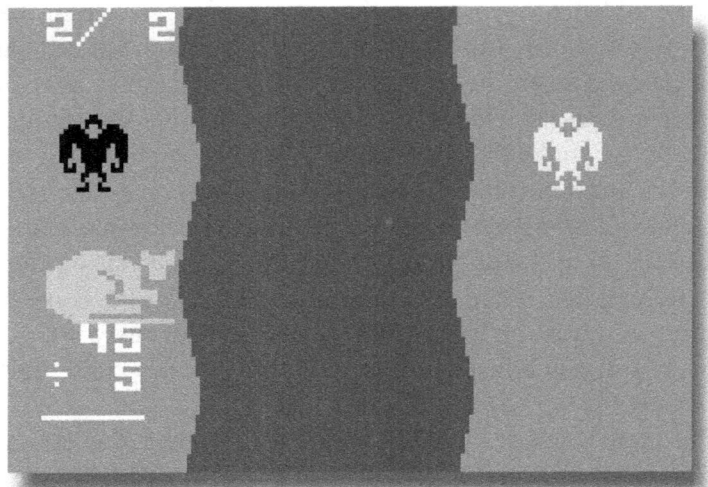

Figure 1.13: Educational software didn't have to be boring, as the charming *Math Fun* showed.

I showed it to my seven-year-old daughter to see if this was still true. I'm always impressed whenever she likes an old game I'm playing. She has an iPad containing games with mind-blowing graphics, sound, and voice-over narration. If something like *Math Fun* holds her attention, I consider it a success. (It did for a few minutes, but she much preferred *Thin Ice*.)

Game Networks

Each Intellivision cartridge at launch came in a gatefold box that opened to show a cartridge inside a white plastic reinforcement tray. The tray sat in a cavity in the cardboard. The left side had a folder pocket to store the manual, overlays, and often a Mattel game catalog. Intellivision box artwork depicts a detailed, imaginative interpretation of each game's action. Many of the creations were in an idiom similar to those found on Atari game boxes. I'd love to see a sequel to Tim Lapetino's excellent *Art of Atari* book that covers the Intellivision.

The first several years of Mattel games shared a graphic design motif. Mattel grouped its early Intellivision cartridges into color-coded "networks," with sports games in the Sports Network, arcade-style games in the Action Network, and so on. There were five networks at launch: Sports (10 games), Strategy (two games), Children's Learning (two games), Action (three games), and Gaming (three games, and with the word "gaming" in a gambling context). It was a cute play on the concept of television networks, and each network got its own box color. Mattel called the Intellivision networks an "ever-changing variety of play situations" where "player decisions are yours." It would soon go on to fill out these lineups further.

Mostly, I won't pay much mind to the game networks in this book. They're more of a historical curiosity important for collectors than they are crucial to our discussion of how great Intellivision gaming was. Back then, you had whatever cartridges you had. You didn't typically think, "Today, I'll play a game in the Strategy Network." (If you did, please write and tell me.)

Keyboard Component

From the beginning, Mattel also made its plans for the Keyboard Component public. It ran national television commercials showing the two components together and docked and a family using the system in various ways, along with narration that highlighted the system's combined potential:

> Soon, the John Guyer family will be using their TV to help compute their federal income tax, learn French, improve math skills, and quarterback an NFL team. Introducing Intellivision, the new home video system from Mattel Electronics. Two components each sold separately start with the Master Component available now for super games like NFL Football, and for learning fun from The Electric Company. And when you add the keyboard component available this summer, Intellivision can change your family's life. It simplifies financial planning, it even custom designs a Jack La Lanne exercise program for you. There is an entire library of Intellivision programs designed to grow right along with your family's interest. Discover Intellivision...it can change your family's life.

The commercial concluded by saying the Master Component was available at Macy's, and that the Keyboard Component would be available in the summer of 1980. Similarly, the first Intellivision retailer catalog released that same year featured the Master Component docked with the Keyboard Component on the cover. The catalog describes the Intellivision on the first page not as a game console, but as part of the Intellivision Intelligent Television System:

> Intellivision is a system of modularized hardware components and a broad spectrum of software that offers consumers benefits for now and in the years to come. The heart of Intellivision is the Master Component. By itself it provides a variety of entertainment and gameplay through the use of preprogrammed ROM game cartridges. These are true to life in visual appeal, simulated sound effects, and variability…
>
> The addition of the Keyboard Component expands the system's capabilities…through the use of preprogrammed software featuring an expert consultant who actually talks to the consumer. The user responds in English using a familiar typewriter-like keyboard. There is no requirement for knowledge of a computer language. Truly, a computer for the home.
>
> Intellivision…the Future Today!

The Keyboard Component did look like a desirable piece of gear. It had the same brown-and-gold plastic and metallic accents as the Master Component. It featured an MOS 6502, the same powerful 8-bit processor in the Apple II, the Commodore PET, and the new Atari 400 and 800 home computers. The Keyboard Component also contained 16KB of RAM, several times more than the Master Component, a full-size QWERTY typewriter-style keyboard, and a built-in cassette deck for saving programs. The main portion of the keyboard had cream color keycaps with black lettering. Bright red, blue, and black keycaps and white lettering designated special keys such as cursor control, Shift, and Return.

The cassette deck featured a block-addressable cassette interface, an audio track you could synchronize with a program and its graphics, and a microphone that let you rerecord and play back audio timed with the program's requests.[56] The Keyboard Component included a cartridge port to insert games, as the Master Component's port would become inaccessible when docked. It featured a printer port for output

Figure 1.14: The Keyboard Component was the second half of Mattel's strategy to conquer the video game and home computer markets simultaneously. (Credit: Daniel McConnell/CC BY-2.0)

to a 40-column thermal printer, alternately dubbed the Printer 40 and Sprinter 40 in various company materials.

Mattel promised retailers a full array of advertising and promotional support for the Keyboard Component. This included television saturation with 60-second commercials and prime-time ads, three-page ads in national magazines such as *Time*, *People*, and *Newsweek* with toll-free numbers that customers could call to locate their nearest retailer, and "substantial co-op advertising funds, ad mats, and slicks." For dealers who purchased a large amount of stock, Mattel promised a display unit with a demonstration cartridge, a carousel-type counter merchandiser to display cartridges, full-color consumer brochures, and in-store support training sessions.

The demonstration cartridge alone must have seemed like a revelation. It played a three-voice rendition of the opening of *Also sprach Zarathustra* as heard in *2001: A Space Odyssey*, while showing *NFL Football*, *Armor Battle*, and *Las Vegas Poker & Blackjack* (still without the "Las Vegas" in the name). It also clearly said on the screen: "Later, you can add the Keyboard Component, and expand your system into a powerful home computer."[57] A companion Keyboard demonstration cassette featured human narration over some of the screens from the above software for exercising, monitoring the stock market, and learning conversational French. A promotional video expanded on this with B-roll of the Master and Keyboard Components.[58]

The catalog promised the Keyboard Component even sooner, in March 1980.[59] But it was nowhere near ready. Worse, the projected retail price of the Keyboard Component would skyrocket as development continued.

2 | Launch

The Intellivision may have been unique and groundbreaking, but one system released around the same time looked like a copy. In the late 1970s, Bandai was selling its own TV Jack line of dedicated Pong console clones in Japan. In December 1979, it unveiled the Super Vision 8000, its first microprocessor- and cartridge-based game console. The wedge-shaped system looked like it took a wrong turn off a *Star Wars* set. It featured a powerful 8-bit NEC D780C processor twice as fast as the Atari 2600's MOS 6507 chip.[1]

The Super Vision 8000 featured a new controller design, a flat rectangle with a 12-button keypad, a side Fire button, and a 16-direction disc instead of a paddle or joystick. The console accepted cassette games and stored the controllers in recessed cradles on either side of the cassette deck. The front panel also featured giant Power and Reset buttons. In other words, just like what you got with the Intellivision Master Component. The controller had one side action button instead of four, and the keypad wasn't recessed and couldn't accept overlays. Although both consoles used different CPUs, they shared the same three-voice sound chip, the General Instrument AY-3-8910.

Despite the striking similarities, it's believed Bandai and Mattel engineers designed both these systems unaware of the other. As both appeared within weeks of each other in late 1979 on opposite sides of the world, it suggests a giant coincidence more than corporate espionage. The Super Vision 8000 cost too much money, and it had fewer than 10 games. Bandai discontinued the console within a year and, ironically enough, went on to distribute Mattel's Intellivision in Japan within a matter of months.[2] Bandai did just fine—it became a leading toy and game developer throughout the 1980s and 1990s. You may know the name today as the behemoth Bandai Namco, one of the world's biggest publishers of video games for Xbox, PlayStation, and Switch consoles.

A bit later on, Emerson released the Arcadia 2001, a similar compact console with two included controllers that also looked just like the Intellivision's. The main difference was that each controller had a small joystick sticking out of the gold disc. A total of 47 games came out for the Arcadia 2001 in the 18 months it was on the market. Various companies cloned and sold the Emerson console worldwide, including Bandai in Japan, Hanimex in Australia, and Tedelex in South Africa. These occasionally surface on eBay and social media. None came anywhere close to the Intellivision in popularity.

The Intellivision Goes National

For Mattel Electronics, the Fresno market test was a success. The company was poised to move beyond handheld electronic games into video game consoles. "Handhelds had established Mattel in the electronic game area, which made it a sensible add-on to go and compete on the console side against Atari," said Mattel marketing director Michael Katz.[3] The stage was set for the industry's first console war—one that Mattel would soon make explicit.

Mattel did let several other vendors sell the Master Component. In addition to the GTE/Sylvania branding deal we've covered, Mattel signed with Sears to sell the Tele-Games Super Video Arcade. The Sears model had an attractive beige housing with a different top design, burled cherry woodgrain accents, and matching controllers. Unlike the Mattel version, the Super Video Arcade's controllers were forward facing and detachable, and the system didn't display "Mattel Electronics Presents" on-screen when you booted up cartridges. Otherwise, the console was the same, just as the Sears Tele-Games Video Arcade was the same as the Atari 2600. Sears sold games in its own box designs, as it did for the 2600, although here Sears generally didn't rename the titles except for removing license information (e.g. *Baseball* instead of *Major League Baseball*).

After an expanded early-1980 test in more department stores around the U.S., Mattel launched the Intellivision nationally in August 1980.[4] Cartridges retailed at $39.95 each, and the console still included the pack-in game *Las Vegas Poker & Blackjack*.[5] Reports differ slightly in timing and number, but *Video* magazine said in its August 1980 issue—figure a two-month lead time to print—that Mattel started selling the Master Component with seven games, and two months later it had increased the number to nine, with 20 expected on sale for the 1980 holiday season.[6] The lineup was packed with sports games, and early on, they came to define the console. Mattel blanketed the country with advertising for its new game system, and the company planned to discount cartridges as newer ones hit the market. In its advertisements, Mattel showed the "running man" sprite—found in its top sports games—in the logo as a series of frames bracketing the Mattel Electronics name.

The national launch meant the public would finally get to see the rest of the console's launch lineup—and why, if you were a sports fan, you simply had to get an Intellivision. Let's look at the console's first smash hit.

Major League Baseball (APh/Mattel, August 1980)

Developed by David Rolfe and the first game programmed for the Intellivision,[7] *Major League Baseball* features two nine-man teams, nine full innings, and grand slams. It packs in stolen bases, bunts, walks, extra innings, cheering crowds, and grumbled "Yer out!" calls from the umpire. You can pick off a base stealer if they become too daring. The game carried the official Major League Baseball license and logo, although it didn't have actual team or player names.

Compare *Major League Baseball* with *Home Run* on the Atari 2600, and it's not even close. You can't tell *Home Run* is a baseball game from a static screenshot because the diamond is missing. The 2600 lacks a proper character set, displaying a disjointed "B" for balls and "S" for strikes. Worse, not only do you only have three men on each team, but you also *can't throw the ball*. You can only run to tag out a baserunner.

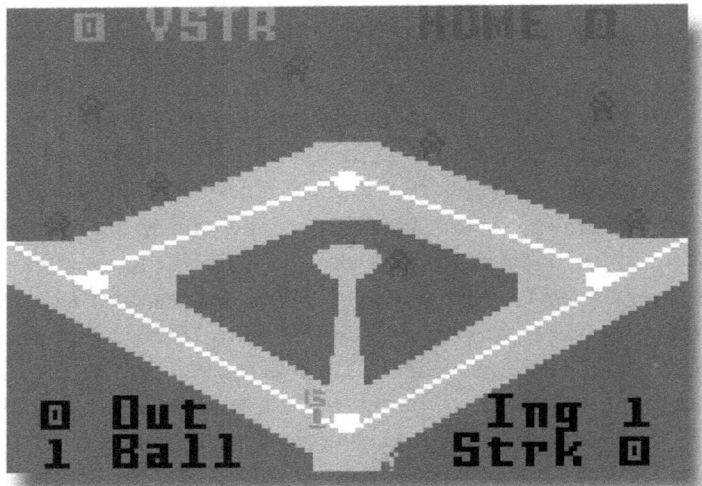

Figure 2.1: Mattel hit one out of the park with *Major League Baseball*, a stunning, sophisticated interpretation that gave players something genuinely new.

In contrast, the Intellivision cartridge depicts a proper baseball diamond on screen, with all nine team members in the right spots and a scoreboard for the home and visitor teams. Start a game, and the blue home team players run onto the field to the sound of a cheering, whistling crowd. The smoothly animated sprites look like real people, right down to their baseball caps. All take their proper positions, the catcher tosses the ball to the pitcher, the first visiting red batter runs to home plate, and the game begins.

Pitching is quick, with plenty of ways to mix up your strategy and confound whoever is at bat. Fastballs, inside and outside curves, and slow balls are thrown depending on where you press the disc. You can control every man on the team by pressing the corresponding key on the keypad, which was impossible to do on other systems. Say you're pitching, and the batter hits the ball into right field. Press the top-right key to call up the right fielder, and then you can maneuver him to catch the ball and throw it to one of the bases. Fielding grounders by running to where the ball is going and throwing them to pick off a runner before they reach base is fast and satisfying—your player turns from black to dark blue or red once you have the ball. Sneer at the Intellivision's direction disc for maze games if you must, but it is perfect for this.

Realism abounds. When at bat, crack the ball into left field and the opposing player must activate their nearest player, who turns black and runs to the ball. Basemen will automatically cover their bases when activated. Have the pitcher throw to second base, and it's faster than throwing to first or third. Go after a daring baserunner taking too much of a lead off the base by pitching to the catcher—who will then try to trap the runner between two basemen. The game makes a few concessions for speed and simplicity: All batters are right-handed, errors are possible but not recorded, and there are no fly balls. None of this matters; hit a home run, listen to the crowd go wild as you run the bases, and you'll be in the stadium. It was the first baseball video game to make us feel this way.

A full nine-inning game of *Major League Baseball* didn't last as long as a real one, but it lasted much longer than the average video game and required real determination from the two players. Mattel went on to sell more than a million copies of *Major League Baseball*. It's still fun to play today, with the only hindrance being the same one we all had more than 40 years ago—you need a buddy to play it. This was something I felt acutely, as I was an only child. I had the same problem with the Atari 2600 and the *Combat* pack-in cartridge, but almost all the other cartridges could be played solo. Today, finding a friend to play *Major League Baseball* with is well worth the effort. Even if you can't, a newer version takes care of the problem, as we'll get to later in this book.

NBA Basketball (APh/Mattel, August 1980)

NBA Basketball, the Intellivision's entry into an already-crowded video game genre, had the first official endorsement (although no NBA teams or player names, the same as with *Major League Baseball*). It depicts a real basketball court from the side with three players on each team. You control one player while the computer controls the other two, and you switch between all three as you pass the ball across the court.

The sprites are about twice the height of those in *Major League Baseball*. The home team is red, and the visiting team is green. Whoever has possession dribbles the ball, and currently activated players turn black. The disc moves your player around, and you pass by pressing one of the nine keypad buttons for the appropriate court position. But you must make sure someone is nearby. A teammate will automatically run into position to receive it, but it will go out of bounds if they can't make it to the ball in time. Each game has four regulation quarters of 12 minutes each, although the actual seconds pass faster than in real life. You score two points per basket; in the event of a tie, the game goes into 5-minute overtime periods.

You can choose between four speeds when you first start the game. Pressing the disc plays at the default fastest speed; otherwise, you can press one of the top three court position keys (1, 2, or 3 under the overlay) to choose "college" (fast), "high school" (medium fast), or "playground" (slow). Then everyone moves into position for the first jump ball, which the computer decides randomly. Whenever you possess the ball, you have a 24-second shot clock. Running into a defender means the ball can get stolen, and if you pass near a defender, they can intercept. Passing is key to the game and vastly increases the likelihood that you'll score baskets. Fast breaks and double passes work even better.

The bottom of the keypad has buttons for set shots, jump shots, and blocking. Set shots give you a better chance of sinking baskets, but nearby defenders can block your shot. Jump shots can't be blocked but are less reliable than set shots. They can still work if you're surrounded

Figure 2.2: You could shoot and dribble with the best of them in *NBA Basketball*, a realistic game that presents the court from the side.

by defenders close to the basket. Either team can land a rebound; you must contact the ball above the waist. When your opponent has the ball, you can block their shots with the Block button and get in their way as much as humanly possible.

Even the sound effects are awesome in what fast became an Intellivision trademark. Dribble the ball and it bounces realistically. Land a basket and the crowd cheers. A buzzer sounds whenever the 24-second clock expires or a period ends. *NBA Basketball* is missing three-pointers, fouls, and foul shots, and you can't dunk. Unlike *Home Run*, Atari's *Basketball* cartridge for the 2600 isn't bad. Although it's only a one-on-one game with simple, blocky graphics, it's fast and offers a one-player mode with an AI-controlled computer player. *NBA Basketball* is for two players only, but it's better in almost all other respects. Like *Major League Baseball*, *NBA Basketball* set the template for console sports games in the following decades.

NFL Football (APh/Mattel, August 1980)

A high point of early sports video games, *NFL Football* is also a sophisticated simulation. Each player controls one player of a five-person football team on a regulation-length 100-yard field with end zones on either side. True to life, the game view is zoomed in, showing 20 yards at any time with two-thirds of the field in front of the offense. The view then scrolls to follow each play, like how a television camera pans the field. The sprites look like real football players wearing bulging uniforms, with the quarterback being the largest. All run smoothly across the screen in various plays, which include dropping back for passes, interceptions, broken field runs, and more. The crowd's cheers, the gun sounding at the end of each quarter, the referee's whistle—it sounds like you're watching and playing a real football game.

The home team has four computer-controlled orange players and one active red player you control; the visiting team has four light-blue players and one black player. Games consist of four quarters of 15 minutes each. After each quarter, the teams automatically change sides of the field. The score and clock sit at the top of the screen; a separate display below the bottom sideline shows the current down, yards to go for a first down, and the yard line the ball is on. Touchdowns are worth seven points; the extra point is automatic, and the end zones lack goal posts. The game also supports three-point field goals and two-point safeties. If the ball carrier steps over the sidelines at the top and bottom of the screen, a referee's whistle blows, and the clock stops. It also stops for time-outs, incomplete passes, and when the score changes.

The level of realism was breathtaking for the time. *NFL Football* has a larger-than-usual 28-page manual to begin with. But the bundled playbook makes the game; it details an incredible 160 offensive and 10 defensive formations and plays. As the team captain, you select plays using the keypad during the huddle. On offense, you choose the type of play (run, kick, or pass) and one of nine formations. For passing, for example, you press the Pass key; choose the alignment (1–9), the receiver (1 or 2), and the zone (1–9); and press Enter to execute. On defense, you can choose from an array of defensive sets. The overlay covers keys 1–9, with 7, 8, and 9 doubling as Run, Kick, and Pass keys.

The top side Hike button snaps the ball from the center to the quarterback; the P/K (pass/kick) bottom side buttons release the ball (on a pass play) or punt or kick a field goal. The disc, of course, determines where you run on the field and allows for smooth, precise control of the player in 16 directions. You control the quarterback until he passes, at which point control changes to the receiver.

"*NFL Football* will make video arcade lovers think they've died and gone to Super Bowl heaven," Bill Kunkel and Arnie Katz (under the assumed name Frank Laney) wrote in the August 1980 issue of *Video* magazine.[8] Two years later, they wrote, "[*NFL Football*'s] scrolling playfield and great number of offensive and defensive play possibilities are without peer in the video-game field."[9]

"Before writing about games for a living, I worked full time as a technician at a cable TV company in Connecticut and was a game hobbyist on the side," former TeamXbox editor-in-chief Andy Eddy said in an interview with IGN. "When the NFL went on strike in 1982, we thought it'd be a goof to offer a 'replacement' to *Monday Night Football* by getting some local kids to play Intellivision *Football* on our public-access channel and do play-by-play over it. When *[Monday Night Football]* came back on after the strike ended a couple of months later, the public-access director started getting calls asking where our 'show' went, so we started doing a sports-based video-game show as a regular thing for a while, taking calls and demonstrating some of the new games. We had no idea people would be so into it."[10]

Figure 2.3: The striking *NFL Football* offered deep play management and a view of the field that mimicked television cameras at real games.

It's somewhat embarrassing to admit, but I had no idea how football worked when I was eight. I remember on what must have been the first day I had the cartridge, I rang up a long game full of safeties—again by myself, so I just controlled one team at a time. I assumed I was supposed to be getting two points for every touchdown. Only when I had friends over to play did I realize how the game worked. I don't know why I retained this memory, but *NFL Football* was and is an unforgettable experience. Even if you swear by *Madden* on today's consoles, *NFL Football* is where it all began.

Space Battle (APh/Mattel, October 1980)

In the brilliant *Space Battle*, one of the Intellivision's defining launch games, you must protect the Mother Ship from incoming alien squadrons using your own three home squadrons of three fighter ships each. The game starts with the Radar Screen, which shows the lonely Mother Ship in the center of a small, oval-shaped Direct Attack Zone. Three rectangular zones fan out from there to the edges of the screen. Five alien squadrons in the outermost zone are slowly closing in, each at a different speed and with multiple spaceships, shown as clusters of dots.

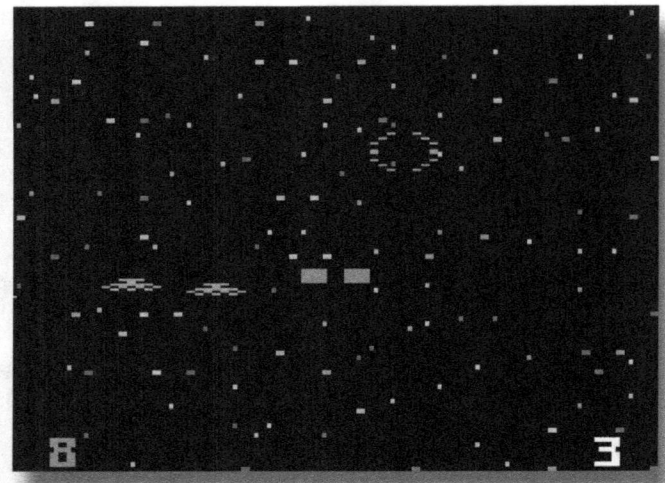

Figure 2.4: Exidy's *Star Fire* meets the *Star Trek* television series in this intense battle for the federation.

Attack the closest alien squadron first by selecting it with the Alien key on the bottom right of the keypad, and then press the blue, white, or gold Squadron button. The chosen home squadron appears on the screen near the Mother Ship and makes its way toward the alien squadron. Once they meet and begin flashing, press the corresponding Go to Battle button to enter the Cockpit Close-Up view.

Now you're in deep space with a view of the stars. Alien fighters soon come into view, performing evasive maneuvers; you aim the laser cursor with the direction disc and then fire with any side action button. Vaporize one and it will explode colorfully, but they also return fire; if their incoming lasers collide with your crosshairs, you'll lose one of your spaceships. Blasting all the alien fighters away means you win that battle, but then you must return to the Radar Screen and intercept the next group.

If an alien squadron reaches the Direct Attack Zone near the center of the Radar Screen, a loud, red alert klaxon sounds. The Mother Ship is under attack! You must immediately deploy a home squadron to it. The game ends, complete with a shattering red explosion and sound effects, if you lose the Mother Ship or all your home squadrons. From there, there's no way out but to hard reset the console. But if you destroy all five alien squadrons, you'll hear a victory fanfare; the game will display "All Clear" on the Radar Screen. That you can finish and win a game in about 10 minutes distinguishes *Space Battle* from nearly all space shoot-'em-up games of the period.

To this day, *Space Battle*'s dual modes give it a nice balance between strategy and action. The pace really picks up when you're maneuvering multiple squadrons while you're fighting a different battle. Deciding which battles to take on and which to let the computer fight for you is a big part of the strategy, as the computer won't fight for your side as well as you can. Four game speeds allow for a spectrum of difficulty levels that make a real difference; I've never beaten the game on the fastest speed. And a fun cooperative mode lets two players control different aspects of the combat experience.

Hal Finney initially developed *Space Battle* with a *Battlestar Galactica* license in mind, in case you've wondered why the enemy fighters look like Cylon Raiders. *Mattel* subsidiary Concept 2000 already produced electronic *Battlestar Galactica* toys and assumed Mattel would also license the video game. It recalls how Exidy designed its 1978 *Star Fire* coin-op, the one David Rolfe had worked on, in anticipation of securing a *Star Wars* license from Lucasfilm. Neither effort panned out.[11]

Regardless of whether you've seen the television series, *Space Battle* was much more than a simple space shooter. Thanks to the red alert klaxon and losing sequence, it was one of the scariest and most fraught games I grew up with. It's still hair-raising to play today and provides a slower paced but still intense counterpoint to the terrific *Star Raiders* on the Atari 400 and 800.

Sea Battle (APh/Mattel, October 1980)

Sea Battle pits you against another player, each of you commanding a naval fleet that must defend their home port while invading your opponent's. It's one of the first strategy games that takes place in real time, even if it's not commonly recognized as what we'd consider a real-time strategy game. Play it, and the sonar's distinctive two-step "ping" sound puts you in the mood for strategic naval battles. The game takes place on a map of an ocean dotted with islands, and in several phases. You need the overlays, as each key corresponds to a different ship and reminds you of the total number you get. Additional keys engage with or retreat from an opponent, create and deploy naval units, and stop ship movements. The side action buttons let you aim the cursor and fire your guns and torpedoes. You move each fleet or ship using the directional disc.

With its singular map, *Sea Battle* looks relatively simple compared with computer-based wargames. Each navy consists of 13 ships in eight types: one aircraft carrier, one troop transport, two battleships, one submarine, three destroyers, two patrol torpedo (PT) boats, one minelayer, and two minesweepers. The game plays in two main phases. In the strategy phase, all units are roughly the same size and look similar; your units and your opponents' units all face each other. You deploy your fleets from harbor, lay mines, maneuver units into combat positions, and repair and regroup fleets after battles. A fleet can consist of one, two, or three different ships. If a unit reaches an island or the map edge, it pauses and stands by for your next command.

Maneuver within firing range of your opponent's fleet, and a klaxon sounds, allowing you to engage in combat. Do so, and the game switches to the combat phase, a zoomed-in battle view where you assume control of your ships. You must aim the cursor using the direction disc and the top side action buttons and then fire using the bottom ones. Your opponent, of course, is trying to do the same thing. In this phase, ships take on damage either from cannons or by running aground on land (unlike in the strategy phase, where touching land isn't dangerous).

Each unit type has different armor, weapons, acceleration, top speed, maneuverability, and other characteristics. It's in the combat phase where the various attributes for each ship come into play. A large battleship can travel at 35 knots, has 30 armor ("very heavy"), long-range shots, and does 12 damage on a strike, but only average acceleration and maneuverability. Compare that with the PT boat, which can travel even faster (40 knots) and has the fastest acceleration and maneuverability but has 15 armor ("light") and short-range attacks; a single shot can sink one. Meanwhile, accelerating an aircraft carrier to its top speed (30 knots) or turning it to face a different direction can take several additional seconds.

The invisible mines are the worst. You and your opponent can each lay up to four. A mine detonates when a ship cruises over it. The mine continues to do damage until the ship moves out of the way or

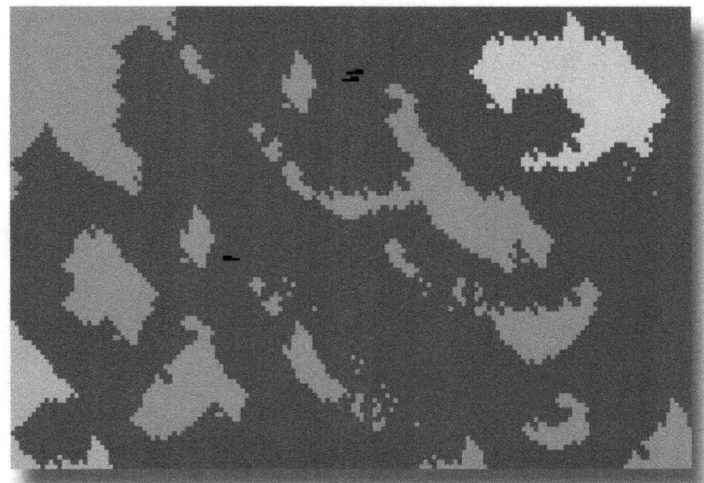

Figure 2.5: The brilliant *Sea Battle* mixes equal parts action and strategy between two naval powers.

sinks. Minesweepers can locate and deactivate mines, but they move very slowly. After the battle, you can send any damaged ships back to the home port for repairs. To win the game, you must navigate a troop transport or aircraft carrier into your opponent's home port. The 20-page manual walks you through all the options and offers a tutorial.

Between the different ships in combat, the ways you can assemble fleet units, the different paths you can take to the opposing harbor, and the wild card mine locations, *Sea Battle* contains enough layers of strategy for serious engagement—and replayability. Another game that no other console at the time could pull off. More than any other two-player game, I played *Sea Battle* by myself out of frustration in not having a sibling. I loved it, and I distinctly remember losing the two white-and-blue overlays early on and being frustrated that I couldn't remember which buttons deployed which ships or how many I was allotted. These were big first-world problems when I was eight.

Auto Racing (APh/Mattel, October 1980)

Mattel's first handheld LED game was *Auto Race*, so it's only fitting that the company translated it into an Intellivision cartridge. With its massive scrolling tracks that took up many screens, *Auto Race* marked

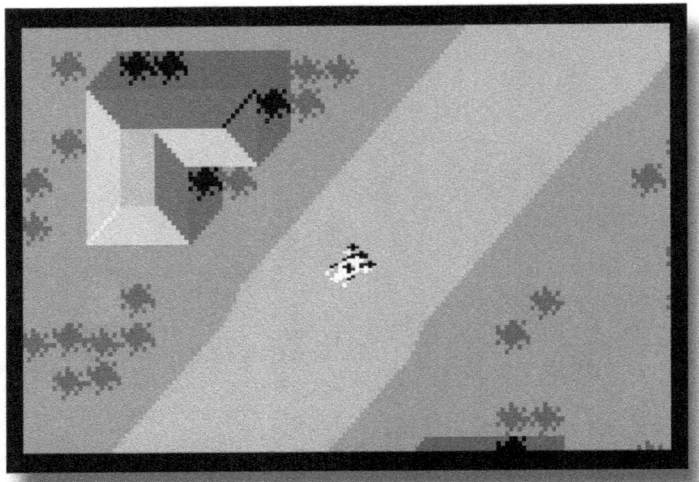

Figure 2.6: *Auto Racing* marked a milestone in the evolution of driving games even despite its flaws.

a notable advance over fixed-screen racing games such as *Gran Trak 10* and *Speed Race* in arcades and *Indy 500* on the Atari 2600. It adds a pronounced element of suspense because you can't see what's coming up ahead until you are almost right on top of it. Depending on your viewpoint, *Auto Race* is either a terrific attempt at a driving game or a confounding, frustrating title that should have never left Mattel's development studio.

The game presents a zoomed-in, overhead view of the track, which weaves in and out of a landscape full of buildings, trees, rivers, and other features. You can race against another human player or by yourself against the clock. The game contains five tracks, each increasing in difficulty; all are mapped in the instruction manual. You can choose from five different Formula One race cars, each with its own color, acceleration curve, top speed, and cornering ability.

Two versions of *Auto Racing* exist, and it's impossible to know which one you have until you start playing. One features "realistic steering," meaning that if you want the car to turn right, you press right on the direction disc (toward 3 o'clock). That sounds reasonable on paper, but on screen, if your car is traveling downward, pushing right means it will turn to its right, which is left on screen. This is the version I remember playing, and that I remember comparing a few years later with *Rally Speedway* on the Atari 800 (which is a much faster game). Pushing farther up on the disc's edge (say 2 o'clock) makes the turn more gradual, pushing straight up (12 o'clock) straightens out the steering wheel, and pushing down (between 3 and 6 o'clock) turns much more sharply and can easily induce oversteer, where the rear end of the car comes around, and you spin out on the track. With practice, light touches of oversteer can help you harness your car's momentum from acceleration and get around corners quickly and smoothly.

The second version uses what's referred to as "intuitive steering," meaning that if you wanted to turn left on the screen, you pushed the disc left regardless of which way the car was currently facing—even if it meant the car was technically making a right turn. This is like playing *Rally-X* in the arcade, if you're familiar with the coin-op. The theory is that Mattel introduced a running change in manufacturing for *Auto Racing* as people wrote in to complain, although there is some debate over which version was first. Compounding the issue, and what I always thought was the worst aspect of the game, is that you turn slowly—you need to start before you get to a turn if you want to have any hope of making it, and by the time you figure out which way to press the disc and see your choice register, it's already too late to course-correct.

In two-car races, the mechanics are different and don't work as well. First, choosing the tan and blue cars is best because they're evenly matched. Each time one car crashes, the opponent gets two points. If one player takes a commanding lead, to the point where the cars become too far apart to fit on the screen properly, that player gets one "ahead" point, and the cars are restarted together again. This skids the racing to a halt each time and feels disjointed. *Auto Racing* has not aged well but was a revelation in 1980. It's worth a play today to see the contrast between typical racing games of the 1970s and this one's much larger playfield and increased sophistication.

NHL Hockey (APh/Mattel, October 1980)

Mattel continued its first run of licensed sports games with the two-player, four-on-four *NHL Hockey*. In this game, you control the puck handler, while the computer controls the other team members and goalie. The object is to score more goals than the other team in three

20-minute periods, and unlike other sports, there are no tiebreakers. The game displays the entire rink from one side on screen at once, with the scoreboard and period clock on top, penalty clocks to either side, and both goal nets visible with the face-off circle in the center. The rink contains regulation lines: red in the center and blue to either side.

Each game opens with the team skating onto the rink to the sound of a cheering crowd. Everyone assumes position for the face-off, with the tan Home team on the left and the light green Visitor team on the right. A random call decides the face-off; as soon as the puck appears, the period clock starts counting down.

The overlays are simple, especially next to the other sports titles I covered earlier. The disc lets you skate forward and accelerate in any of 16 directions. The keypad is only necessary to select one of four game speeds at the start. On offense, the Shoot side action buttons launch the puck across the ice; the lower Pass buttons send it at a lower speed to your teammates. To swing your stick, you must push the disc in the direction you want to send the puck and then press the Shoot or Pass buttons. On defense, you control the defensive captain. The defensive captain and the man with the puck are both darker colored when you are in control.

You and your opponent can each steal possession of the puck at any time. Whenever you've got it, you must either pass the puck to someone closer to the opposing goal or skate toward the opposing net and go for a shot. There's even a slight delay to account for the swing time as the stick connects with the puck (unless you're trying to steal it and you miss). Once another team member receives the puck, you assume that player's control. The best strategy is to wear down the goalie with repeated attempts; you'll see him fall onto the ice and struggle to get up in time—now's your chance! But the goalies are both very competent and rarely miss an incoming puck. They'll both come out to steal or intercept the puck whenever possible.

The best thing about the game, of course, is the checking. You can do it legally if your opponent has the puck; you'll steal it and send him to the ice, dizzy for a few moments. Do it to someone without the puck and you could end up in the penalty box for two minutes while your team plays with one man down. Or the "referee" (who isn't visible) may not catch what you did and let you go. All the cheering,

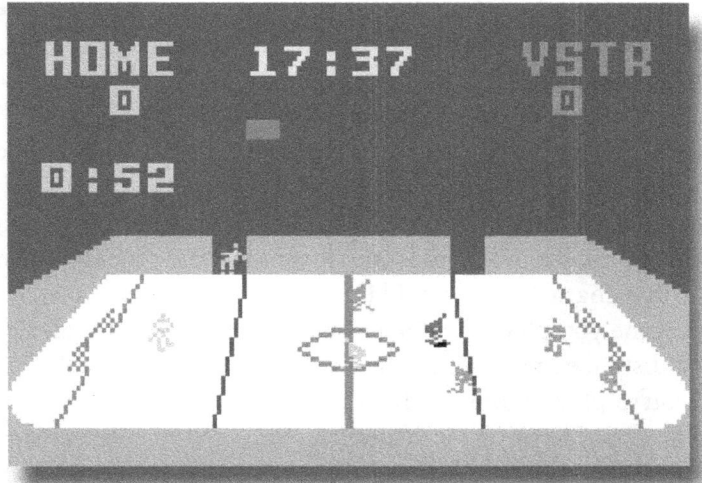

Figure 2.7: *NHL Hockey* **brought all the fast skating, shooting, and penalties of real hockey to your television screen.**

referee whistles, buzzers, and other sound effects from the other sports games are also present and accounted for here.

The Atari 2600 didn't get a hockey game until Activision's 1981 release *Ice Hockey*. It's an excellent game but much simpler, with a barren gray vertical rink devoid of details, two-on-two play, and no checking or penalties. *NHL Hockey* remained one of the best console hockey games for over a decade, only being truly shown up with *Blades of Steel* on the Nintendo Entertainment System and, later, *NHL '93* and above on the Sega Genesis. It's still fun to play now.

Horse Racing (APh/Mattel, October 1980)

Now here's something Mattel wouldn't market to kids today. *Horse Racing* brought equestrian to the Intellivision, complete with a gambling component. The title screen plays "William Tell Overture" to get you in the mood. The object is to beat your opponents by skillfully handicapping races with simulated wagers during a 10-event race day.

From one to six humans can play. Each starts with $750, and races are three to 10 furlongs. On the betting screen, each player enters a bet for the current race (up to $250). After all humans have placed bets, the following screen shows the current race length and the track conditions, plus which four horses are running in the first race. The top two are computer controlled, the left controller corresponds to the jockey for the third horse, and the right controller affects the bottom horse. Or you can let the computer control all four horses.

Each furlong in the race is marked with a black post and a gong sound. Horses tend to slow in the middle of the race. They have different racing patterns that you learn over time, such as speeding up down the home stretch or running faster than the others on a muddy track. These characteristics hold for the current 10 events and change the next time you play. The horse traveling closest to the rail rides the shortest distance in a race, as the course is slightly curved.

If you're playing one of the jockeys, the disc lets you maneuver the horse closer to or farther from the rail. The top side buttons coax the horse during the race's first half for a little extra speed; don't use this too much, or the horse will run out its ability to be coaxed and slow down more. The bottom side buttons crack the whip to hit top speed for the final dash; do it too soon, and the horse will tire out and barely walk the rest of the way. I'm pretty sure this breaks some kind of rule about a jockey betting on themselves.

For all successive races after the first, you can switch between the Past Performance screen and the betting screen to examine the

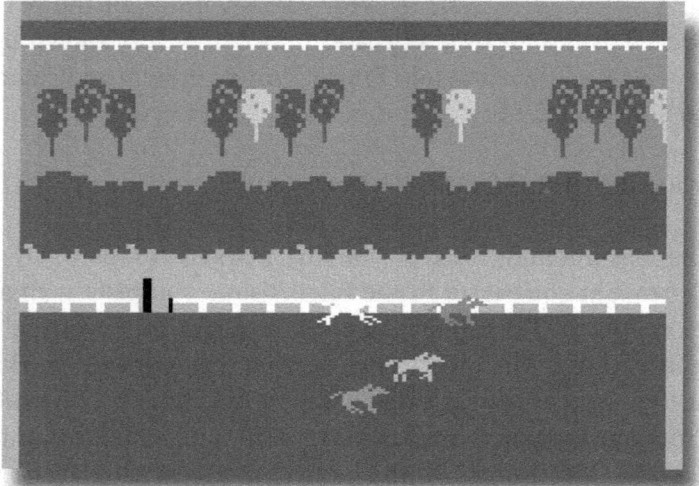

Figure 2.8: A surprisingly deep strategy game in the guise of gambling, *Horse Racing* **even let you control one of the horses during each race.**

tentative odds for each horse in numbered pairs. For example, a 5–2 on "Blu" means that you'd win $5 for every $2 you bet on this horse if it won. You can make two kinds of bets: W means a bet to Win. E is an Exacta bet on the first and second horses in their finishing order. Exacta bets are much riskier but pay off at a high 15 to 1.

The more you play, the more you figure out how to strategize your bets and get the hang of learning the horses. The Past Performance screen is hard to grok—it looks like a jumble of symbols and letters—but it shows how each horse has performed, which horses it has beaten, in what conditions, and how long the tracks were each time. Based on that data, you can sense the odds and place your bets accordingly. The manual even recommends tracking this on paper so that you retain info on every single race and not just the last. If any player runs out of cash, they're out of the game. It's a surprising and satisfying amount of strategy for what amounts to a game of chance.

I used to wonder what my uncle Tony did whenever he entered the store with the giant OTB letters on Sheepshead Bay Road in Brooklyn—the letters stood for Off-Track Betting, and he was gambling, of course. I don't think I realized then that *Horse Racing* let me do the same thing in front of our console television at home, albeit without real money at stake. Mattel did tag *Horse Racing* as part of its Gaming Network instead of Sports Network, but I doubt retail store clerks paid that any mind, and my dad had no problem buying it for me when I was seven.

While I'm looking back, it's a little odd to think I used to play *Horse Racing* and *Las Vegas Poker & Blackjack* at that age. I didn't grow up to develop a gambling problem, but it's hilarious to me now how much time I spent essentially gambling as a little kid. These wouldn't be the first games I'd teach my daughter today, aside from a feeling of nostalgia for my (dearly departed) grandmother's heyday in the 1940s and 1950s. Her friend Kay used to come over in the late 1970s and early 1980s. I'd play Intellivision or the Atari 2600 in the den while they sat in the living room on overwrought couches with plastic covers, watched *Barnaby Jones* and *Kojak* reruns, and drank Budweiser. (Go, Nana!) Anyway, I'm sure my wife would have me committed if I bought my daughter a horse racing app for her iPad. I guess it was a different time.

NASL Soccer (APh/Mattel, November 1980)

Association football has seen a surge in popularity in the U.S. in recent years, elevating it to a status it always deserved and already had worldwide. Mattel nailed the video game formula for the sport more than a decade before EA launched the top-tier FIFA series in 1993. Visually, Mattel's *NASL Soccer* takes a similar approach as *NFL Football*. It features a horizontal-scrolling field and shows about a third of it at any one time; the difference here is that the field is presented in a three-quarter perspective, rather than straight on from the side. The "television camera" pans to keep the player with the ball in view as they move across the field. One player has the yellow team and the other the purple team; each team has four players including the goalie.

The top portion of the display shows the current score and the time remaining in the half, although it disappears momentarily whenever the camera pans across the field. You play two 45-minute regulation periods, and each goal is worth one point, the same as in real life. The crowd roars as the players take the field. The computer randomly decides which yellow player takes possession during the kickoff; then that player turns orange, indicating he's the one you control.

Figure 2.9: For the "other" kind of football—or, if you're European, "real" football—*NASL Soccer* delivers the goods.

The direction disc lets you run offense and defense players in 16 directions. Dribbling the ball is automatic as you run. The top side buttons shoot the ball across the field on offense, if the direction disc is also held down, and moves the goalie upward to lunge on defense whenever visible. The bottom ones send the ball across the field more slowly or send the goalie in a downward lunge. The button layout means that when on defense, you simultaneously control the defensive captain and the goalie whenever he's visible.

The game also sounds realistic; you hear occasional light "thump" sounds as the active player repeatedly touches the ball in front, and there's a healthy "thwack" for shots and passing between players. The impressive physics means the ball slows down as it rolls across the field. You can pass to players that aren't on the screen; the computer adjusts play so that when one player leaves the screen, it wraps around, and a "potential player" is ready for the ball when the camera pans over. It gives the effect of a team with more players than are shown at any one time. Of course, you can manipulate this and intercept your opponent by "wrapping around" the edges of the screen on purpose.

Shoot the ball out of bounds and you'll hear the referee blow his whistle; from there, you can throw in, go for a goal kick, or set up a corner kick. There are no penalty kicks in this game, and a buzzer signals the end of each period. A "Sudden Death" overtime kicks off if the score is tied at the end of the second half; this period lasts seven and a half minutes. The only strange thing is that you can never stop to pass; you can only pass while running. Four skill levels are available: rookie, collegiate, semi-pro, and pro, all of which only affect game speed. No soccer video game was as good as this one when it came out; it was another soaring achievement for Mattel. "The three-quarter perspective and the scrolling playfield make this game fascinating even to those who don't care for the real sport," Kunkel and Katz wrote in *Video*.[12]

PGA Golf (APh/Mattel, November 1980)

Years before *Mean 18* and *Links* redefined the sport for the computer age, Intellivision showed us the future with *PGA Golf*. It's a strikingly realistic simulation given the confines of an aerial view of single-screen holes. Each game consists of nine consecutive holes. Unlike many Intellivision games, *PGA Golf* has only one skill level. The difficulty increases as you progress through the nine holes. You can choose Medal Play (total strokes, low score wins), Match Play (total holes won, high score wins), or Best Ball (in partner play, the best score by either player for each hole is used as the team score). You start by choosing how many players (from one to four); whoever's ball is farthest from the hole takes the next stroke on each turn. The player that completes a hole in the fewest strokes gets to tee off first on the next hole.

PGA Golf takes full advantage of the Intellivision's sophisticated controller design. Before each shot, you must judge the distance required and then choose the club and type of swing using the controller. Your club options include a driver for teeing off, two woods (#3 and #5), four irons (#3, #5, #7, and #9), a wedge, and a putter for the greens. The manual shows the approximate distances in yards for each club and swing in a table, and it says that the full width of the screen is approximately 580 yards, which helps you judge the distances in context. Later diagrams show the ball's trajectory with various irons and woods. The game also models each type of club's effectiveness in various terrains; for example, the #3 and #5 woods are unpredictable in the rough, whereas the irons work as if they're two sizes smaller in the rough (a #5 becomes a #9, for example). In sand traps, only the wedge works well; the #3 and #5 woods are ineffective and even the irons are unpredictable. Choosing the right club each time makes a huge difference in how well you do in the game.

For the swing, you aim using the 16-position direction disc—a white bar moves around the ball in play to show where the right-handed golfer is standing in relation to the ball and which way the stroke will aim. Press one of the action buttons to swing away. Which side button you press determines whether you want a short swing (bottom-right side), a medium swing (bottom-left side), or a long swing (either top side button). Then, press the same action button a second time while watching the figure in the screen's top-left corner. You want to press the button before the bottom to hook left, at the bottom to send the ball straight ahead, or after the bottom of the swing to slice right. If you forget to press it a second time, the computer will choose randomly, and you can even change a hook to a slice mid-swing with a third button press. You'll hear a swish sound and see the golfer perform the selected swing (short, medium, or long).

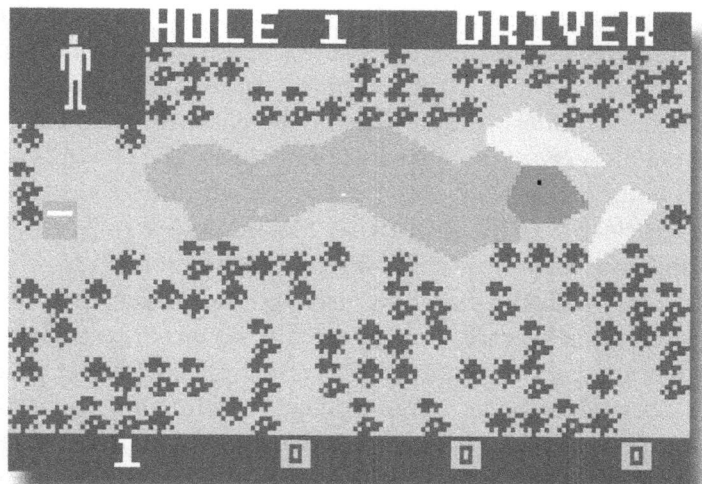

Figure 2.10: *PGA Golf* was a milestone in the development of sports games, thanks to its nine-hole courses and complex swing and ball physics.

Each hole contains various hazards, including yellow sand traps that slow your progress, dark green trees that deflect the ball and cut its distance, and blue water pools that add a one-stroke penalty. You also earn a one-stroke penalty for hitting a shot out of bounds. Holding the Enter key changes the score readout to display the cumulative score for each player. When the ball lands in water, pressing the Choice key lets you choose between playing the ball from either the position on the shore right before it traveled over the water, or from the starting position of the prior stroke. Neither is desirable, so pray that you don't hear a splash sound. Whoever has the lowest score at the end wins the tournament. Programmed by Scott Bishop, *PGA Golf* rewarded repeat play, with nuanced strategies in the physics of the swing that added to your sense of accomplishment as you got better at the game.

Skiing (APh/Mattel, December 1980)

This vertical-scrolling title by Scott Reynolds puts you on the slopes of a treacherous mountain course. It's also an early example of a video game with multicolor sprites—just two colors, in this case, but it's something we only saw for the first time in the arcade with *Galaxian* just a year prior. Using the controller, you must steer your skier through a series of pylons while jumping over icy moguls and avoiding crashing into trees. *Skiing* offers a choice of four speeds, two courses, and 15 different slope grades—the steeper the slope, the faster you ski. Up to six human players can compete by taking turns. The Downhill course is easier and quicker, with wider spaces between the gates and some moguls to clear. The tougher, twisty Slalom course moves the gates closer and runs longer, although it removes the icy moguls.

You steer with the direction disc, and your skier turns in a circular motion the longer you hold the disc down. Pressing left steers clockwise, and pushing right steers counterclockwise. Let go of the disc to ski straight once more, in whatever direction you're facing. You gain speed as you ski downhill and lose speed in turns. Whenever you clear a gate, the left flag changes color. Miss it and you lose credit for that gate; crash into it and you'll destroy the gate and lose speed. The upper side buttons let you turn more sharply—careful, or you'll slip—while the lower-left buttons jump over moguls. You want to time the jumps so you land just beyond the mogul; forget to jump or time it incorrectly, and you'll slip and fall. Reach the finish line and the crowd cheers and whistles for you.

Skiing puts up a good challenge; the only thing wrong with it from today's perspective is that it's a little slow to get going and

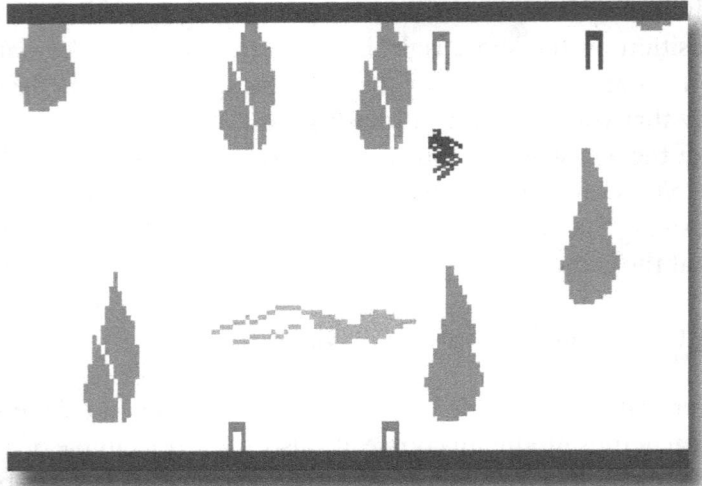

Figure 2.11: Play a game of *Skiing*, and it's all downhill from there. (What?)

build momentum. Which, of course, really puts the incentive on you not to mess up because then you must start from a standstill again. The manual says you're a "safety hazard" if you take more than 150 seconds, a "hot dogger" if you score 51 to 75, and an "Olympic gold medalist" if you can finish the course in under 38 seconds. I am not a gold medalist. For the longer Slalom, a score under 150 seconds is good, and under 105 is Olympics-grade. Emblematic of the style of most Mattel cartridge instruction booklets, *Skiing* starts off with breathless prose: "The slopes are groomed. Skiers are at the top of the course…Blitz through the downhill gates! Jump the moguls and look out for the trees! Race the clock…compete with other skiers! Best time in 3 heats — wins!"

The Intellivision's *Skiing* cartridge landed around the same time as Activision's quality 2600 version, one of the first games the new company released after the four founders famously broke away from Atari in a salary and programming credit dispute. Legend has it that a Mattel programmer needed to look at the original APh source code a few years later. When he did so, "he was startled to find that all variables and subroutines were named with the vilest (and most creative) obscenities."[13] There wasn't much policing back then, as we'll see throughout this book.

Tennis (APh/Mattel, December 1980)

Most tennis video games show a vertical perspective view from one end of the court; the Intellivision's version is distinctive with its horizontal side view. It features larger-than-usual sprites—roughly twice the size of those found in *Football* and *Baseball* and about the same as in *Basketball*. Each sprite is in two colors as in *Skiing*, with the black racquets standing out next to the red and blue players. I won't recap all the rules of tennis, but few differences separate this cartridge from a professional match. If you have the cartridge, the game's detailed 32-page manual gives you plenty of strategies and reveals the depth of gameplay this title offers on the Intellivision.

Tennis takes a stronger-than-expected advantage of the controller design. The disc moves the player in any of 16 directions, always while facing the net. The top upper side buttons swing the racquet hard for deep, powerful serves and low, fast ground strokes—these are tough

74 | Space Battle: The Mattel Intellivision and the First Console War

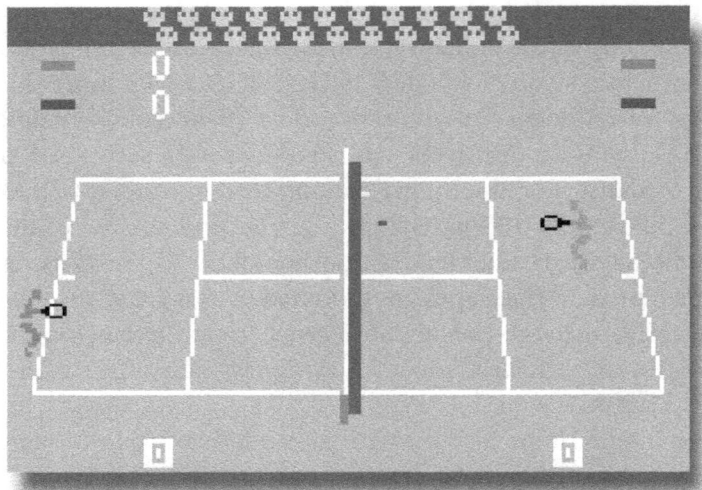

Figure 2.12: An unusual horizontally oriented take in an already overcrowded genre (since Pong!), *Tennis* still manages to feel fresh.

to get right and take practice. The lower buttons allow for a softer serve with an upward curve and a return lob higher in the air, which are easier to get the hang of when first playing the game. In addition, the top three buttons on the overlay, called Service Keys, direct the ball to land in your opponent's inner, center, or outer court.

Timing your serve is key; you press the side button once to toss the ball, and again depending on where you want to place the ball. When returning an opponent's serve, you must let the ball bounce in your court at least once. You can then rush the net and swing hard before the return bounces. Whenever the ball is in the air, keep an eye on its shadow, an unprecedented feature for the time; following the ball's shadow is how you anticipate where it will land. Faults occur if you swing and miss while serving, or if it doesn't bounce the first time or within the lines on a serve. You're allowed one fault when serving. When a ball hits the net and falls to the opponent's side, you play a Let.

One wonderful touch in this game is how the crowd watches the ball as it travels back and forth across the court. The game's biggest downside is that it's another two-player-only title. I would have played this one much more as a kid with a one-player option—even playing today means I must convince a family member to join in, which isn't easy. In comparison with Activision's simple-but-solid 2600 *Tennis*, this one offers more options, deeper strategies, and nicer graphics at the expense of that treasured one-player option. The 2600's version of this sport was halfway decent—something you couldn't say about its bizarre, distorted *Home Run* and *Football* cartridges—but the Intellivision still wins even here.

George Plimpton Ads

The Intellivision's somewhat troubled and extended launch led to some big departures at Mattel Electronics. These included sales director Malcolm Kuhn, marketing vice president Tim Huber, and in what must have seemed earth-shaking in the fall of 1980, both Jeff Rochlis and Ed Krakauer.[14] Mattel Toys and electronic handhelds veteran Joshua Denham became president of Mattel Electronics in September. He brought in Frank O'Connell, a former executive he used to work with from the food industry as his sales and marketing vice president.[15] Chandler had described console sales then as "not moving—people don't know about Intellivision."[16] O'Connell's first job was doing market research, and he found that consumers didn't care so much for the Intellivision's potential as a computer but thought it was superior to the VCS at games.

O'Connell and Denham decided to double down on this. They planned a new series of head-to-head television commercials showing the Intellivision next to the 2600.[17] They landed the perfect spokesperson. In December 1980, Mattel launched the first of many spots featuring the writer George Plimpton. Plimpton compared the Atari 2600's weak sports games, such as *Home Run* and *Football*, with the much superior titles on the Intellivision, which showed realistic players on screen that looked like actual people and baseball and football fields that looked like the real thing. In each commercial, Mattel showed the actual games playing on two televisions to let viewers compare with their own eyes.

"I'll try almost anything," he says from a living room set in one of the first spots, "So when Mattel Electronics asked me to compare their Intellivision games with Atari, I gave it a try. I compared Atari *Baseball* with Intellivision and found Intellivision played much more like real baseball. Then I compared Atari *Football* with Intellivision. Again, Intellivision played more like the real game. In my opinion,

Figure 2.13: Would you trust this man? Many already did, which is why landing George Plimpton for its national advertising campaign was such a coup for Mattel.

if you try them both, there's only one conclusion you can come to: Intellivision." Additional spots show him in baseball and football stadiums, and again in his living room but this time comparing basketball and soccer games between the two systems.

In the commercial for *PGA Golf*, Plimpton is shown walking on a Pebble Beach golf course before going inside to play the Intellivision and Atari 2600. The Intellivision game looks far more realistic, with more complex course designs, expansive fairways and greens, true representations of rough terrain and trees, and better sound effects. And because Mattel secured a license from the Professional Golfers' Association of America for its game, it also sounds like it has an endorsement from the world's top players. Plimpton talks up the Intellivision's high-quality graphics and realism and takes more direct shots at Atari: "With Atari *Golf*, on the other hand, the gameplay is rather simplistic, and the course...not quite up to par."

It was an incredibly effective campaign. None of the Atari games looked like the real thing the way the Intellivision titles did. "Plimpton was well known for his participation in sports," Mattel programmer and later Intellivision brand steward Keith Robinson said later. "What was wonderful about that is he could come out and he

Figure 2.14: George Plimpton had a suave, measured presence that paid dividends for Intellivision marketing as he systematically showed its games looking superior next to Atari.

could show an Atari game screen, and he could show an Intellivision game screen, and people didn't know at that time what a video game really was. It was a brand new item, but people knew what a baseball diamond looked like. On Atari, they didn't see a baseball diamond. On Intellivision, they did. So that really sold our games…you could see the realism because people knew what a sports game should look like, and our games looked like that."[18]

Mattel also featured Plimpton in national magazine ads showing the baseball game comparison under the headline, "Two pictures are worth a thousand words." The general idea was that the Intellivision was a more sophisticated machine than the Atari 2600, with more realistic and complex games. A spokesperson like George Plimpton only accentuated the Intellivision's appearance of sophistication. The phrase "Intelligent Television" spoke to this from the beginning, but the concept was beginning to come into its own—both in the system's expanding game library and consumers' perception of it.

"Two things made Intellivision good," said Al Nilsen, then electronics buyer for JCPenney, in a later interview. "The graphics were superior, less stick figure-oriented, with more bright and vibrant colors. The second thing was the lineup of sports games. Baseball, football, hockey, soccer, backgammon, bowling. Mattel wanted to have every single sport under the sun, all licensed from the right organizations, from the American Backgammon Players Association to the U.S. Chess Federation, to Major League Baseball. Sports really brought new players to video games."[19] Some of the most popular Intellivision cartridges even feature slight variations on the running man character. *Major League Baseball* adds a cap, for example, while *NFL Football* adds a helmet and shoulder pads. The attention to detail was remarkable.

Where's the Keyboard?

What was less good was that Mattel had begun advertising the Keyboard Component nationally, on television and in newspaper ads. A full-age Gottschalk's ad on December 11, 1980, in the *Santa Monica, Calif. Times* presented it right at the top: "Gottschalk's Announces the World Premiere of the Intellivision Keyboard Component by Mattel Electronics…add it to Mattel Electronics' Intellivision Master Component to help learn French, analyze your stocks, lose weight, and more! The most advanced and sophisticated computer-based system ever offered for your home." The advertised price had ballooned to an insane $699.95. The entry fee included Physical Conditioning, Conversational French, and Stock Analysis cassettes "at no charge." The Intellivision Master Component was listed below, still at $269.95. The box for Sylvania's version of the Intellivision showed an inset picture of the Keyboard Component with the Intellivision docked. Retailers continued to add the Keyboard Component to their catalogs. But you still couldn't buy one. In September 1980, Mattel test-marked the unit in Fresno the same way it did the year prior for the Master Component, but it remained unavailable at retail otherwise.[20]

JCPenney was more cautious in its *1980 JCPenney Christmas Book*, advertising in full color the Intellivision Master Component ($269.95) and 10 games ($29.95 each) without mentioning the Keyboard Component. Instead, it advertised the Atari 800 system ($1,080), the 410 Program Cassette Recorder ($89.95), the 820 printer ($599.95), and the 810 disk drive ($699.95). JC Penny also sold the Atari 2600 ($144.95), with cartridges ranging from $19.75 to $35.95. Other local ads of the day showed the Intellivision at $239.95 and the Atari 2600 at $139.95. The only saving grace was that mainstream families weren't yet convinced they needed a computer. Competing full-blown computers from Apple, Atari, and Commodore remained even more expensive, with only the Radio Shack TRS-80 approaching affordability that year.[21]

A Strong First Year

Fortunately, consumers didn't care about the delay. Video game reviews were still a niche business, but Bill Kunkel and Arnie Katz praised the Intellivision in *Video*'s "Arcade Alley" column in the July 1980 issue. "Mattel's recent introduction of its Intellivision computer system has turned the video game world topsy-turvy," they wrote. "A single session at the controls of this second generation programmable game-player will convince even hardened skeptics that home arcades will never be quite the same...It won't be possible to fully assess Intellivision as a modular computer until the rest of the components, including a full keyboard and a cassette tape deck, become available later this year. However, the performance of Mattel's 'master component,' the heart of the system, leaves no doubt about Intellivision's worth as a home arcade. It may not be perfect, but it's certainly the best unit offered so far to players of electronic video games."

The article went on to say that the system will deliver "the most sophisticated games this side of the complex simulations designed for high-level computers right in their own living rooms." It evangelized the hardware and controllers, which it called a "bold departure from the standard joystick." It praised *Las Vegas Poker & Blackjack*, *Armor Battle*, and the rest of the initial cartridge lineup: "[The Intellivision has] some of the most fascinating games ever displayed on a TV screen," Kunkel and Laney Jr. continued. "This home arcade won't necessarily make rival machines obsolete, but every cartridge in the Mattel line is at least marginally superior to all other games of the same general type. At present, there's a definite lack of solitaire games, but there's already a fair selection of head-to-head contests with more to follow soon."

Mattel sold out its entire first production run of 175,000 Intellivision consoles in 1980, thanks in part to the first Plimpton commercials. Combined with its electronic handhelds, Mattel Electronics brought in skyrocketing revenue for the company. The Intellivision's higher price next to the Atari 2600 proved a sticking point for many consumers. But the main problem Mattel faced wasn't pricing or the delayed Keyboard Component. It was demand for a new game from Atari, the long-awaited 2600 conversion of Taito's wildly popular *Space Invaders* coin-op. The 2600 cartridge wasn't a perfect replica of the arcade game, but it was excellent, and everyone wanted it.

Mattel would soon have to address this. APh Technological Consulting had already programmed 19 Intellivision games, but the company realized it needed more firepower to remain competitive. It formed an internal development team headed by Don Daglow, a seminal game programmer who had written *Dungeon* and *Baseball* for mainframe systems. "We absolutely felt we could catch up with Atari because the Intellivision was next generation compared to the Atari 2600—it was that much better," said Daglow.[22] For that, though, Mattel's game library would have to expand.

3 | Smash

At the 1981 Consumer Electronics Show, Mattel reiterated its plans for conquering the rapidly expanding home computer market. "By adding the keyboard component to the Intellivision 'master' game unit," *InfoWorld* reported, "Mattel has given computer capabilities to Mattel Electronics games." It added that the console cost $300, the keyboard cost $700, and the keyboard was slated for release in the second quarter of 1981.

Marketing vice president Frank O'Connell said in the article that the company had no plans to encourage third-party software development and had been testing training methods for salespeople in department stores. "With a large consumer following in the areas of games and toys, and the merchandising experience in the consumer arena, Mattel may prove to be a strong player in the race for sales."[1]

The Mattel Intellivision and its sports games were selling well. But many of the system's first titles were two-player only, and there was a dearth of action games. The fabled toy company had to release compelling arcade-style shooters and racing cartridges to grab the attention of people who gravitated to the Atari 2600 to play home versions of their favorite coin-ops. But Atari owned the rights to many of the most popular arcade machines. Mattel had to course-correct and create its own one-player action games. Some were obvious clones of hit coin-ops; a kinder way to put it was they were "unofficial ports."

Others served as hybrids of two existing games, creating a third one that was equally compelling.

It turned out to be a winning strategy.

Astrosmash (APh/Mattel, October 1981)

In Astrosmash, a frenetic, fixed-screen space shooter, your job is to destroy as many objects falling from the sky as possible. They include multicolored meteors falling from the sky in two different sizes, two kinds of white spinning bombs, an attack flying saucer, and pulsating homing missiles. Shoot a large meteor and it splits into two smaller ones that must be destroyed (each for double points). Whenever a meteor hits the ground, it disappears and you lose points. If anything collides with you, or a spinning bomb hits the ground, your cannon explodes dramatically, and you lose a life. Unable to license *Space Invaders* or *Asteroids*, Mattel decided to smoosh them together to excellent effect.

The controls are simple; you move the laser left and right with the disc, while all four side buttons act as triggers, so you can use whichever one is the most comfortable. The overlay depicts a giant laser cannon with three buttons across the top. Single-shot firing mode, the default, is set with the top-left button on the keypad; you shoot one laser each time you press a trigger. The center button activates automatic firing mode, where the computer shoots three times per second for you all the time—quick, but not as quick as you can manually in single-shot mode if you are fast enough. The Hyper-Space button on the right immediately relocates you to a different part of the terrain, which can be good or bad, just like in *Asteroids*.

At the start of the game, the sky is black. When you score 1,000 points, the sky changes to blue and a 2x multiplier goes into effect. The sky is purple at 5,000, turquoise at 20,000, and gray at 50,000. The game gets faster the further you progress. At 100,000 points, the sky returns to black and stops changing color, but a 6x multiplier activates; play gets progressively tougher after 200,000, 500,000, and 1 million points. It seemed like a big deal whenever the screen changed color, especially when playing on a big television (which meant a 25-inch set then). I first encountered the phenomenon in arcades with *Missile Command*. In this game, it had a similar "wow" effect.

Figure 3.1: The terrific *Astrosmash* gave the Intellivision the kind of space shoot-'em-up it desperately needed.

The guided missiles are tough; they act like smart bombs and seek you out. After 20,000 points, attack UFOs appear; these are worth the most points. Although *Astrosmash* seems challenging at first, the computer is generous with free lives: You get one every 1,000 points. More significant is an impressive feature coded into the AI: The game adapts to the player's skill level. Whenever you die, the game becomes temporarily easier; something similar happens with Activision's *Kaboom!* on the 2600. Regardless, *Astrosmash*'s difficulty level always seems just about right for whomever is playing.

The similarity to *Asteroids* and *Space Invaders* was obvious, but there was even more to it. The game began life as *Meteor!*, an outright clone of *Asteroids*. Programmer John Sohl had plenty of room left, so he coded a variation called *Avalanche* with the same graphics and sound effects. That one turned out to be more fun. Mattel's lawyers ended up nixing *Meteor!* to avoid a lawsuit with Atari, so Sohl modified the code to run the *Avalanche* version on bootup each time.[2] (Rumor has it that if you hit the console's Reset button just right, very rarely, the *Meteor!* version comes up; I've never been able to make this happen.)[3]

I'm glad I was too young to read reviews describing the pacing as "plodding" (as *Video* said) in the early stages. I never noticed that then, although I suppose I can see now how one could think that. But

I had zero problems with the pacing when the game came out. I was a lucky kid; I remember receiving *Astrosmash* on Christmas Eve and then several *Star Wars* ships, including the Millennium Falcon, for Christmas that year. As much as I loved *Star Wars*, I remember asking when I was done opening presents, "Is it okay if I go play *Astrosmash*?" I don't know why I remember that so clearly, although it was obviously an awesome Christmas morning. But I became addicted to the game, and only after I realized some months later that I could seemingly play forever did I lose interest.

In late 1982, Mattel replaced the pack-in *Las Vegas Poker & Blackjack* with *Astrosmash*, a wise move by all accounts. By June 1983, the company had shipped 984,900 copies of *Astrosmash*, making it the third most distributed game for the Intellivision after *Major League Baseball* and *Las Vegas Poker & Blackjack*; the game went on to sell some 2 million copies.[4] To give you an idea of the game's popularity, Sheldon wore an *Astrosmash* T-shirt in an episode of *The Big Bang Theory*. So did Cisco in *The Flash*. The Atari 2600 already had some excellent space games by 1981, but none were like this.

Snafu (Mattel, October 1981)

Atari's *Surround* may have been the first *Snake*-like game, where each player left trails on the playfield and aimed to cause the opposing player to crash first. But Mattel's *Snafu* improved the concept in numerous ways. It plays Mattel's *Arkanoid* to Atari's *Breakout* and is one of the best games on the Intellivision. The object is to create a maze and trap the opposing players before they do the same to you. The entire time you're moving, you leave a trail that you can use to block opponents. The problem is you can't escape through it either. A beep sounds when you're about to crash, a high-pitched one for blue and a low-pitched one for red. Whenever a serpent is eliminated, the others remaining receive one point each. If two collide, they're eliminated, and the remaining each earn two points.

Twelve of the 16 games are variations of the trapping mechanic. Any trail that hits the edge of the screen or contacts another trail, an obstacle, or itself will be eliminated. The other four (4, 8, 12, and 16) are biting variations for two human players with just two serpents. You must connect your serpent's head to an opponent's tail to bite off one link at a time. Each snake starts with 10 links and periodically grows new ones (up to 20), depending on the speed of the game selected; it takes anywhere from 20 to 40 seconds. Whoever is left at the end wins.

The overlay is unnecessary, although it looks nice (like all the overlays do). It's simply artwork for the numeric keypad, and the side buttons don't do anything. You start by choosing one of four speeds, as in many other early Intellivision games. Then choose one of 16 game variations and how many rounds you want to play. Some variations enable diagonal movement, some are for two serpents instead of four, in some trails remain even when eliminated, and some contain obstacles. For all games, all you need to play is the direction disc, which functions as a four- or eight-way pad depending on the variation selected.

The obstacle variations are fascinating, as they scatter various different-colored objects around the screen. And in variations with diagonal movement, you can cross another serpent's trail if both are diagonally moving when it happens, and it's in one of the spaces between the links. Whenever the game is down to you and one other serpent, or if it's a variation that starts with only two serpents, you'll hear music to signify "showdown" mode. One of two multivoice, snakelike songs will play, with clever delay and rattling effects to liven up the tracks. Hissing and rattling are occasionally audible as the snakes travel around the board. For such a simple game, *Snafu* is colorful, sounds good, and is an excellent head-to-head title. It's also notable in that it's the only game released during the Intellivision's heyday to use STIC's Colored Squares mode, where each tile had four different color 4x4 blocks.[5]

"I really enjoyed *Snafu*, that was my favorite game, I worked on that by myself, and the only thing I didn't like about it was the name marketing picked for it," said Mike Minkoff in a company headquarters video. "I had no idea what Snafu had to do with it. I originally called it 'Snakessss' with a bunch of esses on the end. All I could see that was similar was that it started with SNA, and…" He shrugged. "*Snafu*. It was a fun game."[6] Anyone familiar with military history knows "SNAFU" is an acronym for something. Curiously, the game's manual never mentions this.

The game dynamic inherent in *Snafu* and *Surround* had staying power. Early Nokia cell phones became famous for including *Snake*, a

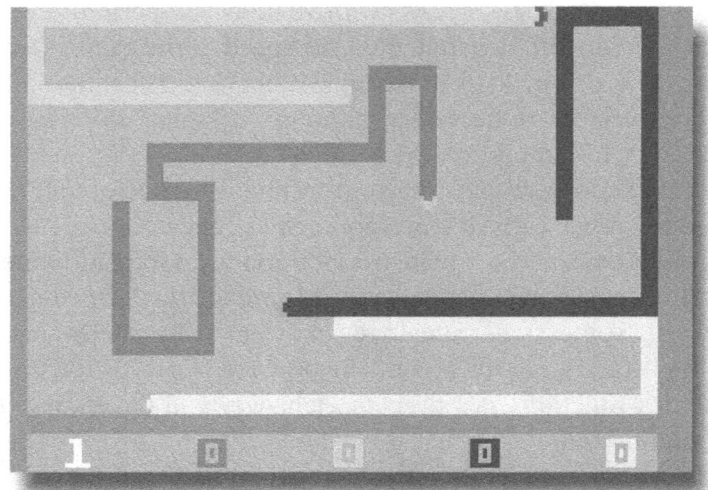

Figure 3.2: Why does it always have to be snakes? Just don't show this one to Indiana Jones.

simpler game playable on many of the company's handsets beginning in 1997. But nothing beat two human players going after each other on a big screen.

PBA Bowling (Mattel, July 1981)

The startlingly realistic *PBA Bowling*, developed by Rich Levine and Mike Minkoff, depicted a huge sprite for the player, actual multilane graphics, and a visual frame-by-frame scorecard. The graphics practically jumped out of the Intellivision game catalog. Each time you tossed the ball and it began rolling down the lane, the game switched to a vertical perspective showing the pins and the approach and angle you took. Levine was a bowling enthusiast and had already programmed Mattel's *Bowling* electronic handheld; this was the duo's first Intellivision game.[7]

At the start, you choose '5' for a regular bowling game or '6' for a Pick-Up Spares game, and then choose from one to four players. Each player uses the keypad keys to select three key attributes: the alley slickness (from 0 to 10, with 0 being the slowest and 10 the fastest), the ball weight (from 7 to 16 pounds, with heavier balls offering more pin action and lighter weights delivering more ball deflection), and their bowling hand (left, which curves the ball to the right, or vice versa).

The game presents a three-dimensional side view of the alley and bowler. Tap the disc on any edge to pick up the ball. The left side buttons move the bowler at the line up and down. Pressing the bottom-right button starts your toss; you hold it while watching the white spotter ball that sweeps back and forth across the alley. This spot shows where the ball will pass about a third of the way down the alley. Once you have the right location, release the button and the bowler moves up and release the ball. At this point, you press the edge of the disc that corresponds to how you want the ball to curve. The right edge directs the ball straight, and to the lower right indicates a slight reverse curve. The rest of the way around, from 2 o'clock backward to 6 o'clock, increases the curve. If you leave the disc alone, the game will randomly choose your curve which you do not want to happen.

One final option is to cue up a sharp breaking curve at the far end if you're trying to nail a split and knock out pins on both sides. You do this by waiting until your arm has begun its downward swing. At that point, you press the top-right side "Loft" button; how late you press it determines how pronounced the final curve of the ball is. You can alternate which scores are showing, and which set of five (the

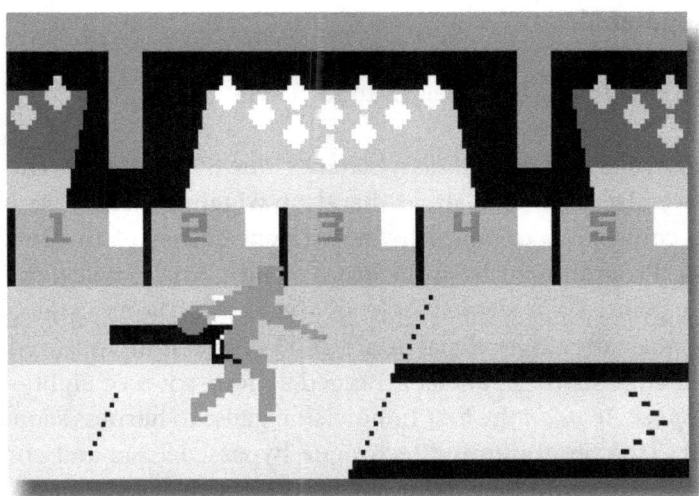

Figure 3.3: *PBA Bowling* **combined excellent graphics with surprisingly deep gameplay.**

first five frames or the last) by pressing the appropriate keys on the overlay. The manual also details several key strategies that help you refine your throw and control the variables involved, and how they change in different kinds of alleys and with different ball weights.

Once the release is complete and the ball passes the spotter marks in the lane, the view shifts to a top-down presentation of the alley. The ball rolls realistically, with the holes turning—try that on the Atari 2600!—and the view goes into slow motion to show the pins move and tumble. Then the sweep comes down to clear the way for the next round. The "Pick-Up Spares" game gives you two chances to knock down the pins on 32 randomly occurring pin configurations, all of which are technically possible to "make," although some are exceedingly difficult. The game plays a multivoice musical fanfare (Tchaikovsky) if you score above 200, or 75 in the Pick-Up Spares game.

"*PBA Bowling* achieves greatness by boldly striking out in a new direction that departs markedly from all pin games on the market today," Kunkel and Katz wrote in *Video*. "[It] sets graphics standards for games of this kind. Multiple views of the action give us a feeling of realism and involvement unmatched by any other bowling cartridge."[8] I never had this one as a kid, but I certainly play it now. So do many other people, if the various forum threads about Intellivision bowling leagues on AtariAge are any indication. Maybe I'll join one on the next go-around...

Space Armada (APh/Mattel, October 1981)

The colorful *Space Armada* is a blatant clone of *Space Invaders*. It features oversize, animated aliens that drop wiggling laser shots like the arcade coin-op, as opposed to the straight dashes of the 2600 conversion. Programmed by John Brooks and Chris Hawley, the game filled a giant, alien-shaped hole in the Intellivision's catalog more than a year after the official Atari 2600 conversion appeared. Each armada consists of 32 aliens arranged as four rows of eight—which made *Space Armada* the first Intellivision game to harness sequencing GRAM. This programming technique bypassed Exec and conveyed the illusion of more than eight objects on screen at once.[9]

You start *Space Armada* with six laser guns and three bunkers. The massive armada advances slowly, crawling across the screen. Each

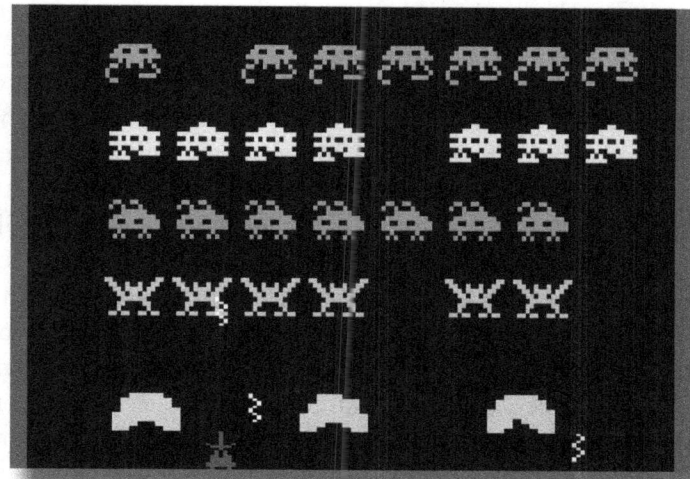

Figure 3.4: Mattel couldn't license *Space Invaders*, so it did what countless other video game developers did and cloned it.

time it reaches the edge, all the aliens drop down a level and then march in the other direction. You must clear them all before a single alien lands. Succeed, and you move on to the next, tougher board; fail, and you lose a life. Each time an alien bomb vaporizes you, your score and reserve cannons briefly show before the action continues.

Interestingly, you can control the position of where you appear by holding the disc left or right; otherwise, your next cannon appears in the center. The game is a bit more musical. It sounds different tones as you blast away each alien against the *Jaws*-like familiar beating backdrop that speeds up as you near the end of each board. A red flying saucer periodically soars silently across the top of the screen. Shoot it, and you hear the trademark Intellivision "gunshot" sound. It's tough to squeeze a shot between the columns of giant aliens, though.

Between the slow pace, large target sizes, and starting with six cannons, *Space Armada* seems easy compared with the 2600 version, at least on the lower levels. When you get to the last two aliens, the pace isn't as fast on screen, and if you kill the first alien in the "lead," the second one plows into the explosion of the first one and dies. On the flip side, because the aliens are so much larger, they only traverse the screen five times before they reach the ground. Get to the third board, though, and things become more challenging as the aliens begin dropping longer, brown bombs that explode on landing. Later, purple guided missiles are even tougher to avoid. Worse, some aliens become invisible—meaning you must remember the armada's structure and not accidentally forget to destroy one before it lands. Aliens are worth 10 points each on the first screen, 20 on the second, and so on. The flying saucer is worth a random multiplier of 1x to 32x the current alien value, and shooting it also repairs your most damaged bunker.

Another interesting quirk is Practice mode, which lets you play the last level you got to at a slower pace and with six new cannons. Choosing Practice mode when you first insert the cartridge means you play the first level at a slower speed. Aside from the minor gameplay differences, the only real issue with *Space Armada* is the stiff, side-mounted Fire buttons on the controllers. Playing for long periods isn't as comfortable as the arcade and 2600 versions. Get past that—we all did—and you'll have a good time with this one, even if *Astrosmash* is superior.

Triple Action (APh/Mattel, October 1981)

One of the most enjoyable early cartridges, *Triple Action* defines "pick-up-and-play." It was conceived as a quick way to bring six Atari

Figure 3.5: *Triple Action* **puts you and a friend in tanks, biplanes, or cars, depending on your mood.**

coin-op games to the Intellivision at once to give the console some action games that weren't about sports or gambling. Hilariously, APh programmers referred to it internally as "Some of Theirs."[10] The cartridge wouldn't have enough room for six, so they dropped it to five, only to then jettison "Brickout!" (a *Breakout* clone) and "Hockey" (a *Pong* clone) because Mattel's legal department thought they were too close for comfort.[11]

The three remaining minigames still make for a fun time. Plug in the cartridge, power up the console, and you'll see a menu displaying "Battle Tanks," "Car Racing," and "Biplanes." The controller overlays are simple; depending on the game, the top side buttons either accelerate the car or fire the gun, and the bottom side buttons brake the car or move the tank and plane. Otherwise, you only need the top four numbers to select in-game options; the rest of the buttons do nothing.

"Battle Tanks" is essentially a lightweight, faster version of *Armor Battle*—you stalk your opponent's tank while avoiding their shots, hiding behind walls for cover, and steering clear of shots that ricochet around the board. You can shoot three shells at once and must wait for at least one to disappear off the screen before you can fire again. Whoever gets 15 points first wins the battle. Four options let you toggle long and short-range bouncing shells and whether they bounce.

In "Car Racing," you compete against another player as you each drive up two-lane roads, like *Street Racer* on the Atari 2600. The first player to drive 100 miles as indicated on their odometer, while avoiding slowpoke, weaving computer-controlled cars, and steering around wrecks wins the game. Options are available for normal traffic and heavy traffic. As much as I love car racing games, this one is the weakest of the three, as there's not much challenge to accelerating and sometimes switching lanes; you don't feel like you're driving.

"Biplanes" is the best of the lot. You each fly a plane around the screen, doing loop-de-loops, diving, flying upside down, and otherwise soaring among the clouds as you try to shoot each other out of the sky. Whoever gets 15 points first wins. You can't climb too fast, or your plane starts to stall and drift downward; then you must build some momentum by heading straight for the ground on purpose to pull up at the last minute and save your plane. Periodically, a balloon sets off; you can shoot it for extra points. Options are available in this one for short or long-range bullets. Contemporary reviews agreed. *Computer & Video Games* said, "There's real skill when you take to the airways in *Triple Action*,"[12] and *Video* magazine called both the "Biplanes" and "Battle Tanks" games "pure arcade action" and "delightful in many respects."[13]

This game doesn't get a lot of love because of its simplicity, and you need two players for all three games to get the most out of the cartridge. The "action," such as it is, becomes compelling with the competitive element added. I spent many hours playing "Biplanes"; that was the only one I didn't mind playing alone, as it was fun to soar through the clouds and try all kinds of tricks. But when a friend came over, it was so much better.

Star Strike (APh/Mattel, December 1981)

This technically impressive nail-biter of a game was ahead of its time. The object is to destroy an alien base station before Earth passes over its launch trench and becomes vulnerable to destruction. You must take out scores of deadly enemy fighters, specifically five red spaceships, to destroy the station. If you take too long and Earth aligns with the trench, and then you miss a red spaceship, it turns into a missile that blows Earth to pieces.

You fly your ship through a massive, three-dimensional trench. The game conveys a sense of speed by alternating the trench's dark and light green sections while the starry sky above shows you're in deep space, with a giant, cratered moon to the left. As the game progresses, the Earth peeks from behind it and begins crossing the sky over the trench. The controller overlay shows the same image; the direction disc controls your ship, and the top three buttons on the keypad set your ship's speed to Warp 1, Warp 2, or Warp 3. The side action buttons on the top fire lasers, while the bottom ones bomb targets.

Enemy fighters appear in pairs behind your ship and fire white lasers at you as soon as they're in range. Once they fly in front, they turn from dark blue to light blue—which means you can shoot them now. Keep an eye on your shadow in the trench. It gives you an idea of your altitude, which is helpful for shooting enemies and avoiding collisions. When the all-important red targets appear, a warning alarm beeps just before it's time to release a bomb—nail the shot and the screen will shake from the explosion. You can't fire your air-to-air lasers while a

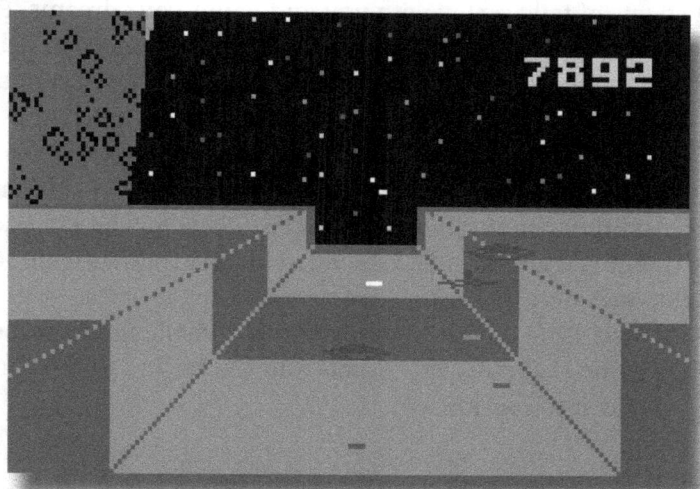

Figure 3.6: In *Star Strike*, it's you against the aliens and the clock in a race to save civilization.

bomb is falling. Destroy the fifth target, and the alien station explodes, trench and all. Congratulations—you just saved the Earth!

If you get hit, your ship catches fire and becomes momentarily more challenging to control. You'll climb slowly, bank left or right sluggishly, or fly at a fixed speed. Sometimes your radar malfunctions, or your lasers go on the fritz and only produce white noise when fired. The game has six difficulty levels, not the usual four; in addition to pressing the disc to start a game at the default level 4, you can choose one of three easier and two harder levels, denoted by stars on the keypad. On the more challenging levels, you'll have less time to bomb the five targets, and on the hardest, you can't miss even once. In a twist, you start with 8,000 points, and your score decreases rapidly as you play. Shoot an alien ship to add 250 points (or fewer at higher difficulty levels). Miss a red target once the Earth is fully in view and aligned with the trench, and that's it—the game treats you to a cinematic display of the Earth's destruction.

When I first went to play this game again after many years, I felt a little nervous, like I did when I recently replayed *Space Battle*. This one had even more of an effect on me when I was a kid. It was just tough, and like *Missile Command* when it flashes "The End" and then the words blow up in a sea of nuclear explosions, the images and sound effects of failure stay with you and haunt your dreams. Part of the problem is that if you accidentally crash into another fighter—something you can easily do, even within the first few seconds—the game ends right then and there. It forces you to watch the Earth destruction sequence, which you can't exit without pressing the Reset button or turning off the console. The game makes you sit there and contemplate the loss of billions of people. Okay, maybe I'm taking it too hard. But is it any wonder why it felt almost traumatizing when I was eight years old?

With that little caveat, *Star Strike* is a challenging, somewhat repetitive game that nails the visuals and the feeling of tension. Just try not to take it too seriously.

PlayCable

Around the time of the Intellivision's national release, Mattel began experimenting with a new online service that let Intellivision owners download games. It was the first of its kind, a Mattel and General Instrument joint venture that required the use of an adapter manufactured by Jerrold, a maker of cable television equipment General Instrument had acquired in 1967. Cable subscribers used the service with the PlayCable adapter to download games and play them on the Intellivision. Inklings of it were reported before the Intellivision even got its name, in the May 21, 1979, issue of *Weekly Television Digest With Consumer Electronics*, albeit with a lowercase "c":

> Mattel executives weren't on hand to comment at demonstration of Mattel-Jerrold cable-game system in N.Y. Playcable is a system allowing cable TV systems to market video game software to subscribers who own Mattel programmables. Game is connected to the headend computer of a one-way CATV system through a $50 Jerrold "emulator," which fits in game's cartridge slot. User selects a program from library of 20-40 games in the headend computer, punches in a number, and the program is loaded into the video game [system] in 5-7 sec. Playcable will begin a six-month market test on four cable systems in October…Individual cable systems will market emulators to subscribers and charge $5 to $10 monthly for Playcable service. Game (and later, education

and home finance) programs in the headend unit will be rotated monthly, and can't be recorded by the user. The company to market Playcable will be a 50-50 joint venture of Mattel and Jerrold parent GI.

The above is pretty much how it went. In 1980, PlayCable was test-marketed in four cities—Rochester, Minnesota; Jackson, Mississippi; Moline, Illinois; and Boise, Idaho. GI added nine more cities across the U.S. the following year, including Fayetteville, New York. PlayCable cost between $6 and $10 to subscribe at first, depending on the regional service.[14] You needed to buy the $48 PlayCable adapter, which plugged into the Intellivision's cartridge port and connected to your cable box. The package also came with a small brown cardboard box with modified game instruction manuals that replaced the standard play setup steps with those for accessing the game on PlayCable.[15]

On the other end of the line, a $12,000 DEC PDP-11 minicomputer broadcasted the service through a dedicated data channel in the unused FM band (88–108MHz) in the cable.[16] Players tuned their cable box to a channel that displayed a menu of available titles. By keying in a number on the Intellivision's keypad, you selected the game you wanted to play. Downloading a title took up to 20 seconds; 15 were available at any one time, and it would say "PlayCable Presents" instead of "Mattel Electronics Presents" on the title screen. The games disappeared once you turned the console off because it had no internal or external storage.

The program expanded nationally in late 1982. It cost more by then—$8 to $13 per month[17]—but PlayCable expanded the number of games available simultaneously and continued to add more games to the service. As it did so, it mailed out new instruction manuals and overlays to PlayCable subscribers to ensure they could play the new games.[18] Sometimes it removed older, less popular titles. The company signed up Mickey Mantle as a spokesperson. At least four commercials featuring Mantle ran in different parts of the country, advertising how with PlayCable, you could play any game you want for $12 per month—"Make one call and you'll play 'em all without cartridges," and that to gain access to more than $500 worth of games, it cost less than half what a single game cartridge cost (typically $25, as shown in the on-screen text). One of the commercials recalled

Figure 3.7: The PlayCable adapter and a monthly subscription gave you access to several dozen games you could download and play whenever you wanted.

the earlier George Plimpton spots. It showed Mantle next to a cardboard cutout of a Plimpton likeness, standing behind two TV screens comparing Atari and Intellivision. Mantle says, "PlayCable: Only a millionaire would want to play any other way" while tweaking the cardboard cutout's ear.[19]

By 1983, some 650,000 households in America could access PlayCable—still a small number, as cable TV in the home didn't go mainstream until the 1990s. But of that select group, only 3 percent subscribed to PlayCable.[20] Part of the problem was that the commercials omitted the part about needing to buy the PlayCable adapter, which cost $48 to $57 depending on the provider. The adapter had only 6KB of RAM, so later titles didn't work, and Mattel also blocked third-party companies from participating. By the time the system shut down in 1984, 47 Mattel titles had worked over PlayCable, but the requirements and service costs kept most people from subscribing. It would take decades before the technology caught up and people became more amenable to subscription-based streaming services. Even now, few love the increasingly high monthly fees and the necessity of subscribing to multiple services to get everything they want.

TV Powww

The Intellivision factored into another innovative if short-lived technology, although Mattel had nothing to do with it. Starting around 1980, many television stations across the country began to offer variations of *TV Powww*, a franchised television game "show" with competitive video game playing from home, but usually shot in brief episodes of just a few minutes long. These ran as filler between two different shows in the schedule. These programs started with Fairchild Channel F games but soon upgraded to Intellivision titles.

I grew up in New York City, so our local version was TV PIXX, which ran on WPIX channel 11 on weekday afternoons. When you called into the station, they'd put up a customized version of a familiar Intellivision game such as *Space Battle*, but with only the action sequence and an oversize crosshair designed just for the program. You had to say "PIX" whenever you wanted to fire the lasers. If you scored high enough, you'd win a prize.

I never called in, but I loved watching other people compete. I watched to see if they got the timing right, as if they were pressing a Fire button for real. It looked correctly timed to viewers, but the person playing the game experienced lag if the station lacked the necessary

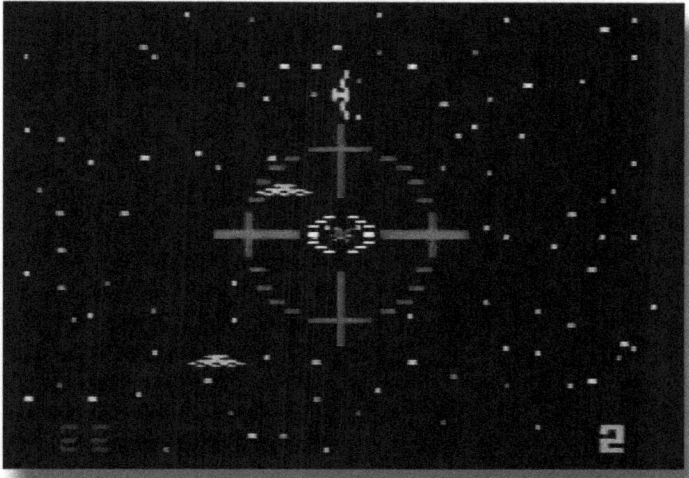

Figure 3.8: Call your TV station and you may get a chance to win prizes when playing one of several console games with TV Powww, including this tweaked version of *Space Battle*.

special voice-activated controllers. In those cases, the station had an employee just manually press the Fire button whenever the person said "PIX" over the phone.[21] Maybe I should have thought of starting my own company like Twitch back then. I could have been a zillionaire.

The 1981 Holiday Season

Mattel's national ad campaign with George Plimpton sparked a battle with Atari as the 1981 holiday season approached. The Intellivision was clearly superior in sports games, and it was holding its own in other genres as well. Atari soon responded with commercials showing its wide variety of arcade games such as *Missile Command* and *Asteroids*, pointing out that you couldn't compare them with the Intellivision because the Intellivision didn't even have those games.[22] Atari also spoofed George Plimpton, showing a child wearing glasses "who speaks in adolescent high-brow tones," *The New York Times* wrote, only to admit that "nobody compares" with Atari. In turn, Mattel ran more commercials where Plimpton showed its titles were better than the 2600's genuine arcade translations and spoofed the kid in glasses.

Atari filed complaints with the television networks, and newspapers covered the back-and-forth with some zest. "Atari, a division of Warner Communications Inc., owns the television video game rights to many familiar arcade games that focus on outer space and intergalactic battle," wrote *The New York Times* on December 14, 1981. "The interloper, Intellivision, a unit of Mattel Inc., is trying to break into a market where Atari has been the leader."[23]

It got ugly quickly. "We went to the networks because the Intellivision commercial is misleading," said Atari president Ray Kassar. "NBC and ABC reviewed all the facts and decided that Intellivision was indeed misleading the facts." CBS continued to run the ads, but ABC and NBC pulled them from both companies.[24] Controversy aside, Mattel Electronics more than quadrupled its Intellivision sales in 1981, with 900,000 units sold and a 27% market share.[25]

More Keyboard Trouble

By the end of 1981, you still couldn't buy the Keyboard Component in stores. One of the most famous bits of trivia about the Intellivision concerns the Keyboard Component, a holiday party, and a particular up-and-coming comedian named Jay Leno. Mattel hired him to entertain employees at its 1981 Christmas party. He tore the house down with this line: "You know what the three big lies are, don't you? 'The check is in the mail,' 'I'll still respect you in the morning,' and 'the Keyboard will be out in the spring.'"[26]

The reasons for the delay were complex. Mattel engineers continued to run into technical problems with the design of the Keyboard Component. It worked, more or less. But it cost way too much to produce, so management held back the release to give the team more time to tinker with the design and bring costs down. They didn't have much success. Since Mattel Electronics employees used to carry business cards with the slogan, "Talk to us…We hear the signals," you would think someone higher up would get wind of the ongoing issues.[27]

Unfortunately for Mattel, consumers noticed the Keyboard Component's absence at retail. They began to file complaints that they had purchased the Intellivision with the explicit expectation the Keyboard Component would soon become available and they could use the system as a computer. The Federal Trade Commission picked up on this and began investigating Mattel Electronics for fraud.[28] The commission eventually concluded Mattel had made claims that constituted "deceptive advertising" for failing to release the promised upgrade and ordered the company to pay $10,000 per month in fines until it was released.[29] Mattel defended itself by saying they were already test-marketing the Keyboard Component in cities such as Seattle and New Orleans (although scant evidence remains of this). But Mattel immediately began to sell the Keyboard Component and thermal printer to consumers via mail-order.[30] You could order some software programmed in CP6160 assembly for the Keyboard Component, such as Conversational French, Jack LaLanne's Physical Conditioning, Jeane Dixon's Astrology, and Spelling Challenge. The rest, including Guitar Lessons & Music Composition and Speed Reading, were BASIC programs that also required a BASIC cartridge that you could use to write your software.[31]

The FTC was satisfied, but this defense didn't hold for long. It wasn't looking good inside Mattel Electronics, either. An internal "Keyboard Overview" document from Feb. 8, 1982, detailed the following issues under "Present Keyboard Status:"

Manufacturing costs $506 to $530 per unit
Highly labor intensive (10 hours per unit)
Difficult manufacturing process
Incomplete and inadequate test programs
Poor quality of finished product (30% return test toy)
Complexity is approximately 10 times greater than Master Component

The letter listed the fixes made to date and suggested further changes. It said to "motivate control of the assembly process," management should "install a quality attitude" and "provide assembly feedback on a timely basis" as well as several ways to "improve the test function" and "install a TEST DISCIPLINE." It also detailed a "4,000 Unit Build Strategy" to be executed by June 1, 1982, with new burn-in and testing steps and an updated comprehensive build component list.[32]

Magazines Cover the Intellivision

Soon, it wouldn't just be television commercials highlighting the new console war. Along with the launch of the computer industry in the mid 1970s came the arrival of dedicated computer magazines such as *Creative Computing, Byte,* and *InfoWorld.* Some of these had scattered articles showing early efforts at computer games. Nothing comparable covered the arcade and console industries despite their inaugural launches in 1971 (*Computer Space,* and soon *Pong*) and 1972 (with Magnavox Odyssey). It went on for most of the rest of the decade.

Bill Kunkel and Arnie Katz, of *Video*'s "Arcade Alley" fame, penned an article for *The New York Times* summarizing the available consoles ahead of the holidays. They wrote that the Mattel still retailed for $299.95 and had 15 games available (though it was almost certainly closer to 20 by that point). They noted that Mattel still hadn't released the computer keyboard and cassette but that "meanwhile, gamers don't mind all that much since it's a fine home arcade as it stands." The story called attention to Mattel's recent efforts to add new action games like *Astrosmash,* "but slower on-screen movement makes such efforts only partly successful." They concluded that "those who enjoy simulated sports and head-to-head competition should definitely consider Intellivision despite its higher price." Katz and Kunkel recommended

Space Battle, *Auto Racing*, and *NASL Soccer* as three standout cartridges to consider purchasing as gifts.[33] In the 1981 Arcade Awards in *Video*, they awarded *Auto Racing* "Best Sports Game."[34]

These two characters were up to something else, though. Around the same time, they launched the world's first consumer video games magazine, *Electronic Games*, which began with the Winter 1981 issue. *Electronic Games* soon went monthly and became popular, igniting a market for critical video game coverage. A competing magazine in the UK called *Computer and Video Games* also launched, although it was more focused on computers. Numerous other publications launched to cover video games directly or expanded their existing sections in computer magazines in 1982 and beyond.

Mattel Electronics Diversifies

Despite the Intellivision's increasing market share as 1982 wore on, Mattel began to hedge its bets, training its eye on competing systems

Figure 3.9: Bill Kunkel and Arnie Katz led the way in critical video game coverage, culminating in the launch of the influential *Electronic Games*.

for potential new revenue streams. Its Mattel Electronics division started prepping 2600 conversions of its best games to sell under the M Network brand. The ports had slightly different names, such as *Armor Ambush* (a port of *Armor Battle*). These 2600 cartridges proved quite good, with an early highlight being *Astroblast* (a conversion of *Astrosmash*). The effort may have unintentionally highlighted the strengths of the 2600. Although the Atari console's graphics and resolution didn't compare well with the Intellivision's, the 2600 played faster and was more challenging in reflex-intensive titles.

Intellivision engineers were already working hard on their next system, a follow-up to the Master Component. An internal video shows a series of graphics tests for the so-called Super-STIC (STIC 1B). The idea was that this new video chip would support much finer on-screen resolution with smoother animation and running-man-style sprites with additional colors. The test video showed improved scenes from *NFL Football* and *Auto Racing* as example footage.[35]

Space Hawk (APh/Mattel, April 1982)

A game that can genuinely make you feel adrift (paging Major Tom), *Space Hawk* puts you in the role of an astronaut hunter alone in deep space. You must pursue white space hawks, shooting them with your ray gun and vaporizing the colorful gas bubbles each emits. Programmer Bill Fisher picked up the unused code for *Meteor!*, the *Asteroids* clone, and was able to develop an entirely new game sufficiently different from Atari's. The result is that *Space Hawk* plays *Asteroids* to *Space Armada*'s *Space Invaders*, with more detailed graphics, background sky objects of various sizes and colors, and even shooting stars.

You start the game with five lives. Space surrounds you, and you're in immediate danger. You can either move out of the way with your jetpack, shoot the incoming obstacles, or enter hyperspace. Three shots take out a space hawk; the bubbles and wandering comets give you additional points, although they're dangerous and can take *you* out if they hit you.

Numerous control options let you customize the game mechanics on the fly. What makes *Space Hawk* interesting is that you can switch between these control options whenever you want. That means you can change up how you're playing to suit whatever challenges you're facing. From the keypad, selecting Direct thrust means you quickly start and stop whenever you apply and release the thrust buttons. Drift gives you momentum; you continue to drift in space even when you take your finger off the thrust. The direction disc controls which way you're heading. In Smooth Aiming mode, you gently rotate to the next position you choose with the disc. In Quick Aiming mode, you immediately snap to the next direction. The top side buttons fire your ray gun, and the bottom buttons apply thrust from your jetpack (regardless of whether you're in Drive or Direct mode).

Your ray gun can fire one shot at a time with the Fire buttons in Single Shot mode or continuously with Auto-Fire, which is less precise but makes the game easier to learn and lets your finger rest up. Either way, emissions from your gas blaster spread out as they fly farther away, letting you hit more distant targets with somewhat less precision. And the Hyperspace button on the keypad blinks you out of existence and back again in a different position—possibly safer, possibly more dangerous.

In what fast became an Intellivision trademark, four game speeds are available. I enjoyed playing this one at the fastest speed, with direct thrust and quick aiming. And, as with *Astrosmash* and *Star Strike*, the scoring is weird. You start the game with 500 points, and the score

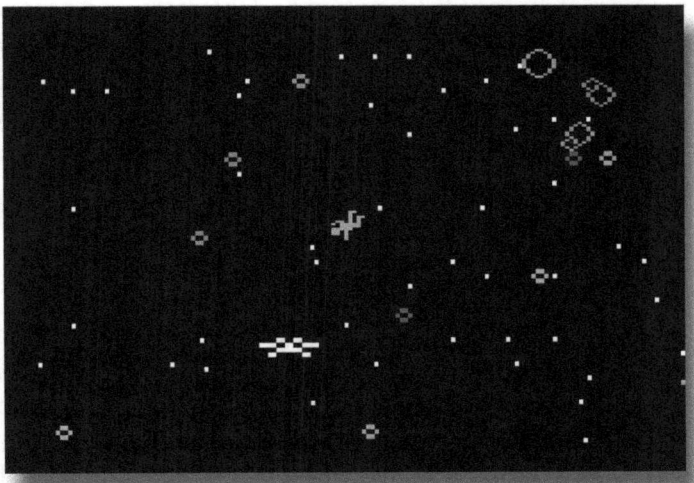

Figure 3.10: Space is vast, lonely, and cerebral, and *Space Hawk* plays this for maximum effect while delivering *Asteroids*-like action.

goes up or down depending on what happens. Shoot bubbles, double-bubbles, big hawks, comets, small hawks, and rainbow bubbles, and your score will increase; the last three objects don't appear until your score passes 10,000, 20,000, and 100,000, respectively. Your score goes down whenever you are hit or go into hyperspace. Six score multiples serve as level markers from 1x to 6x, and whenever you hear a two-note fanfare, it means you scored high enough to advance to the next multiple, which increases scoring but also means the game is getting that much harder. Later in the game (after 40,000 points), pulsating gray amoebas appear that you can't destroy; you can only evade them by thrusting away or entering hyperspace.

Though this is nominally a one-player game, the manual suggests that two players can take turns or work together with both controllers, with one person flying and shooting while the other aims and controls hyperspace. It also mentions a "sabotage" idea where one player plays normally while the other uses the second controller to mess everything up, which is as ridiculous as it sounds. These ideas sound suspiciously like "we didn't have enough memory to program a two-player mode," and I've yet to meet someone who preferred to play *Space Hawk* together with another person. It gets better: Sometimes you'll fly near an invisible black hole that sends you into hyperspace as a precautionary measure. The black hole bit is a bug in disguise, as the programmers couldn't figure out why hyperspace occasionally triggered on its own, so they made it a part of the game. And when it happens, it's certainly a surprise. *Space Hawk* may seem a little hacked together—and it was, given its origin from the remnants of *Meteor* code—but it's a fascinating and memorable take on *Asteroids* and doesn't feel like an ordinary clone.

Night Stalker (Mattel, May 1982)

The nightmarish *Night Stalker* is a simple maze shooter and one of the most addictive games on the Intellivision. You're running for your life, trapped in a single-screen maze of shrubs. Evil robots track you down relentlessly while dangerous spiders and bats wander the pathways. You must destroy as many robots as possible and stay alive as long as you can. *Night Stalker* is memorable for its classic "running man" sprite and its distinctive control scheme, which employs the numeric keypad for shooting in four directions instead of the side action buttons. The cartridge is creepier and more minimalist than *Berzerk* but evokes a similar feeling of foreboding, while its pulsing, deep background sound recalls *Space Invaders* and *Asteroids*.

You start inside the central bunker and without a weapon. First, go get your yellow gun, which is flashing for attention somewhere else in the maze. Each gun contains six bullets; use all six and you must grab the next loaded gun when it appears in one of five possible spots. Crucially, the game doesn't let you run in one direction while shooting in another—you must stop first, fire, and then run again, the same as in *Berzerk*. Plus, there are no boards to clear or defined levels besides whatever robot is on the screen. The action never pauses or says "great job!" to denote progress. Although this is also true of *Astrosmash* and *Space Hawk*, here it seems especially intense without a periodic breather. The only rest you get is whenever you return to the bunker. At least the walls aren't electrified.

The spiders and bats are mostly distractions. The brown spider (100 points) crawls slowly but paralyzes you if you touch it. Shoot it and a new one emerges in the top-left corner web, a safer zone that only some bullets can penetrate. The two black bats (300 points each) also paralyze you on touch. Shoot one and another materializes, hanging down and resting momentarily before taking flight.

The real challenge is in shooting the robots, and five types stalk the passageways. Gray robots (300 points) are the slowest and have poor aim, but they're smart enough to shoot ahead of where you are running to. They're worth 300 points. Blue robots (500 points) start appearing after you score 5,000 points; these are more cunning. At this point, as you shoot the bats, they'll each be replaced with gray robots, which means that soon you'll have three robots and a spider chasing you. White robots (1,000 points), which appear after your score passes 15,000, are aggressive and take three shots to kill instead of one. Normally, you're safe in the bunker, but even that's in doubt once the dreaded Black robot (2,000 points) appears. These join the fray after you score 30,000 points and fire scary white energy bolts that shoot away your bullets. Score 50,000 and they start shooting yellow energy bolts that will slowly destroy the bunker. Finally, invisible robots (4,000 points) come after you once you score above 80,000. These are the worst because you can see the bullets but not them.

Figure 3.11: The creepy *Night Stalker* became one of the Intellivision's best-remembered games and it's still fun to play today.

One trick that works well: hiding in corners, waiting for robots to come out into the open to shoot them. This works even when you're not positioned right in the center of a hallway, so you can fire off a shot that hews close to a wall and nabs a robot right before it can return a shot. You can start a new game at one of four speeds—the fastest is the most fun—and you get six lives plus another every 10,000 points. *Night Stalker* became one of Mattel's most successful Intellivision games, so it was a natural choice for the M Network division to port it to the Atari 2600 (as *Dark Cavern*). Intellivision high score competitions to this day feature *Night Stalker* as a top title, where gamers battle to see who can last the longest and score the highest. With the benefit of 40 years of hindsight, the game could have used even more speed and some extra mazes. Fortunately, an enterprising homebrew programmer already thought of this, as we'll soon see.

Frog Bog (APh/Mattel, May 1982)

You couldn't walk 10 feet in 1982 without stumbling on a frog game, and *Frog Bog* was Mattel's contribution to the genre. This one drew inspiration from the 1978 Sega coin-op *Frogs* and is as simple as it looks: Two hungry frogs must compete to catch delicious bugs by jumping up from lily pads to swallow them with their super-long tongues. Jump into the pond by accident—you'll see and hear a nice "splash"—and you'll have to climb back onto a pad before you can resume eating bugs.

Frog Bog offers the option to play during the day, where the game continues until the sun goes down, or at night, when bugs twinkle like fireflies, as the manual puts it, until the stars come out and the frogs go to sleep. The game lets you play against the computer or a human with three difficulty levels. Selecting Day mode puts you in Easy, meaning you're just jumping; you choose the kind of jump, but that's it. Jump up and get near enough to a bug and you automatically stick your tongue out and swallow it, which earns points. Each jump puts you on the opposite lily pad.

Night mode is harder, giving you control of the frog's direction and arc on each jump. Press the left and right edges to jump; how long you hold down the disc determines the jump's distance, letting you catch bugs farther away and ones right next to you. The Direction & Tongue mode is the hardest; it means you also have to time sticking out your tongue with the side buttons. All games are precisely three minutes long. Interestingly, you can swap difficulty modes during play just by pressing the appropriate button on the overlay.

Figure 3.12: Sometimes a game can be exceedingly simple and still tremendous fun, as *Frog Bog* shows.

There are four kinds of bugs to eat, which are not named. Each is worth 5, 10, 15, or 35 points. The 35-point bug looks like a dragonfly; these are the hardest to catch. At night you also hear crickets, a sound effect that does fantastic work to convey the setting. The top of the screen displays each player's score in different colors.

Frog Bog is a basic game, but it's suitable for all ages—mainly because you can select different difficulty levels for each player. At the end of each game, you're stuck until you reach for the console and press Reset, as with many other Intellivision titles. Eventually, this mechanic (or lack thereof) went away, and every cartridge let you cue up new games with the controller. But it's a reminder that something so basic for the user interface still wasn't a given. At least it was good exercise; otherwise, you could just sit on the couch for hours eating bugs.

Sub Hunt (APh/Mattel, May 1982)

This tense submarine simulation and strategy game puts you in control of a fleet of four submarines defending your nation against imminent attack. You begin the game by stalking six convoys on open waters. The ships are attempting to reach a safe harbor, where they will form an invasion force and attack your home base. Before they reach the harbor, you must dispatch your submarines, navigate to them, sight them through the periscope, fire your torpedoes, and hopefully sink them one at a time—all while evading depth charges and deck guns. The destroyers are the toughest, and you can't outrun them, so you need to outsmart them instead.

The game begins with the deployment view consisting of a map of the ocean showing the safe harbor on top, your submarines and home base on the right, and the location of the first of six convoys on the left side and heading east. Your selected submarine is red. You can send each out separately by selecting an engine speed and direction, keeping in mind that you travel a bit faster on the surface than being submerged at the same engine speed. The overlays let you select from five engine speeds, dive, surface, and toggle sonar. You can also stop one or all submarines at once. The top side buttons fire torpedoes, and the bottom ones reverse engines. The direction disc steers the rudder port (left) or starboard (right).

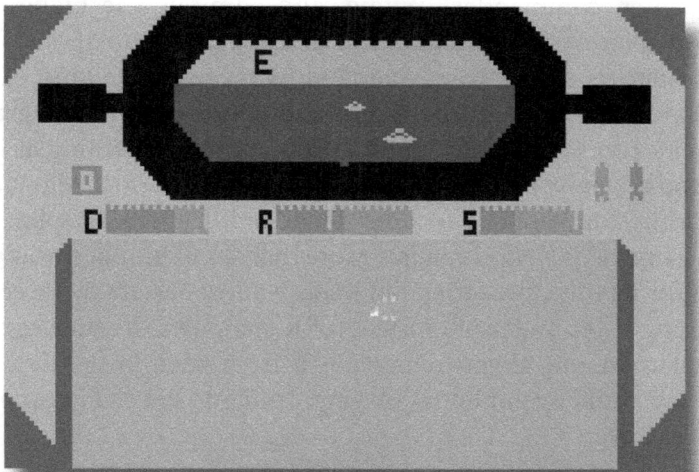

Figure 3.13: The cerebral *Sub Hunt* was more simulation than action game, with its cerebral play and tense moments in combat.

When a sub meets the convoy, the battle is joined, and you drop to the periscope view. Three horizontal meters monitor depth, rudder position, and speed. An indicator to the right shows you when your two torpedoes are green (armed) or red (not yet reloaded). The main view through the periscope shows you the open ocean and whether any ships are in view, which should correspond with their position on the sonar map. As you approach ships shown in the periscope view, they get larger and larger until they disappear, signaling that you have passed them by. You must be at or near the surface to fire a torpedo. It takes a few seconds to reload. You can turn off your engines and sonar to sneak up on a convoy or hide your position. Take on too much damage and the periscope view fills up with water as you sink; say goodbye to that sub.

Sink 36 ships—six convoys of six boats each—or sink enough ships in each so they can't form the invasion force, and you'll hear a victory theme because you won the game. If the worst happens and enough convoys reach the safe harbor, they will join forces with three additional destroyers and troop transports, form an invasion force, and head for your home base. This is much harder because sinking three destroyers is no picnic, and if the force reaches your home base you lose the game. Five difficulty levels exist: lieutenant, lieutenant commander, commander, captain, and admiral. The higher levels mean the convoys each contain two destroyers instead of one.

Despite its slower pace, *Sub Hunt* is precisely the kind of game that showed off the Intellivision's additional power and graphics capability compared with the Atari 2600. If you're coming at it cold from today's perspective, it may seem hard to get into. Many newer submarine simulators offer more detail and deeper gameplay, and a single game of *Sub Hunt* can last more than an hour. But it was one of a kind for its time, predating Sid Meier's *Silent Service* by three years and doing it on a console instead of a computer. It's an impressive piece of code and, if you remember it from back in the day, a taut game you could spend hours playing, trying to get the jump on one more destroyer.

Utopia (Mattel, June 1982)

Before *Civilization*, before *SimCity*, before just about any world-building, real-time strategy, or "god" game, there was *Utopia*, a technical and game design marvel developed by Don Daglow that punched far above its weight. Daglow began in the early 1970s designing mainframe games, such as early examples of baseball and *Star Trek*. In 1975, he created *Dungeon*, the first known computer role-playing game. He was a fan of mainframe computer simulation games and decided to build one for the Intellivision. *Utopia* packs world-class strategic gameplay and action into a cartridge, with a finely balanced roster of rules that fit inside a small 10-page manual. It didn't sell incredibly well. But it upended what everyone knew about game design and released shockwaves that reverberated in the industry for many years to come.

In *Utopia*, you govern an island state. You control the treasury, agriculture, infrastructure development, and the military. You make decisions that boost the economy and improve the welfare of your citizens, such as providing housing and food, diversifying crops, building factories and fishing boats, and building new hospitals, schools, and housing projects. Make your citizens unhappy, and rebels appear and take over. Your decisions affect your island state's population, productivity, wealth, and well-being. Text-based strategy games came and went in the years prior. But the difference with *Utopia*—aside from being fully graphical, and on a game console—is that it was a strategy game set in real time.[36]

At the start of each game, you select the number of rounds (from one to 50) and how many seconds each round is (from 30 to 120). Shorter rounds mean you earn money faster. The object is to score the most points possible during your term of office. If you're playing against someone, you must do better than they do with their island. (If you're playing alone, the other island sits idle.) The main screen displays both islands in the ocean, along with numbers across the bottom denoting (from left to right) player 1's treasury in gold bars, the number of rounds left, the time left in the current round, and player 2's treasury.

Each player starts with 100 gold bars. The money lets you build or plant crops; you select the area you want to improve with the direction disc and press the appropriate key on the keypad. You'll want a fishing boat first, as it generates income and feeds 500 people. Soon, you'll need to house them and build a factory so they can be productive. Other options include schools and hospitals, which make your people happier; a PT boat to block pirates or attack your opponent; or even rebel soldiers you can send in to reduce your opponent's income. You can also plant crops, which generate food but also need rain and require frequent replanting. Eventually, you'll want to build a fort, which protects everything in a one-square radius around them. You make all these decisions in the spur of the moment because it's in real time, and pausing doesn't help because it blanks the screen.

The lower-left action button displays your island's current population; as it increases, you'll want to build additional housing and food sources. Weather patterns spin up random rain showers, tropical storms, and hurricanes. It helps to plant crops where it rains a lot. Schools of fish appear and disappear, crops wilt, and pirates roam the seas. It's a living, breathing world. As each round ends, the game pauses momentarily. It sounds three tones in succession, adding earned money to the treasury (10 gold bars is automatic) and displaying your last-round and total scores. The game ends when you complete the number of rounds set at the beginning and your total score is displayed.

I didn't get *Utopia* until a couple of years after the Intellivision was discontinued; I picked it up in a stack of 10 99-cent Intellivision games I found at Kay Bee Toy & Hobby in a mall in Brooklyn, maybe around 1985 or 1986. (That was a good day!) I remember being puzzled over how the game worked, putting it off for a few days while I played the others, and finally figuring it out and becoming hooked. Even playing by yourself can be fun, although it's a little slow without a second player to compete with and attack or defend against.

Utopia sold some 250,000 copies, even though Mattel Electronics marketing had no idea how to push it and didn't.[37] It received rave reviews, including a "Video Game Hall of Fame" nod in *Playboy*. A blurb in *TV Guide* called it "splendid" and said, "*Utopia* should delight anyone who enjoys *The MacNeil/Lehrer Report* on PBS."[38] It was a weird time. *Utopia* spawned the construction management simulation genre, which led to hits such as *SimCity*, *Civilization*, *Caesar*, and *The Settlers*.[39] In 2012, the Smithsonian Institution's The Art of Video Games exhibition included *Utopia* in its collection of 80 historically significant titles.

Daglow went on to produce or supervise the production of many famous computer games from Electronic Arts, Brøderbund, and his own Stormfront Studios in the 1980s and 1990s. He designed *Neverwinter Nights*, the first graphical MMORPG that paved the way for *Ultima Online*, *EverQuest* and *World of Warcraft*. Today's gamers

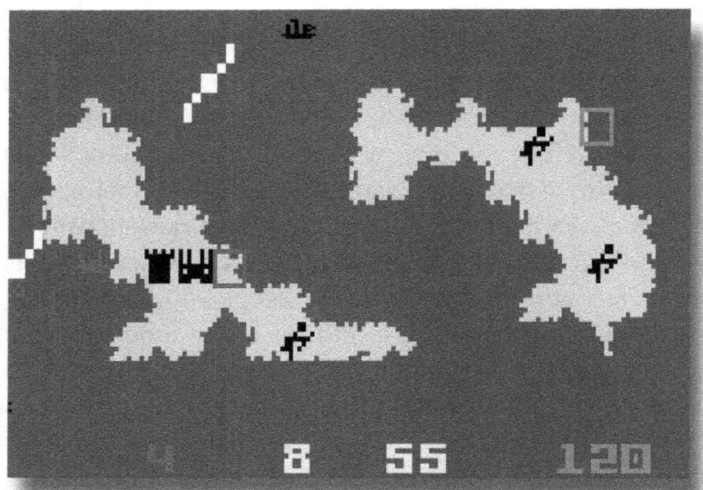

Figure 3.14: The groundbreaking *Utopia* laid the groundwork for construction management and real-time strategy games while being addictive all on its own.

know much more about MMORPGs than *Utopia*. But every major city-building game, especially one with a real-time element, owes some debt to this fabled Intellivision cartridge.

Lock 'n' Chase (Mattel, July 1982)

Data East's *Lock 'n' Chase*, a dot-eating maze game like *Pac-Man*, hit arcades in 1981, and it proved popular enough that Mattel developed home conversions for both the Intellivision and the Atari 2600. As with many coin-op games of the era, they stretched out the square boards to fill rectangular television screens at home. But here, the maze still looks good because of its simpler features—not distorted the way the more distinctive *Pac-Man* maze does in most home conversions.

The hook with this game is that you're a thief robbing a bank vault, and the police are chasing you. You must collect all the gold coins on each board and run through the escape door without getting caught. When each maze starts, you get a few seconds' head start before the police come barreling in. The disc moves you around the maze. Occasionally, treasures appear in the center of the screen, either a cash bag (shown with a dollar sign) or one of 10 others, such as hats, crowns, and briefcases.

Some of the rules differ from *Pac-Man*'s because, well, this isn't *Pac-Man*. For example, four green doors open and close independently in the maze. You can press a side button to lock one behind you as you run; this turns the door red for a few seconds to signal it's holding shut for a moment before unlocking on its own. You can also accidentally get stuck in a door while it's closing, but you'll be released when it opens again. The side tunnels don't slow down the police, and all four seem to have the same personality. Four money bags appear per maze and are worth progressively more points, up to 4,000. Score 20,000 for a free life, and after 100,000 points, the game speeds up. You can also select one of three game speeds at the start.

What makes *Lock 'n' Chase* work, aside from the general appeal of dot-eating maze games, is its high amount of polish. The graphics are colorful and well-drawn. Multivoice music plays at the start and whenever you're caught or complete a level. The game runs relatively quickly for an Intellivision cartridge. The Intellivision didn't get a proper *Pac-Man* translation until it was too late to sell many copies;

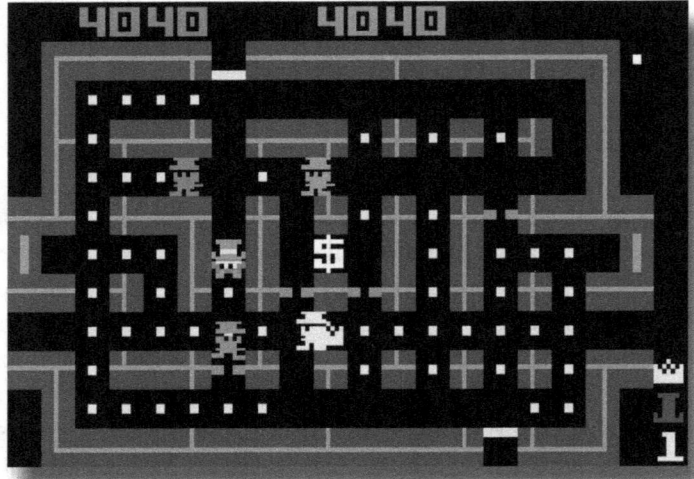

Figure 3.15: Don't call it *Pac-Man*: *Lock 'n' Chase* may look like the typical dot-eating clone, but plenty of innovations set it apart.

we'll cover it later in this book. Suffice it to say no Intellivision owner was looking at the poor Atari 2600 conversion of *Pac-Man* and wishing they could play that one instead.

Lock 'n' Chase, programmed by Mike Winans and Julie Hoshizaki, was the first of a series of Data East conversions on the Intellivision.[40] Some may complain that the direction disc is the opposite of ideal for maze games. I was used to it from many other games, and it was never a problem. An early 6KB version of the cartridge *was* difficult to control. If you accidentally press one of the diagonal directions, you won't make the turn; you need to be deliberate and push either up, left, right, or down, and steer clear of the disc's other 12 positions. Most sales were for an improved 8KB version. You can tell which one you have by whether Lupin collapses into his hat when he's caught, just like in the arcade—that also happens only in the 8KB version.[41]

Mattel Electronics advertised *Lock 'n' Chase* in at least three separate television commercials. One was a sly dig at Atari and featured George Plimpton and an eleven-year-old Henry Thomas, the star of the 1982 Steven Spielberg blockbuster *E.T.: The Extra-Terrestrial*. At the end of the commercial, Plimpton asks the boy his name so he can autograph his new game box, but he doesn't say it. Instead, he asks, "My name?" and leaves the question unanswered. It seemed funny at the time—George Plimpton doesn't know who Henry Thomas is? One of the most famous kids on the planet?

It turns out there was more to it than that. After Atari spent $20 million to license *E.T.: The Extra-Terrestrial* for its upcoming 2600 cartridge, Mattel went and hired Thomas, the star of *E.T.*, to appear in Intellivision commercials. Word has it that Atari threatened to sue Mattel if it identified Thomas in the commercials, so Mattel got around it with the above call-out at the end.[42] The line was a tongue-in-cheek reference to the lawsuit—and how Mattel pulled one over on Atari.

The *E.T.* cartridge didn't work out all that well for Atari, either.

Continued Strength in 1982

By the middle of the year, the Intellivision continued to make a compelling case for itself on its own, even without the Keyboard Component. In addition to the above titles, other games landed as well. *Reversi* offered well-done rendition of the classic board game where you must take control of the board before your opponent. *Boxing* featured striking graphics, even compared against other Intellivision titles. But it fell short thanks to sluggish gameplay that amounted to a lot of button mashing, and little of the strategy and reflexes that Activision's simpler *Boxing* game brought to the 2600.

Some third parties began to get into the fray by building accessories. Compro Electronics sold the Videoplexer, an attachment that plugged into the Intellivision's cartridge port. On the top panel were eight cartridge slots; the idea was to fill them up and leave them alone, using the Videoplexer's touch membrane keyboard on the front panel to cue up whatever game you wanted to play next. Many vendors began selling cartridge holders that could hold either 2600 or Intellivision games in their slots.

During one promotional campaign, Mattel sent out some market research mailers with Plimpton's likeness, promising a rebate check for $2.50 on their next Intellivision cartridge purchase if recipients answered basic questions about their household—and they did deliver the checks as promised.[43] Bigger plans were also in the works, and soon, Mattel would be selling its own high-powered accessory for the Intellivision. It seemed as if there was nowhere to go but up.

4 | Soar

In 1982, Mattel commissioned an extended two-minute commercial called "Intellivision Galactic News Update" that played in movie theaters across the U.S. In it, three animated newscasters cover eight segments, each one corresponding with footage from Intellivision cartridges: *Space Battle*, *Night Stalker*, *Utopia*, *Tron: Deadly Discs* (coming soon, it says!), and moving to the "sports desk," *Boxing*, *Tennis*, and *Skiing*. At the end of the commercial, the newscasters cheer as the Earth is saved from incoming alien fighters in *Star Strike*. It's striking and effective in a way that only the future as seen in 1982 could deliver. The commercial effectively showed how good the games looked. Notably, the ad made no mention of the Keyboard Component; no further TV commercials ever did, even after its release.

The Intellivision's critical and commercial reputation continued to soar. Ken Uston, who wrote the popular *Guide to Buying and Beating the Home Video Games* that year, called the Intellivision "the most mechanically reliable of the systems." Uston wrote, "In many, many hours of experimentation, the Intellivision system performed exactly as it was meant to...Not once did a cartridge fail to load or a game fail to appear on the screen. The controller worked with perfect consistency. The unit never had overheating problems, nor were loose wires or other connections encountered."[1] Strategy guide writer Jeff Rovin wrote, "Intellivision is the unchallenged king of graphics" among the seven top video game systems of the time.² "The images being highly detailed—down to the shifty eyes of the blackjack dealer—the colors no less varied than those of Atari but much less garish."³ Neither Rovin nor Uston liked the Intellivision's controllers and overlays, but an alternative for providing that level of detailed player control didn't exist. It came part and parcel with the Intellivision experience.

The console was selling well—in June 1982, *The New York Times* called Atari and Mattel together "the two leaders in producing hardware for home video systems," and most estimates pegged Mattel as commandeering 25 percent of the home video game market.⁴ In May, Atari face-planted with its horrendous 2600 conversion of *Pac-Man*, the game that shattered the company's image of invincibility. Not every Intellivision game was a success, even despite being high-quality. For example, *Utopia* was one of the best made for the Intellivision. But its complex rules and two-player orientation (if not an outright requirement) prevented it from becoming a bestseller. But sales soon began to slip next to the 2600.⁵

It didn't matter because the console would soon achieve even greater heights. In addition to its coveted sports licenses of professional organizations across America, Mattel was savvy enough to gain the rights to other key properties. Let's start with the one that applies to what many believe is the console's best cartridge. It was also the first video game to feature TSR's coveted *Dungeons & Dragons* branding.

Advanced Dungeons & Dragons (APh/Mattel, August 1982)

This incredible action adventure puts you in control of a three-person expedition. The object is to retrieve the two halves of the Crown of Kings, located inside the distant Cloudy Mountain. To get there, you must traverse a dangerous forest and survive deadly, randomized caves inside the mountain, armed with only a bow and arrows. A deadly Winged Dragon guards each half of the crown.

At a whopping 6KB, *Advanced Dungeons & Dragons* was another one of the first Intellivision cartridges with more than 4KB of ROM. It's also notable for its brilliant use of sound and its fog-of-war effect. It doesn't use AD&D rules, and it's not an RPG. But it's an absolute blast to play and one of my favorite games on the console. Perhaps it's one of yours, too.

Each game begins with the outdoor strategy map. You start at home on the left, and three blinking squares mark your location. The map contains grasslands, forests, rivers, castle walls, gates, and mountains in two colors. Eight arrow keys on the overlay move your expedition in the corresponding direction. Brown mountains are impassable. Black ones indicate peaks with caves you can explore and pass through. Move next to one or two of the black mountains and they turn color to show their difficulty, from easiest to toughest: gray, blue, red, or purple. The color also denotes whether you'll find tools inside. Blue mountains contain a boat for crossing rivers. Red ones have the axe, which chops down forests. Purple peaks have a key that lets you pass through gates.

Enter a mountain and you'll discover a series of dark caves, controlling one of your three warriors equipped with a bow and arrows. The game presents the caves with an overhead perspective, and you can only see so far ahead. As you explore the dungeons, the fog of war clears and the map gradually fills out. Some mountains are four rooms by eight rooms, and others are four by four. Rooms can be different shapes and sizes, and narrow, winding passages connect them. The maps loop around, so you'll eventually cross the same areas repeatedly.

The overlay arrow buttons shoot arrows in any of eight directions. Three buttons at the bottom of the overlay pick up objects, count how many arrows you have—you'll hear a rapid series of clicks, one for each arrow—and exit the mountain. The direction disc controls your adventurer's direction, and the controller's side buttons make your adventurer run instead of walk. Occasionally you find quivers, which replenish your supply of arrows. Stock up early because you only start the game with three arrows.

Sometimes you come across different kinds of tracks or skulls. Sometimes you hear hissing, wings flapping, or growling. These are all clues as to what monsters lurk nearby. You'll run across rats, snakes, bats, spiders, dragons, demons, and sluggish, gelatinous blobs you can't kill. You can kill monsters you can hear but not see, and sometimes you'll startle them and wake them up. You must stop moving before you can shoot an arrow. Get hurt and you'll turn blue, and then red when you're seriously hurt. You also shouldn't shoot arrows indiscriminately. Aside from wasting them, if an arrow hits a nearby wall, it ricochets, and several times in close passages. It can quickly

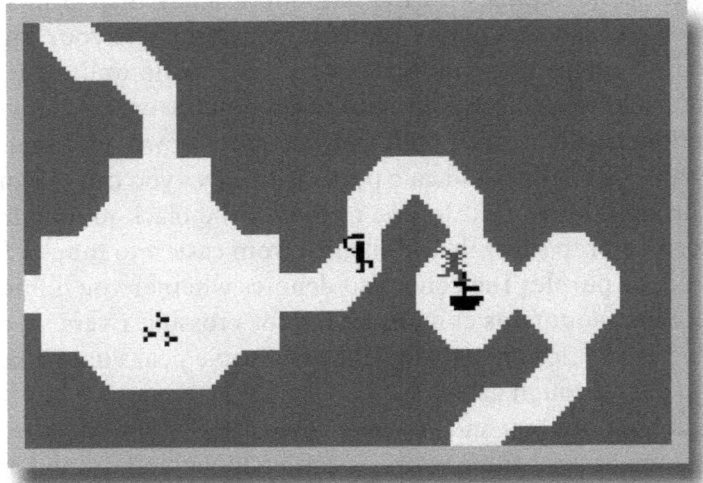

Figure 4.1: A stunning achievement in a console game, *Advanced Dungeons & Dragons* offered exploration, action, treasure, and the chance to fight dragons.

return and hit you for damage. You can use this to your advantage, but being careful is the order of the day.

In each mountain, you must find the ladder, kill the monster guarding it, and exit. Do so and you complete the mountain and pass through it on the outdoor strategy map. It's possible to cross through the last three mountains you completed without re-entering it. Enter a fourth and the earlier one will respawn, and you'll have to clear them again if you need to go back through (though normally you shouldn't). Each time you lose an adventurer, one square disappears from your expedition, which you'll see when you're back outdoors. Lose all three warriors and the game ends with a tombstone marking your place of death on the outdoor strategy map.

When you finally reach Cloudy Mountain, go inside, find and kill both winged dragons, and pick up the two crown pieces. Grab the second one and you'll hear a loud, low synthesizer tone indicating that you've won. The crown will appear assembled. The game returns you to the strategy map, where you'll see a crown become part of the mountain. Victory is yours.

Oddly enough, this game was also responsible for some early disappointment. Mattel's 1981 dealer catalog showed a title dubbed *Adventure* with a blue screen and some seriously impressive-looking sprites. The Intellivision catalog with many Mattel cartridges showed the same screen and called it *Dungeons & Dragons*, raising hopes. The game we received looked nothing like that screenshot. But it didn't matter in the end because the cartridge we got was still excellent. Contemporary reviews were uniformly positive in what amounted to one of the first full years of critical analysis in mainstream magazines. *Electronic Fun With Computers & Games* wrote, "The graphics are terrific...each creature has its own distinctive behavior and charm." *Electronic Games* said, "*Advanced Dungeons & Dragons*...proves to have been worth the wait,"[6] and awarded it Best Adventure Video Game the following year.[7]

Four difficulty levels are in the game: 1 is Sightseer (easy), 2 is Weekend Adventurer (medium), 3 is Soldier of Fortune (medium hard), and pressing the disc cues up Hero (hard). On the more challenging levels, monsters move faster, and fewer arrows are in each quiver you find. You can also tell which level you selected by Cloudy Mountain's color on the outdoor strategy map: gray, blue, red, or purple, the same as for the smaller mountains. Only you'll know it the entire time you're playing. As was often the case back then, simple color changes alone could raise your blood pressure once you knew what it meant. And if that didn't do it, the deep snoring sounds coming from the mountain certainly did, letting you know what was in store when you finally made it there.

With Mattel's *Advanced Dungeons & Dragons*, TSR flexed its muscle. It allowed the use of the same font as its flagship Advanced Dungeons & Dragons products but forced Mattel to put "Cartridge" in the title on the box to distinguish it from actual TSR books.[8] I'm refraining from that here because it's redundant, but it shows how every video game license deal can be a complex negotiation from the earliest days of licensed games.

Intellivoice

The timing was ripe for speech-enabled games. The Texas Instruments Speak & Spell was one of the hottest toys of the era. It taught spelling to young children by speaking out loud whatever letter a child pushed on its surface-mounted keyboard. Talking arcade coin-ops such as *Vanguard* and *Berzerk* had just begun to land in arcades. The 1981

Datsun 810 Maxima became the first "talking car" available in the U.S., thanks to sleight of hand rather than any futuristic technology: a small, phonograph-based module containing a miniature record and a stylus. The car let you know if you forgot to turn the lights off by saying "lights are on" when you tried to exit the vehicle. Later models included additional grooves on the miniature record for more phrases, such as "right door is open." (In 1985, the newly renamed Nissan stopped cheating by using solid-state chips to store the voices digitally.) Sci-fi movies and television shows had talking computers for years, but one of the biggest debuts of 1982 was Glen A. Larson's *Knight Rider*. The NBC television series featured a young David Hasselhoff piloting K.I.T.T., the Knight Industries Two Thousand, a talking black Trans Am voiced by William Daniels.

It turned out General Instrument had just the thing to go with the Intellivision's CP1610 CPU and support chips. The SP0256 speech synthesizer chip worked directly with the CPU. Mattel designed a new attachment around it for the Intellivision. The Intellivoice did what it said on the tin: It added speech synthesis capability to the console. The chip's 2KB ROM contained a database of common words that games could connect to say things, spoken in an adult male voice. The Intellivoice was styled to resemble the Master Component but in a smaller housing that plugged into the console's side-mounted cartridge slot. The right side held another cartridge slot for inserting games.

Figure 4.2: Mattel's futuristic Intellivoice module was the first popular speech synthesis add-on for playing video games. (Credit: Evan Amos)

"Just attach the new Intellivoice voice synthesis module," Mattel's two-page magazine spread promised. "Plug in any one of our new talking cartridges. Then, concentrate on the visual action. While Intellivoice gives you up-to-the-second verbal status reports. Feedback. And instructions which are essential to your game strategy."

The Intellivision wasn't quite the *first* console with human voice capability—that honor goes to the Magnavox Odyssey^2's The Voice attachment, which arrived a couple of months earlier. The difference with The Voice was that Magnavox focused on education instead of arcade or strategy games. In addition, none of the programs that supported it *required* it, leading Danny Goodman to write in *Creative Computing Video and Arcade Games,* "that eliminates any incentive to buy the $100 voice module."

In contrast, you needed the Intellivoice to play games that supported it. With the Intellivoice attached to the Master Component, you could insert any cartridge from the rest of your collection, but only Intellivoice-enabled games would speak. Retailers generally sold the Intellivoice for between $80 and $100. Mattel released three Intellivoice cartridges simultaneously: *Space Spartans*, *B-17 Bomber*, and *Bomb Squad*. In the vein of Stern's popular *Berzerk* coin-op, all three used speech as a key game mechanic.

In a brilliant commercial, George Plimpton introduced the Intellivoice to television viewers from his living room: "I'm about to show you something new for Intellivision that will revolutionize the way games are played and compared. First, here's a popular Atari game. Now don't look." He then covered the camera with his hand, blacking out the screen, as 2600 *Asteroids* played audibly in the background. "And here's new *Space Spartans*, for the Intellivoice module." He covered the screen a second time; viewers heard "Hello Commander" in a female voice. A different robotic voice said, "Starbase One Under Attack," and a deeper third voice said, "The battle is over." Plimpton then closed the commercial: "New Intellivoice—now that Intellivision talks, you can tell the difference with your eyes closed."

Space Spartans (Mattel, August 1982)

Space Battle gave the Intellivision a space combat game in the vein of *Star Raiders* for Atari home computers—and, later, for the 2600 version, which came with a special keypad for the various extra keyboard commands, something every Intellivision controller already had. But if you want a real *Star Raiders*–type game for the Intellivision, *Space Spartans* is the answer. It's the first game Mattel sold as an 8KB cartridge. Even that wasn't enough memory to pack in the desired number of voice samples.

The manual dispenses with a backstory, and instead says straight out that it's a re-enactment in space of the 480 B.C. Battle of Thermopylae between a small Spartan force and Xerxes and his Persian army. (Points for honesty?) It means knowing you'll die at some point, but that's part of the fun, I suppose. You must stop alien onslaught after onslaught to "give your home galaxy time to prepare for attack," although you never get to see that part. The object is to score as many points as possible by blasting away alien ships before you're destroyed or run out of energy. You can head to a starbase and dock for repairs and re-energizing whenever you're running low, or your ship is too damaged to fight effectively.

The game takes place on two main screens. The Sector Grid shows a grid-based galaxy layout, sector by sector, with your location and the locations of the three starbases; at the start of each game, you decide where to place the starbases yourself. The grid also shows the incoming alien squadrons. The color indicates how many aliens are in a sector: green (1–4), yellow (5–8), orange (9–16), red (17–32), and purple (33 or more!); to start fighting, you must move the cursor to the first alien squadron sector and engage hyperdrive. Then switch to the Battle view, which looks out of your cockpit into space, with crosshairs in the center. It lacks a dashboard or gauges; you'll need to use the keypad to hear important information. Here is where you blast away aliens; get 'em all, and then you'll want to warp to a different sector.

A big part of the fun is to run your ship in combat. The tracking computer locks onto enemy targets, while the battle computer auto-fires your laser torpedoes once a target is locked. Impulse and hyperdrives let you fly within a sector or jump to another sector, which you need to do often to reach the attacking aliens or to dock at or defend starbases. Other keys on the overlay let you raise and lower shields, get a voice-enabled status report, check your energy level, and switch between the Sector Grid and Battle views. Blast away all the aliens in the Sector Grid, and you start over on a new map, where you

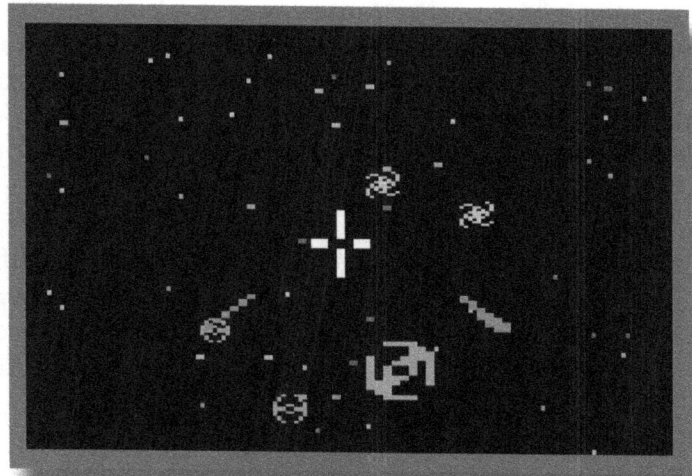

Figure 4.3: *Space Spartans* wasn't your average early 1980s space shooter, and it played the Intellivoice's speech capability to full effect.

can place your starbases in different spots, and where more aliens will attack than the last time.

"The part of *Space Spartans* that I was happiest with was the maneuver language that I wrote," Bill Fisher said, "which was a little tiny set of tables and very compact piece of code that was [still] very long because I had to write so many comments to explain what the heck it was doing because it was totally not obvious…it set up the formation, so you have the ships fly in barrel rolls or coming in from the side or coming in from the top, or looping around like this, or whatever the maneuvering they would do. It would mirror them back and forth and turn them upside down so they wouldn't all look the same every single time you played the game."[9]

"I'm writing the tracking computer at the same time that he's making all these motions the ships are doing," Stephen Roney said. "I had no idea what the ships were going to be doing, so the tracking computer really is tracking the alien ships and it doesn't know."

Three different computers speak to you in the game. The male voice is the central computer, which reports the energy level and how many aliens remain in the current sector. The female voice is the ship's computer; it reports system conditions for the shields, impulse drive, hyper drive, battle computer, and tracking computer. The starbase computer sounds like a robot and delivers attack alerts, which are as nerve-wracking as you would expect. Eventually, you'll hear one more distinctive voice: When your ship is destroyed and you lose, the alien commander will tell you, "The battle is over."

Space Spartans lacks the smooth combat animation of *Star Raiders*. You have zero sense that you're flying through space, and the choppy motions of the alien ships make them difficult to track, even if the sprites become pleasingly large as they approach your craft. The best part of the game is the speech. It's thrilling to hear the computer respond "Tracking Computer On" or "Starbase 2 Under Attack" in heavily synthesized voices. It's exactly what we expected the future to sound like in the early 1980s.

B-17 Bomber (Mattel, August 1982)

"Mattel Electronics presents…Bee Seven Teen Bahhhmmmerrrrr." Anyone who had this game in the 1980s has this phrase imprinted in their brains, as it's the first thing you hear as soon as you insert the cartridge and power on the console. This early combat flight simulator is a showcase for the Intellivision. It puts you in the cockpit of a bomber aircraft in a series of Allied air raid missions over Europe near the end of World War II. You must fly to and bomb various key targets, including anti-aircraft guns, factories, airports, and ships at sea while fighting enemy planes. You go in, you bomb the targets, and you leave before your fuel gets too low. Then you must return to England for repairs, rearming, and refueling.

B-17 Bomber took over a year to develop. In the spring of 1981, 10 Mattel employees decamped to a Los Angeles park. They threw frisbees and made jokes about a park custodian, suggesting he was a spy from Atari. They brainstormed new games that would use the Intellivoice and planted the seeds for *B-17 Bomber*, with crew members positioned off-screen talking to the pilot via the Intellivoice. They worked late nights, and the lead programmer spent several days at the Air Museum outside Los Angeles. The curator eventually let one of the Mattel employees crawl through a B-17 on exhibit. He soon learned how the plane worked, where the gunners sat, and what targets must have looked like to them. Soon, his small office was cluttered with models of B-17s.[10]

The resulting game was extraordinary; some Mattel Electronics employees felt it was one of the best home video games ever devised. *B-17 Bomber* begins with a strategic map view, which shows the locations of anti-aircraft batteries, factories, and airfields across Europe. It also shows your B-17's initial location (represented with a white cross) in England and some warships in the Atlantic Ocean. The direction disc moves the square cursor around the map; the side action buttons select a target. To take off, you must visit the Gauges screen by pressing the appropriate keypad button and then press the lower-left action button to spin up the B-17's engine. Once it reaches 2,500rpm and your speed reaches 90 mph, you can take off and gain altitude and airspeed.

While flying, the Pilot button shows the view with the horizon line. The game announces the direction of each incoming attack; for example, "Bandits, 9 o'clock!" You can even pick up a bit of a Southern accent in the speech. You then press the corresponding button to bring up a view, with 12:00, 3:00, 6:00, and 9:00 options. In this view, you use the direction disc to aim—listen for "Target in sight!"—and then press action buttons to fire on incoming fighter planes. Sometimes the ground-based anti-aircraft guns also fire on you, and you must also take them out. Take on damage, and you'll see bullet holes in the gun port, indicating the machine gun is disabled for the rest of the mission.

In bombing runs, once you're under an altitude of 500 feet, you can press the Bomb Bay button to bring up the below view and then use the direction disc and action buttons to aim and drop bombs. The Preview button gives you close-up views of targets. You can also lose the bomb sight but can still complete the mission by dropping bombs blind. If you survive and don't crash, you must head back before your fuel falls too low; fly in low enough and at a slow enough speed, and the computer automatically lands the B-17 for you. Your score reflects how many bandits and targets you take out on the plus side and how many times you've been hit on the minus side. You get bonus points for completing each mission. Bombing England (by accident or on purpose) is particularly egregious.

"*B-17* was the ultimate terror of the release of a product because we were literally told that we had to be finished on a given date, so that they could get the factory going to manufacture the product,

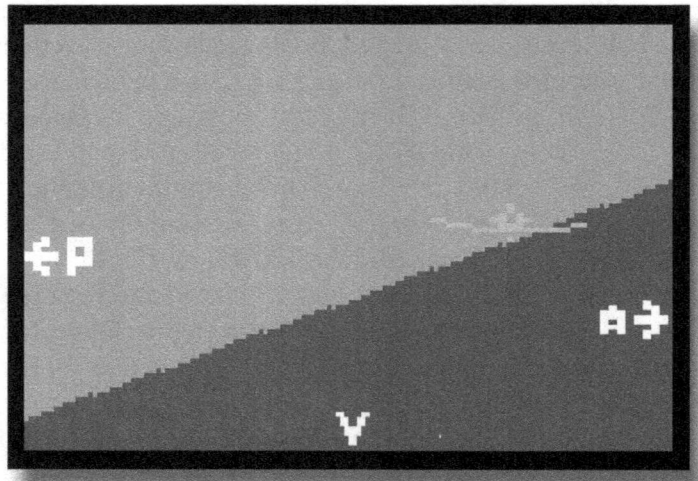

Figure 4.4: *B-17 Bomber* **offered plenty of combat action in the skies and on the ground.**

because if we didn't manufacture it they would lose tens of thousands of dollars and we would all be killed, or something along those lines," Fisher said. "We had one last bug; it was half an hour before we had to [start] burning the ROMs. We had to fix the thing and we had three decles left in the code. [A decle is a 10-bit word, as opposed to a byte, which has eight bits.] We tested it for five minutes—'gee whiz, it looks like it runs, that's fine, we didn't change anything else, it looks like it's not broken.'

"We started burning the ROMs, tested while we were burning the ROMs, and ran down with the ROMs to the people to get it out to the shipment and get it out to the factory so we could make the Christmas date…That was rather terrifying; we had literally half an hour of QA on the product before we shipped it."

"And then we shipped the game," Roney added, "my father-in-law comes over, and I'm showing him this game we just finished, and he's playing it for the first time, and he's played for 10 minutes and he hangs the game."

Even without the speech synthesis, a complex game like *B-17 Bomber* would have been impossible to pull off on the Atari 2600. But as we move deeper into 1982, the 2600 was far from the only thing Mattel had to worry about.

Bomb Squad (Mattel, August 1982)

Another technological marvel for the Intellivision, *Bomb Squad* benefited from the Intellivoice module in a big way. It's a game that, like *B-17 Bomber*, straddles the line between console and computer title in its complexity and sophistication while still being easy to pick up and play once you get the basic idea of how it works.

In *Bomb Squad*, Boris the terrorist has planted a bomb in your city. You have less than 30 minutes to disarm it by deciphering a code number, which you must work to figure out by disconnecting and repairing circuits with cutters, pliers, and a soldering iron. Frank, a demolition expert, will help you by telling you exactly what to do. During this process, Boris occasionally taunts you, saying "You'll never do it in time!"

The code number could have one, two, or three digits. Each code number appears as a four-by-five bank of scrambled LED squares that, when deciphered, will form a giant digit with lit green squares. Each square represents a wiring circuit you must repair. You don't necessarily have to repair all 20 squares to figure out the digit. A pencil and paper help. So does imagining what each digit will look like, and whether you see enough green squares to determine the shape of the number (and therefore the answer). With that in mind, you

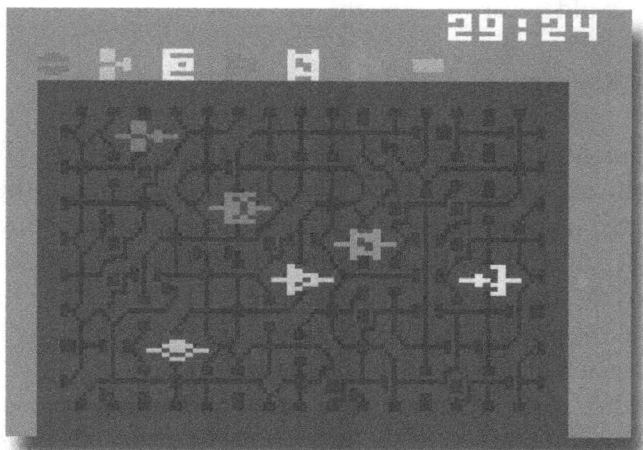

Figure 4.5: *Bomb Squad* **puts you in charge of saving innocent people from a terrorist's bomb by using your considerable skills with electronics.**

choose squares that will convey essential information you need and repair those circuits first.

Once you choose a circuit, the board appears with a clock on the top right. Frank will walk you through what you need to do—whether to cut out or replace a component and in what order. His voice prompts help you move through the game as you maneuver tools with the direction disc and use them with the lower-left side button. Then you drop the tool on the right side next to the board and pick up the next one. Pressing Sequence makes Frank repeat the order. The top of the board has an array of replacement parts in different colors and shapes. You must find the right one and then use wire cutters, pliers, and the soldering iron to install it.

In the higher two difficulty levels, components sometimes burst into flames, along with the chilling sound of a fire alarm whenever it happens. You have just eight or nine seconds to use the fire extinguisher to put out the fire. Worse, if you make a mistake, the clock speeds up, and you must correct it as fast as possible. The top side buttons speed up operations, which you can do more and more of the better you get at the game. Decipher one code digit, and you'll win 1,000 bonus points; get the entire code right for an additional 2,000 points and a fireworks display. Congratulations: You saved the city and have foiled Boris's evil plans. Now you get to try all over again—something we both enjoyed and cursed simultaneously back in those days. We could never get enough.

Blue Sky Rangers

APh Technological Consulting designed and programmed all the earliest Intellivision games. Mattel wanted a larger share of the profits, so it created its own software development group, consisting of Rick Levine, Mike Minkoff, Don Daglow, Gabriel Baum, and John Sohl. Like Atari, Mattel kept the programmers' names secret so that other firms couldn't poach them. At the time, they made similarly low salaries, between $20,000 and $40,000 per year.[11]

It didn't matter because they loved their jobs. In a profile of the Intellivision console in its June 19, 1982, issue, *TV Guide* called Mattel's secret game development staff the "Blue Sky Rangers," a name that stuck.[12] The article's author, Howard Polskin, called them that after the team's formal brainstorming sessions to come up with new game programs, a process known as "blue-skying," as Robinson related at the 1999 Classic Gaming Expo:

> The way they named Blue Sky Rangers came out…we were actually technically application software at Mattel, and *TV Guide* wanted to do an article about us, and it came out, a nice little puff piece on us. The writer wanted some sort of hook, some sort of a name to give us. So he wanted to say we call ourselves the Blue Sky Rangers because we did use the term 'blue sky sessions' for brainstorming sessions.
>
> And so he said, 'You call yourselves the Blue Sky Rangers,' and we said, 'No, we don't call ourselves the Blue Sky Rangers.' 'Yeah, but I want to put in the article that you call yourselves the Blue Sky Rangers.' 'No, but we don't call ourselves the Blue Sky Rangers. That's a stupid name, we don't want it to say that.' Finally, he said, 'how about we say, you ARE the Blue Sky Rangers, because if I say you're the Blue Sky Rangers, then you're the Blue Sky Rangers.' And our vice president said, 'Nahhhh.' And the senior vice president in charge of publicity said, 'Yessss. We want this article.'
>
> So the article said that we're the Blue Sky Rangers. We thought it was a very stupid name, which is why we immediately made up T-shirts, because anytime there's something stupid, we embrace it.

The team soon grew, adding members such as David Warhol. By the time the article came out, the team had 22 members. The article described the hard but often joyful parts of the job, where underslept and overenthusiastic programmers code, playtest their games, and bounce ideas off each other. It could take up to 20 months to develop the average Intellivision game. It didn't matter—despite the hard work and long hours, those Mattel employees discovered what many thousands have found since: Developing games is one of the coolest jobs ever.

Over the following year, the Blue Sky Rangers grew to more than 100 people. Robinson explained why there were so many members: "The 'Blue Sky Rangers' kind of caught on as a name for the Intellivision programmers, but at Mattel, we would also have Atari 2600 programmers, so the Blue Sky Rangers included those programmers," he said. "But then there were also people who were closely involved with Mattel or with the games, in the marketing department; in the personnel department; in Design and Development, like voice—these people who really handled the voice editing were in D&D. So we kind of kept expanding what 'Blue Sky Rangers' were. We finally figured out the Blue Sky Rangers were anybody that we invited to our parties."[13]

Tron: Deadly Discs (Mattel, October 1982)

Disney's *Tron* was one of the most anticipated movies of 1982. This pop culture phenomenon marked the first time a major studio released a motion picture about a video game and the first time live actors appeared in a computer-generated world. In the movie, which hit theaters on July 9, a computer expert who ran a local arcade was trying to prove his former employer stole his game code, only to end up trapped inside a game himself and sentenced to death. *Tron* also marked a point where video game merchandising—already profitable thanks to *Pac-Man*, *Asteroids*, and other hit coin-ops—combined with blockbuster movie merchandising. Disney first made the concept

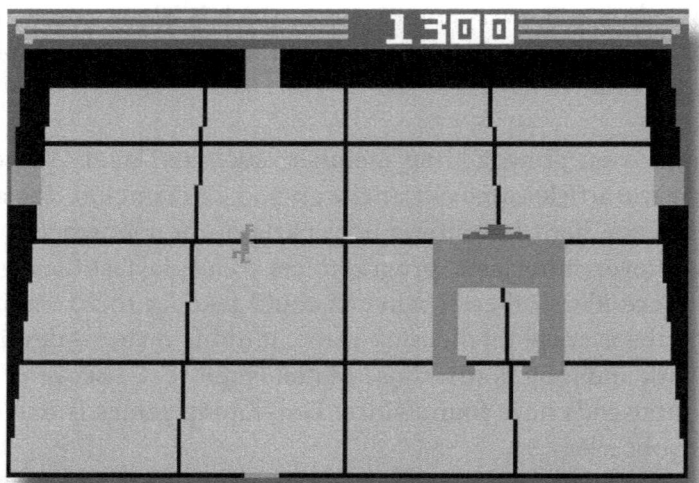

Figure 4.6: ***Tron: Deadly Discs*** **locks you in a arena to do battle with an array of computer-controlled disc throwers and the Recognizer.**

successful with its animated features, but 1977's *Star Wars* propelled it into the stratosphere. For *Tron*, Disney signed with Bally Midway to produce a coin-op of the same name. The resulting machine was excellent, a clever assembly of four minigames depicting various scenes from the movie.

Disney also signed with Mattel to produce three Intellivision game cartridges. *Tron: Deadly Discs*, programmed by Daglow and Steven Sents, locks you in a deadly arena battle against computer-controlled warriors. You must de-rez (kill) them with your flying discs in wave after wave of three against one. The direction disc moves your man around the arena, while eight directional arrows on the keypad throw the disc in the selected direction. The disc returns once it strikes an opponent or hits a wall. Press any throw button, and it will return to you faster. The center "5" button switches from Move to Block mode, which lets you hold the disc as a shield and aim it in any direction to block incoming flying discs.

Your man can take three hits from attacking warriors before the game ends; each time you take a hit, you slow down. Pick off a warrior, and you have 10 seconds to clear the other two; otherwise, the computer will replace the fallen warrior with a new one, although at that point, you can again take three hits. Both you and the attackers regain the ability to withstand additional hits every four seconds. Beginning with 20,000 points, you can take four hits; after 100,000 points, you can take five. Anyone who takes a hit slows down temporarily. Doors at the side of the arena open and close to let warriors in. If you jam opposing doors open with your body or disc, you can use them as an exit like in *Pac-Man* and teleport to the opposite side of the board, recovering one hit in the process. Clear the arena, and you'll earn bonus points before a new wave appears.

The craziest thing is the giant Recognizer, a T-shaped robot that pops out whenever there's at least one jammed door. Its primary purpose is to repair jammed doors, but it can also send out a probe that freezes you for the rest of the time the Recognizer is in the arena. The only way to destroy it is to hit it in the eye with your flying disc. It shoots sparks everywhere and leaves the arena. If you manage to touch it, the game ends immediately, so don't do that.

The higher your score, the more challenging the game gets. Light-blue warriors are the easiest to de-rez and take just one hit. Purple warriors take two hits but are slower and less accurate; dark-blue warrior leaders can only take one hit, but their mere presence makes the other warriors better shots. Orange warriors serve as guards and only appear after you score 1,000,000 points. They take four hits to de-rez and carry white sticks that paralyze you and end the game immediately. It's possible to earn 1,000,000 points on the regular simply by keeping the warriors alive to prevent the guards from arriving and then blocking and shattering their discs until you get bored of playing.

Tron: Deadly Discs is one of the best original Intellivision games and is still fun to play today. The graphics and gameplay hold up, and it's an excellent non-sports use of the famous running man. Usually, the middle of the figure has an air gap. But Mattel programmers joined the top and bottom halves to better represent the "space onesie" science-fiction films and television are known for. The movie was a box office disappointment, meaning less-than-stellar sales and revenue from all the related video games. Even the excellent *Tron* and *Discs of Tron* coin-ops, unrelated to the deal with Mattel, weren't big revenue generators. *Deadly Discs* did the best of the three Intellivision cartridges and landed somewhere north of 300,000 sales, but that was still just one-third of projections.[14]

Imagic

As the Intellivision surged in popularity, it was only a matter of time before third-party developers began to make games for it. Imagic (a portmanteau of "imagination" and "magic") was the first to dive in and the one that dove in deepest. Some ex-Atari employees started the company, including its vice president for marketing and critical developers such as Rick Maurer and Brad Stewart, who were responsible for programming the 2600 versions of *Space Invaders* and *Asteroids*. Imagic games soon became known for their crisp graphics and innovative gameplay. Even on retail shelves, Imagic titles impressed with their beautiful packaging, including silver-foil labels, boxes, and distinctive, slanted black plastic cartridge edges. The company's Intellivision cartridges also came with thicker, matte-coated overlays that have held up better over the years than their glossy Mattel counterparts.

Imagic cartridges marked some of the best games for the Intellivision. Let's start with the company's first.

Atlantis (Imagic, October 1982)

A beautiful conversion of an already-excellent Atari 2600 game, *Atlantis* puts you in charge of defending the fabled underwater lost city from swarms of attacking spaceships. This upgraded version is considerably more advanced. The story goes that the evil Gorgon Fleet is invading the mythical underwater city of Atlantis. You must blast as many Gorgon vessels out of the sky as possible before they can destroy city sectors with giant death rays. Three defense installations guard the city that you can fire from. You use the crosshair sights to aim shots from the two anti-aircraft in the sentry posts on the far left and right. Press the direction disc, and the crosshair sight moves in any direction; the top side buttons fire the left and right anti-aircraft guns, respectively. These have unlimited ammunition, and every ship you destroy in this manner earns 10 points.

You can also launch the Sentinel Saucer from the center by pressing the Saucer button on the overlay. It will take off from the launch pad, and the crosshair sight will disappear. From there, you move the saucer with the direction disc and fire left or right with the corresponding top side buttons. Each ship you destroy with the Saucer earns you 40 points. The Sentinel Saucer has a fuel gauge that decreases by one unit every few moments. A warning buzzer signals it's time to head back and refuel when it gets down to just five remaining. It will explode if it runs out of fuel or crashes into the city. Return to the launchpad, and the crosshair sight will reappear, meaning that your anti-aircraft guns on the sides are once again available.

Each day cycles between three phases: daylight with a blue sky; dusk with a gray sky; and at night, where giant moving spotlights illuminate portions of the sky so you can see where the enemy ships are. They're only visible as black shadows in the spotlight; otherwise, they're invisible, and you only get hints of their locations by whether they're shooting at you.

"[*Atlantis*] opens in mid-day, goes through the evening hours, and then nighttime comes and the sky is black," programmer Pat Ransil said in a 1983 interview in *Blip*. "You see the enemy only by means of searchlights. Lighting the sky in that manner was the idea of Mike Becker, one of our graphics specialists. That's the way games get created. It's a team effort."[15]

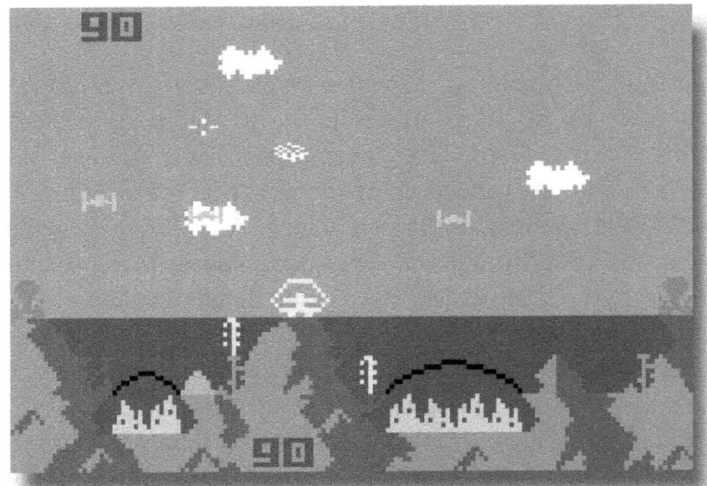

Figure 4.7: The Intellivision's superior port of *Atlantis* from the Atari 2600 made for a stunning introduction to the platform from Imagic.

The Gorgons attack in three waves of squadrons with four ships each, all with varying flight patterns; these include Squid Bombers, Bi-winged Bullets, Rocket Rallies, Spider Fighters, Spar Modules, Recon Rockets, Bandit Bombers, Astro Orbiters, and Cosmic Crawlers. You go through one complete set during each phase of the day. Each full day you survive, the scoring increases by 10 for anti-aircraft guns and 40 for the saucer. So on day two, you earn 20 and 80 points. On day three, you earn 30 and 120 points, and so on. The attract mode shows the different Gorgon ships and how to destroy them.

Squadrons approach from above Atlantis and make four passes across the sky, each lower than the last. In the final, lowest pass, the ships activate their death ray, which destroys the first sector of the city it passes over. The best strategy is to destroy as many of these ships as possible while still high in the sky and not yet low enough to fire their death rays. A nifty two-player mode alternates play at regular intervals, with each player dealing with one wave of three squadrons before the opposite player gets their shot. Each player has their own city, so the layout will change along to the sound of a short musical fanfare when it's time to change players (David Durran handled sound design). The game only ends when both players' cities are destroyed.

Atlantis on the Intellivision is a gorgeous shooter. Although not as smooth as the 2600 version, it offers more complex and satisfying play, and the day-dusk-night cycle delivers a stunning backdrop and additional challenges the 2600 version can't match. Both are worth playing incessantly.

Demon Attack (Imagic, October 1982)

Imagic's launch title for the Atari 2600, *Demon Attack*, received an incredible makeover for the Intellivision. It's closer in some respects to the arcade coin-op *Phoenix* than even Rob Fulop's 2600 version, which had already gotten Imagic in hot water with Atari for its resemblance. It's also more sophisticated, harnessing the Intellivision's superior hardware.

"The [game] designer has to be aware of the pluses and minuses of the system that he or she is designing for," said Ransil, then senior systems engineer at Imagic. "Take Imagic's *Demon Attack*, for instance, which was first designed for the Atari VCS. One of the features of the VCS is that it permits smooth and easy movement across the screen in a horizontal direction. Vertical movement, on the other hand, can

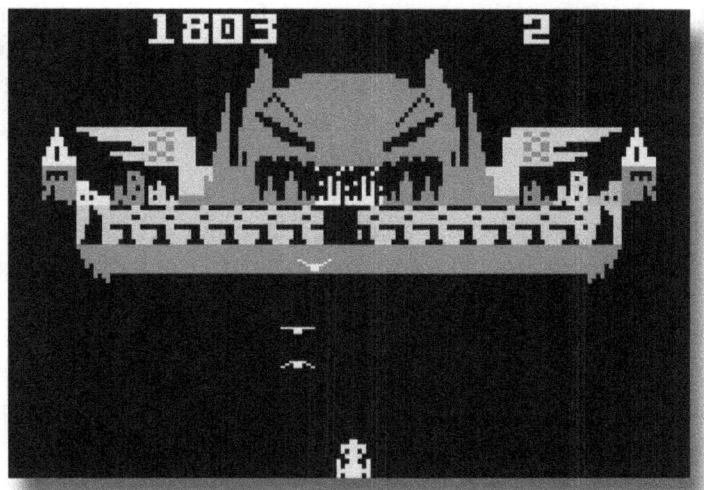

Figure 4.8: Just as with *Atlantis*, Imagic's port of *Demon Attack* to the Intellivision took excellent advantage of the console's improved graphics, sound, and memory over the Atari 2600.

be troublesome. Thus, when Rob Fulop designed *Demon Attack* for the VCS, he programmed the demons to move mostly on a horizontal plane. But when Gary Kato designed the Intellivision version of *Demon Attack*, he was not so limited. He could provide demon movement in any direction—and did."[16] Conversely, the Atari demons are many different colors because the hardware supports it, but the Intellivision doesn't, and the demons are never more than two colors.[17]

The Demon Armada attacks the moon and soon plans to invade Earth. In the Intellivision version, you must defend the moon from incoming waves of suicidal demons and then lift off to face the demon flagship, Pandemonium. The overlay sets the mood with its dark red accents, demon graphics, and black matte backdrop. You use the overlay to select from 12 game variations. These include regular and advanced speeds, the option for tracer shots that follow the location of the laser cannon, and how many players. A confusing two-player co-op game lets you alternate play during the same waves.

The game starts at Moon Station Tranquility, a picturesque scene on the moon's cratered, craggy surface, with a deep starry sky backdrop and the oversized Earth looming in the distance from the right. Your laser cannon has unlimited shots; you move it left and right with the direction disc and fire with the side buttons. Four types of demons attack you: Winged Warriors, Tentacled Terrorists, Bound Bombers, and at the demon's base, yellow Suicide Patrollers. Pressing a keypad number during the game toggles automatic firing. You start the game with three laser cannons and earn an extra one after every wave of eight demons you survive without being hit.

Once you eliminate three waves of demons, you'll reach Pandemonium, a mode the 2600 cartridge doesn't have. Here, you must fend off the Suicide Patrollers, which fly out of the flagship's core. Then you must puncture Pandemonium's flickering shield with repeated laser cannon fire. Finally, you must time your shots to pass through the revolving Window of Vulnerability to destroy the flagship's core. Blast Pandemonium apart, and you get 1,000 points and restart at a higher difficulty level. In subsequent rounds, demons drop bombs that explode and scatter shrapnel, and if you're good and destroy three demon bases, they start letting loose heat-detecting detonators that track your laser cannon. The game also just gets faster and more challenging as you play.

In both versions, *Demon Attack* became Imagic's best-selling game in 1983. Play it, and it's easy to see why. The Intellivision is just as smooth as the Atari 2600 version and almost as fast, and the different enemies make the game feel less repetitive—especially when you approach Pandemonium. The game plays a low, droning synthesizer motif when you reach it, and it takes up the entire width of the screen in resplendent red, orange, and yellow, with its haunting visage and massive flickering shield. It's much more exciting to play than *Space Armada*. I had this game for both systems and enjoyed playing both constantly. Imagic soon ported it to other systems, including Atari and Commodore computers, a joint Tandy 1000 and PCjr version that took advantage of those PCs' upgraded graphics hardware over CGA, the TRS-80 Color Computer, and a slightly different version for the TI-99/4A called *Super Demon Attack*.

Microsurgeon (Imagic, October 1982)

One of the craziest and most innovative video games of the early 1980s, the mazelike *Microsurgeon* puts you in the role of a futuristic doctor at Xenon Medical Center, treating human patients with all kinds of sicknesses following a tanker accident carrying hazardous materials. The striking, colorful graphics present a zoomed-in view of the inside of an ill patient's body, including its bones, organs, and cardiovascular and gastrointestinal systems.

Using the controller disc, you guide a robot probe that shoots medication into each patient to eliminate tumors, clots, disease, and infection and exit the body before the probe runs out of power. You must avoid attacks from invading white blood cells. Nine variations are available at the start: Basic, Intermediate, and Advanced surgical difficulty, and patients with Fair, Critical, or Random statuses. The last option simulates an emergency room where patients come in one after the other with unknown conditions until you begin microsurgery.

The overlay is vital to understanding the game. From the top, the Inside Body button (1) brings up the multiscreen patient view, which shows a frightening view of the patient without skin. The Patient Status button (2) shows a raft of important information, such as the probe's current location, the patient's overall status (good, fair, serious, or critical), the remaining robot probe power, the condition of

Figure 4.9: One of the strangest cartridges ever made, the many-layered *Microsurgeon* turns the typical maze game on its head and shoves it inside the body.

the patient's lungs, gallbladder, heart, kidneys, intestines, and brain, and the level of bacterial infection in the body. You'll also hear the machine beep to the sound of the patient's heart rate.

You control the robot probe with the direction disc and toggle the probe's speed with the Fast/Slow button (0). As you move, the screen scrolls vertically to reveal more surrounding tissue and organs. The probe can safely traverse red, purple, and orange areas. The circulatory system consists of red arteries and purple veins, while orange denotes the lymphatic system. Go anywhere else, such as into white bone, and you'll slow down. Also, roaming white blood cells will begin to attack the probe as a foreign presence in the body, draining it of crucial power reserves. Stationary white blood cells appear as structures in arteries, veins, and lymph nodes. As the probe explores, it loses one power unit every 20 seconds or three units every 20 seconds at a fast speed.

The side buttons dispense medication (shoot), which also costs one power unit per shot; the default is ultrasonic rays (7), which cure many diseases such as cholesterol buildup, gall and kidney stones, tapeworms, tar deposits in the lungs, and tumors. I find tapeworms disgusting in real life and also in the game. You can also shoot antibiotics (8) at green bacteria and aspirin (9) to treat green viruses. Shooting viruses increases your power units by three with the first treatment and one for each additional shot. Take more than three shots to eliminate a virus and you start to lose power. You also gain a unit each time you treat tapeworm, bacteria, kidney, and gall stones. Tumors require up to four shots and you get power reserves for eliminating them in time.

The correct treatment depends on the condition. As you treat each organ, you see the patient's condition improve. The goal is to bring each organ up to Good status, where it will stabilize and no longer deteriorate; otherwise, Fair and Critical organs will continue to worsen until treated. A key strategy is to save the Critical or Serious organs first and then move on to the rest of the conditions. Otherwise, the patient's organs will eventually degrade to Terminal and can no longer be saved. Lose two or more organs, and the patient dies. There are 197 patients in the game, each with a list of conditions and ID bracelet number in the upper-right corner of the status chart. The 24-page manual contains plenty of tips and a detailed glossary of conditions, internal organs, systems.

At the game's end, the hospital calculates your fee (score), and only patients with insurance are billed. You don't make any money if the patient dies or the robot probe runs out of power while still inside the body. Otherwise, the better your job, the more you earn—up to $4,000 depending on the patient's overall status, plus $200 for each "good" organ and $1 for every power unit left in the robot probe. And—here's where the big bucks come into play—if the patient started at Fair, one zero is added to the fee. A Serious patient means two added zeros and a Critical patient means three. Intermediate or Advanced Surgical Difficulty also adds one or two additional zeros. The manual helpfully points out that "microsurgeons, more interested in curing patients than in making tons of money, donate their fees to various disease research foundations," something clearly written before the rise of HMOs.

A two-player game is possible by assigning the second player the ability to select and dispense medications while the first player controls the robot probe and its speed. I'm pretty sure I had at least one nightmare as a kid that this game was directly responsible for. Imagic ported the game to the TI-99/4A and the PCjr, but nothing like it is available for other systems. *Microsurgeon*, programmed by Rick Lavine, won several awards from various computer and game magazines and made it into the Smithsonian's "The Art of Video Games" exhibit in 2012. Not everyone will find the game enjoyable, but it's undeniably ambitious and a key title for the Intellivision.

To this day, *Microsurgeon* is one of the strangest games I ever played. If you'll excuse me, I will now have some ginger ale to settle my stomach. I still can't deal with the idea of tapeworms, even decades later. I guess some people aren't cut out for a career in medicine.

More Competition Threatens Mattel

Several competing systems arrived in the latter half of 1982, threatening the Intellivision and the Atari 2600. The Atari 5200 SuperSystem was ostensibly its intended 2600 successor, despite a complicated and twisting history that led the company to this point. The 5200 was essentially an Atari 400 computer in an oversize wedge-shaped case. Atari promised improved conversions of popular coin-ops that exceeded even what was available on its computer line. Like the Intellivision, the 5200 came with numeric keypad–equipped controllers, complete with Start and Pause buttons and overlay support.

But Atari chose to bundle a conversion of the four-year-old *Super Breakout* that did nothing to show off the console's capabilities. Worse, Atari opted for an odd, stubby joystick design that offered 360-degree control but couldn't self-center. It made playing directional games like *Pac-Man* unnecessarily vague. The 5200 did have a fantastic trackball console accessory for playing *Centipede* and *Missile Command*. Its twin-stick holder made Atari's conversions of *Robotron: 2084* and *Space Dungeon* the best available on a home system. It also didn't play 2600 games out of the gate, which most consumers had expected it could; eventually, Atari sold an expensive adapter. Ultimately, the system had too few games and didn't make a compelling case for itself over simply getting an Atari computer instead.

Meanwhile, Ed Krakauer, who headed up the original Intellivision project, left Mattel in 1981 and formed General Consumer Electronics (GCE). GCE spearheaded the launch of the Vectrex, designed by Smith Engineering.[18] The Vectrex was a compelling, tiny system with a built-in 9-inch, vertically oriented monochrome monitor. You

Figure 4.10: At the time, there was nothing like the Vectrex, a self-contained game system with its own black-and-white screen and tack-sharp vector graphics. (Credit: Evan Amos)

didn't need to hook it up to a television like all the other consoles. The rectangular controller looked like a giant gamepad but included a real joystick on the left and four buttons in a row to the right. The controller folded into the console when you weren't playing. The Vectrex was also the only way to get tack-sharp vector graphics in the home. Vector graphics looked amazing, almost futuristic (and they still do to me!), but color would have been prohibitively expensive. Even then, it couldn't fill in the shapes.

Nonetheless, the systems' vector graphics made it perfect for Cinematronics arcade games like *Star Castle*, *Rip Off*, *Space Wars*, *Armor Attack*, and the built-in *Mine Storm* (a clone of Atari's *Asteroids*). The Vectrex also played interesting interpretations of popular games with raster graphics like *Berzerk*, *Scramble*, and *Pole Position*. Vectrex games came with translucent color overlays you applied to the monitor before play, just like the Magnavox Odyssey (and how many coin-ops of the day were built). The Vectrex sold well during the 1982 holiday season, and soon Milton Bradley picked up the rights to distribute the Vectrex in early 1983.

Figure 4.11: The system that most threatened the Intellivision, the ColecoVision added more power, speed, and color and delivered the best arcade translations of popular games yet. (Credit: Evan Amos)

It was a precarious time for Mattel, even before Wall Street crashed the party. And that's not even counting the Intellivision's most fearsome new competitor—or its worst arcade conversion.

Donkey Kong (Coleco, October 1982)

In May 1982, Atari fumbled the 2600 version of *Pac-Man*, arguably the company's single biggest disaster. It changed the course of the video game industry for the worse, at least as far as how Atari would continue to fit in it. Mattel had a debacle on its hands soon afterward with *Donkey Kong*, which damaged the Intellivision's reputation similarly. This one came from a third-party developer, though. And to understand the story of Intellivision's *Donkey Kong*, it's important to consider the context in which the unfortunate coin-op conversion appeared.

Initially the Connecticut Leather Company, Coleco tried to catch the home video game craze with its Telstar consoles, but Atari proved too tough a competitor. Eventually, Coleco gave up and released the Gemini, a straight-up Atari 2600 clone that played the same cartridges.

But Coleco wasn't done yet. It made a big splash in the home video game market in August 1982 with the ColecoVision, a robust system with more memory and better graphics than the Intellivision and the Atari 2600. Coleco pitched the system and its 12-cartridge launch lineup as bringing arcade-quality gameplay home and even inscribed "plays like the real arcade game" on every cartridge box. And it did, even despite Coleco's inability to secure rights for anything from Atari, thanks to Coleco's stunning conversion of *Donkey Kong* as the pack-in cartridge. Signing up Nintendo for the launch was a massive coup for the company. The console's launch lineup also featured excellent coin-op conversions, such as Konami's *Time Pilot* and Universal's *Cosmic Avenger*, *Mouse Trap*, and *Lady Bug*. There was also a brilliant translation of Sega's *Turbo*, which came complete with a steering wheel and gas pedal controller arrangement unavailable on any other platform.

Simultaneously, Coleco contracted Roklan Corporation to translate coin-ops for competing systems like the Intellivision and the 2600. Coleco had the rights, so it made sense financially, even though it was also a console manufacturer and denying itself potential exclusives. The move made plenty of money for Coleco but didn't go nearly as well as producing cartridges for its own console. The biggest disappointment was the Intellivision's version of *Donkey Kong*, one of the hottest coin-ops of the golden age of arcades. The public was angling to play *Donkey Kong* at home, so having one the year after Nintendo's smash hit arrived in arcades in 1981 was a shoo-in for big sales.

Figure 4.12: Possibly the port that sealed the Intellivision's fate, Coleco's *Donkey Kong* was a huge letdown and only served to cast Mattel's console as not powerful enough for the latest hot games.

It would have been folly to expect older hardware to measure up to the ColecoVision version, much less the original coin-op. But the Intellivision port contains just two of the four boards in the arcade coin-op, just like the 2600 version, and one fewer than the ColecoVision pack-in cartridge. Worse, the graphics are terrible; the girders look accurate enough, but everything is one color (red), including the hammers. Mario looks weird, and Donkey Kong looks nothing like a gorilla. The umbrella on the second board looks like a pickaxe. The whole game plays stiffly; you slow down when you jump, and grabbing and using the hammer is frustrating. When you pick it up, it doesn't even play the arcade's (monophonic!) hammer tune.

Roklan, and by extension Coleco, could have done a much better job with the Intellivision cartridge. Mattel's console was sorely lacking in arcade conversions and desperately needed a good one. *Donkey Kong* sold over a million copies but damaged the Intellivision's reputation. Back then, you took whatever chance you could get to play the hottest arcade games at home. When the cartridge didn't measure up, the disappointment was palpable.

For years, Intellivision programmers suspected Coleco purposely hobbled its conversion so that it didn't show up the new ColecoVision and its blockbuster pack-in cartridge.[19] The Blue Sky Rangers believe it's more likely that Coleco's programmers had a rushed schedule and didn't know the hardware yet.[20] But once the Intellivision received a conversion of another popular game we'll get to shortly—one so good, people think it's even *better* than the ColecoVision's—it only bolstered the theory. So did homebrew, massively improved versions of *Donkey Kong* that have appeared in recent years.

Beauty & the Beast (Imagic, October 1982)

An inspired take on *Donkey Kong* and *Crazy Climber*, *Beauty & the Beast* puts you in control of Bashful Buford, who must rescue his Tiny Mabel from the clutches of Horrible Hank. You must climb up giant skyscrapers, section by section, through open windows while avoiding bats, rats, birds, and whatever boulders Hank tosses down from higher up. Meanwhile, Mabel drops hearts. Catch one to start flashing, become temporarily invulnerable, and gain the ability to zap the boulders, bats, rats, and birds for a few seconds.

Fortunately, the graphics in *Beauty & the Beast* are quite good. The windows have white frames and lights, the platform ledges marking each floor have three bumpers the boulders can bounce off or fall through, and the whole building has a three-dimensional look. Hank, dressed in black, looks like a giant jerk as he holds and throws builders in his right hand and clutches Mabel in his left. Buford looks like Inspector Gadget. You use the direction disc to make him run left and right on the ledges or climb up the open windows; the side buttons cause him to jump, which is useful for clearing rolling boulders. Only one window opens at a time on each floor.

You get three chances at the start and earn an additional chance every two times you reach Hank and Mabel. After the fifth time, you earn them less often. The game progresses quickly as you maneuver up each skyscraper section via the windows. The rocks roll across the platforms and then fall down the openings. If you try and climb up an open window while it's closing, and it closes all the way while you're still on it, you'll fall and lose a chance.

Reach Hank, and the view will zoom out to show you the entire skyscraper, with the parts you've traversed so far colored red. A small biplane flies overhead with a sign containing encouraging words, such as "good job" or "not bad." You earn 100 points for completing a section. Different musical ditties play each time, and the screen displays your current score and chances you have remaining. As you reach the upper levels, the skyscraper thins out, so the boards aren't as wide and the rocks start sliding diagonally (more shades of *Donkey Kong*).

Nab Hank at the top of the skyscraper and the view will zoom back out, showing him falling down the side. Buford and Mabel reunite at last, and you'll earn 500 points. The biplane comes again sans banner, collects Buford and Mabel, and flies them off the screen. Then you start on a new skyscraper with new challenges, including rocks that split into two. And in case you're wondering if you can fall off the side, you can. The game ensures you see the whole thing as you fall section by section until you hit the street back on the first board. Of course, you must start the current skyscraper all over again.

As a platformer, *Beauty & the Beast* is undoubtedly better than the *Donkey Kong* port Coleco "blessed" the Intellivision with. It's a compelling premise, and the fast pace of play makes it fun, if somewhat repetitive.

Figure 4.13: *Beauty & The Beast* **immediately reversed the damage from** *Donkey Kong,* **for those who knew of its existence.**

Tron: Maze-a-Tron (Mattel, October 1982)

Maze-a-Tron is an intriguing if difficult game that's inspired by the movie, with equal parts action and strategy. You're the young programmer Flynn, trapped inside a computer system by the Master Control Program (MCP), which seeks to conquer the human race. The object is to clear the computer's memory chips in the first phase of the game and disable the MCP in the second. This cartridge is not easy to explain, and most people eventually gave up on it. I didn't have this one as a kid, but I most certainly would have given up on it, as that's exactly what I've done as an adult for years. I finally put in the time to understand this one and will do my best to cover it here because it was a hugely ambitious design and absolutely nothing else is like it, even if the results were almost impregnable to gamers of the day.

The first phase is a forced-scrolling Circuit Maze. You run the maze using the control disc. Green trace lines denote the walls. The maze consists of four circuit boards, each with 38 sections; the layout is the same every time and there are only five section layouts, so you can learn it with some persistence. Two of the four boards have sets of RAM chips, and you only need to clear one of the sets. You can travel between the boards by entering I/O Transporter chips, which dematerialize you in one spot, send you flying over the boards, and rematerialize you in another, random place.

To win the Circuit Maze, you must first gather zeros inside Latches, which are chips that have lock icons. The longer you stay inside one, the more zeros you accumulate, to a maximum of 255. Transformers are also helpful; they recharge your energy units (up to 255 as well). Once you have some zeros, you must find the RAM chips and turn the numbers inside each one into black zeros to clear it. Enter a RAM chip from the top to turn the left number black, enter form the bottom to turn the right number black, and if the number is a one, use a stored zero to turn it into a zero. Repeat for the entire set of chips.

Several obstacles get in the way of clearing the RAM chips. The forced scrolling means you're constantly working against being pushed off the screen and sent back to the beginning. Although you don't lose a life when this happens, it's annoying. Helpful Flip-Flop circuits let you change the scrolling direction when you're in a tough spot, if you're lucky enough to be near one. Meanwhile, giant Recognizer guards come after you and are generally impossible to avoid; you can either activate your Force Shield or lead the Recognizer into a ROM Force Field, both of which will disable it. Otherwise, you'll lose a turn if you

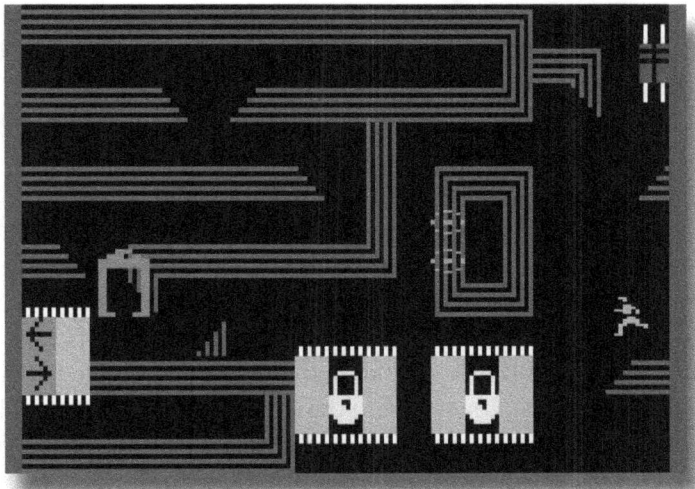

Figure 4.14: *Tron: Maze-a-Tron* proved too baffling for most gamers despite its amazing graphics and unique gameplay.

touch a Recognizer. And zaps, circular electrical impulses that follow the board traces, severely drain your energy units if you touch them.

Clear an entire set of RAM chips and you'll enter the second phase, where you face the MCP in all his ugliness. Whenever his eyes turn from orange to red, he's about to shoot a laser at you; you can activate your Force Shield to deflect the beam. While fending off the MCP, you must find pairs of numbers in the two center columns that match the bit pair at the top of the two outer columns. You use the controller to turn the matching bit pairs black before they leave the playfield. The disc moves the bit gun sight, and the top side buttons fires the gun to turn numbers black. When a matching pair exits the screen on top, the stack pops and the next set of bits is on deck for matching. If you get hit by lasers three times, or when the outer columns leave the screen entirely, you're transported back to the maze. Win and you start over at a higher difficulty level.

The graphics and sound design in *Maze-a-Tron* really stood out at the time, with its attractive, inside-the-computer visuals and menacing synthesizer tones pulsing in the background. Just about everyone who had it remembers it well but had no idea what was going on in it. You can choose from four maze speeds, and a Practice Mode lets you try your hand at phase II at the lowest difficulty level and without scoring. But none of that helped.

Fire it up without knowing any of the above, and all that happens is you start in a maze, the maze starts scrolling, and then either it keeps pushing you off the screen and bringing you back to the beginning, or you run around aimlessly to prevent that from happening but have no idea what you're actually supposed to *do*—and then the Recognizer appears and kills you anyway. Although the game's graphics were striking in 1982, they weren't realistic enough to distinguish the various chips and other elements without the manual's help. Even the score readout only appears for a few seconds at the start of your turn; the left number is your energy units, the middle is how many zeros you have, and the right is how many lives you have left. Which number is which isn't obvious, and then the readout disappears before you can begin to interpret the "25 0 3" at the bottom of the screen. None of them is even your score, despite the zero in the center; your score doesn't appear until the MCP phase, or if you don't make it that far, until the game ends.

Maze-a-Tron flopped at retail, mainly because of the same box office-related reason as *Deadly Discs*, as opposed to anything about the gameplay. Like *Utopia*, *Maze-A-Tron* made the Smithsonian's "The Art of Video Games" exhibit. Like *Tron* itself, this game is an incredible time capsule of 1982 graphic design, perhaps more so than *Deadly Discs*. (If you're curious, the other two Intellivision games included in the exhibit were *Star Strike* and *Advanced Dungeons & Dragons*.)

More Games for 1982

Mattel soon locked down its quality control from APh, thanks to several bugs in *Royal Dealer*, a cartridge that brought Hearts, Crazy Eights, and Gin Rummy to the Intellivision. According to the Blue Sky Rangers, APh was late in delivering *Royal Dealer*. To get it out in time for the 1982 holiday season, Mattel essentially pushed it straight through to production with almost no quality assurance. The result was discovering a bug that crashed the game. Mattel only projected 36,000 sales, so it shipped the cartridge anyway and included an errata slip. After this, the QA department "was given life-or-death authority over future games; nothing was allowed to be released until the official game testers Traci Roux and Dale Lynn had signed off on it."[21]

A late release was *USCF Chess*, which included 2KB RAM in the cartridge. Long delayed so that Mattel programmers could get the AI right and maintain the console's reputation as "Intelligent Television,"[22] *USCF Chess* became the most expensive Intellivision cartridge ever at $55.95 and was well received.[23] *Sharp Shot* packaged the action elements of four existing cartridges, turning them into fun minigames that could be played by younger kids—or older folks just looking for some mindless shooting action.

More third-party games started to trickle in. Coleco released a solid port of the circus-themed shooter *Carnival*, and Activision brought over its I-can't-believe-this-is-fun lassoing game *Stampede* from the Atari 2600. The trickle would turn into a deluge in 1983.

Trouble Ahead

By the end of 1982, though, clouds had appeared on the horizon. Major retailers such as JCPenney, Toys "R" Us, Sears, and others had stocked up on products to sell for the holiday season, but a growing sense was that the wave had already crested. Mattel began offering a $50 mail-in rebate for the Intellivision, something it promoted in several new television commercials featuring George Plimpton. According to John Hillkirk, Gannett News Service, for *USA Today* on November 14, 1982, retailers anticipated a rush and packed their shelves with video game machines and cartridges, but noted that "many could collect nothing but dust…A growing number of observers fear that inventories are too high, and customer interest too low, to empty the shelves."

"I sense a real industry bloodbath," said consumer electronics market analyst Jerry Wasserman, as Atari Inc., Intellivision, and other firms started battling for market share. "It won't destroy all the companies but many will start dropping out." He said the $50 rebate indicated that retailers needed customer incentives to sell their huge inventories.

"The same thing that happened to the CB radio, pocket calculator, and digital watch industries could happen with video games," Hillkirk reported analysts as saying. "Meanwhile, sales of inexpensive home computers that can play games as well as be used for financial planning and other tasks are growing at 110 percent a year."[24]

The biggest problem for Mattel was that it was headed in the opposite direction. In late 1982, it finally brought the hammer down on the Keyboard Component and all related software and peripherals in development. News continued to trickle into 1983 that it would still be released, possibly in a different form, as a suddenly much lower price indicated. *Electronics Magazine* ran a segment in its "Electronic Games Hotline" feature in the April 1983 issue declaring, "Intellivision's Keyboard Is Here." It said the keyboard is "at last ready for release to the general public after extensive testing…The $150 unit is described as being capable of performing the functions of a home computer when attached to the Master Component Console… Test-marketed for the past two years, the keyboard should be fully distributed by mid-83." I sympathize with the magazine's editors, which had to deal with the months-long print lead times common in those days.

Mattel had its reasons to give up on the original attachment. Thanks to the delays, any hope the Keyboard Component would be competitive was squashed. Mattel had been paying daily fines to the

FTC while it scrambled to produce product. Ultimately, Mattel sold just 4,000 units via mail order, thanks to continuing technical issues and difficulties in servicing customer units.[25] Mattel made any customer who wanted to keep their Keyboard Component sign a waiver that absolved the company of all future responsibility for technical support.[26] In the end, Mattel used the platform as a dev kit for future titles. Compro, the company Mattel had contracted out to manufacture the units, sued Mattel for $10 million for breach of contract, fraud, and not paying for the last 1,300 units, a lawsuit Mattel ended up settling out of court.[27]

Although Mattel Electronics was in trouble, Atari ran straight into a wall. On December 7, the company announced that 2600 sales wouldn't meet estimates, causing the stock to fall and ultimately kicking off an SEC investigation. Mattel also missed estimates and lost money during the quarter, leading to a suspension of trading Mattel stock for two days, and further agitation across the rest of the sector for Coleco and Toys "R" Us. Imagic postponed its plans to go public.[28]

Despite the above woes, the Intellivision was still selling surprisingly well—thanks not just to that $50 incentive but also to a slew of excellent titles such as *Advanced Dungeons & Dragons*, *Star Strike*, *Astrosmash*, and Imagic's stellar third-party lineup. To give a small example of how the market looked heading into the 1982 holiday season, an October 22, 1982, Toys "R" Us ad for its new store in Shreveport showcased six systems: three game consoles and three home computers. The Intellivision was listed at $149.97 after a $50 rebate, compared with the Atari 2600 at $129.84 and the ColecoVision at $189.97. On the computer front, the ad listed the Commodore VIC-20 at $179.87 next to the Texas Instruments TI-99/4A for $199.97 (after a $100 rebate) and the Atari 400 at $269.96.[29] Games like *Pac-Man*, *Donkey Kong*, and the long-awaited *E.T.: The Extra-Terrestrial* for the Atari 2600 were also high on everyone's wish lists this season. The problem was that not everyone was discounting the Intellivision so much. And the ColecoVision, Vectrex, and Atari 5200 were about to have their first Christmas.

Radio Shack launched the Tandyvision One, another branded version of the Intellivision with wood trim instead of the top-mounted gold strips. It opened the Intellivision to an existing retail chain with thousands of locations in the U.S. and top-notch brand name recognition. It also gave Radio Shack a game system to sell next to its wildly popular TRS-80 computer line and its then-new Color Computer. But at $249.95, it cost more than a TI-99/4A or Commodore VIC-20, as *InfoWorld* reported.[30] Sears advertised the Super Video Arcade ($199.99) next to the Video Arcade ($124.99) in *Time* magazine that December, along with the Intellivoice module ($69.99). Among the cartridges listed were *Space Spartans* ($34.99), *Demon Attack* ($22.99), and *Lock 'N Chase* ($29.99).[31]

Industry pundits were optimistic about Mattel's chances, speculating that the company was getting close to releasing its own home computer. Its combination of speech synthesis and M Network games would keep the company in the thick of it for the holiday season. But Radio Shack already sold its own TRS-80 computers, so no one expected it to go near the Keyboard Component.[32] *InfoWorld* cited Mattel's Keyboard Component debacle in suggesting that consumers may also balk at the ColecoVision's promised plug-in keyboard and printer, due to be released sometime in 1983.[33]

The Intellivision was still scoring good press. The November 1982 issue of *Video* ran "Video's Guide to Electronic Games," a survey of the market penned by Arnie Katz, Bill Kunkel, and "the editors of *Electronic Games* magazine." It covered what it called "the four major systems": the Atari 2600, the Odyssey^2, the Intellivision, and the Astrocade. It noted how Mattel intended its console as the first module of a multicomponent personal computer system and had so far "failed to put any other components into general distribution since then," but that most Intellivision owners didn't care "since Intellivision has turned out to be an excellent video-game console."[34] The article called it a "senior programmable console" (hey, it was three years old already), but pointed out its "top-flight graphics" that were "still without peer" among the four major systems. "As George Plimpton never tires of pointing out in its commercials, Intellivision games almost always look better than competitors' equivalents."[35] The writers went on to criticize the console's slow on-screen movement speed in arcade games and that the controllers are "either a strength or a weakness depending on who's doing the judging." They added that the Intellivision continued to offer strategy and sports simulations that were "certainly the finest ever produced in video game form," and that the console was sleekly attractive and "the best-looking unit of the big four."³⁶ The article also mentioned the still-upcoming Intellivoice, which hadn't gone into wide release yet. (This makes sense assuming a two-month print lead time and the November issue appearing on stands most likely sometime in October.)

"Remember when you could rent video game systems from mom-and-pop video stores in the early eighties?" wrote Levi Buchanan, the editor of IGN Retro, in 2014. "I was a regular renter of the Intellivision. It wasn't George Plimpton that convinced me, though. It was the screenshots of Imagic (one of my favorite third-party publishers ever) games on the Intellivision that were just not possible on the Atari 2600. *Microsurgeon*? *Dracula*? *Beauty and the Beast*? These were among the first games I picked up when I entered my collecting phase in 1999 and went daffy over buying back my childhood."³⁷

The good news is that everyone could and did have a terrific time with the Intellivision, even without the Keyboard Component ever coming to fruition. Plus, Mattel switched gears and developed a lower-cost alternative for the Intellivision and a separate low-cost computer. In the end, the company eventually did release a proper keyboard attachment—just not the one it had originally promised.

5 | Clouds

At the January 1983 CES, Mattel Electronics revamped its entire Intellivision lineup. First up was the updated Intellivision II, a redesign of the Master Component with squared-off, computer-age styling. The new unit was lighter and smaller at just 10 by 6.6 inches. More streamlined than the original model, it was finished in a chic light gray color with black and red accents. Mattel combined the power switch and Reset button into a single switch and added a red power LED. The controllers were now detachable for easy replacement and featured longer coiled cords. Most importantly, a cheaper-to-manufacture console meant a lower list price.

The Intellivision II had the same 16-bit CP1610 CPU and supporting chipset. The new controllers looked sharp, but they were a step backward. The keypad was completely flat instead of bubbled, and many people missed the feedback from button pushes. It meant that a game designed to be played by the feel of the buttons under the overlays couldn't be played in the same way. The side buttons were easier to press, though.

Mattel also modified the internal Exec OS to lock out unlicensed third-party games. It wasn't necessarily a terrible idea, but to add the lock-out code and retain compatibility with existing games, Mattel engineers moved some portions of the code in a way that changed the timing of their execution. It surfaced in how some sound effects

Figure 5.1: The slick Intellivision II offered new 1980s styling and a gray-and-black color scheme with red accents. (Credit: Evan Amos)

were different in *Shark! Shark!* and *Space Spartans* when played on the Intellivision II. The Electric Company's *Word Fun* wouldn't run at all.[1]

To go with the Intellivision II, the company introduced a redesigned Intellivoice module that matched the Intellivision II's styling. The new version featured a large black volume dial on the top panel. Mattel also unveiled the long-awaited System Changer, a module that added Atari 2600 cartridge compatibility to the Intellivision II, bringing it to parity with the Atari 5200 and ColecoVision, each of which had its own 2600 game adapter. The System Changer included difficulty switches, a game select switch, and a switch for color or black and white, all mirroring elements of Atari's console but with sleeker styling to match the Intellivision II line. The Changer contained a 2600 chipset and only used the Intellivision for its power supply and RF modulator.[2] But it was late to market, and it only worked with the Intellivision II. Original console owners needed a ROM upgrade to support it.

The company announced a slew of new Intellivision games, many of which we'll cover in the next two chapters, including a fourth game for the Intellivoice. But it was another announcement from Mattel Electronics that drew the most attention.

Entertainment Computer System (ECS)

Also at CES, Mattel unveiled the $119 Entertainment Computer System (ECS), which finally delivered on (some of) the Keyboard Component's promises to a national audience. Mattel had previewed its existence in a few holiday 1982 commercials, but the official CES launch displayed all the goods. The Intellivision Computer Adapter was the brains of the system. It included 2KB of RAM, two more controller ports, a second GI sound chip adding three more audio channels, cassette recorder I/O, a printer port, and built-in BASIC. It came with a detachable 49-key alphanumeric QWERTY Computer Keyboard with silent, raised chiclet-style keys and a sealed surround that made it easy to keep clean. The keyboard let you create your own programs and play more advanced games.

Along with the ECS, Mattel introduced the $99 Intellivision Music Synthesizer, a 49-key music keyboard with full-size organ-style keys, and the *Melody Blaster* cartridge for learning to compose and play six-voice music. Play notes on the keyboard, and they'd appear on the television screen. With the ECS attached, the Intellivision also became the first console with a synthesizer keyboard. Mattel also promised an array of additional peripherals. The Program Expander added an advanced 8KB BASIC interpreter in ROM and 16KB of RAM. Extra Hand Controllers would enable three- and four-player games when combined with the Intellivision's first two. The Audio Cassette would save and load your BASIC programs as well as run prepackaged software. It would also store and load your compositions from *Melody Maker*. The ECS works with just about any tape deck, though.

To go with its new product, Mattel jettisoned all the original software for the Keyboard Component and instead announced a new lineup of Computer Adapter cartridges. *Mr. BASIC Meets Bits 'N' Bytes* turned learning BASIC programming into three minigames using the Computer Keyboard and game controllers. *Game Maker* would include graphics and gameplay logic that you could select and assemble to make your own game, and it could read the graphics characters from any Intellivision cartridge you plugged in so you could put them in a new game. *BASIC Programmer* was a more serious package that included lessons, a printed step-by-step manual, and examples of programs you could write. One neat feature was importing the

Figure 5.2: Mattel finally delivered on the promise of a computer attachment with the Entertainment Computer System...

sprites from any Intellivision cartridge and using them in your own programs. Unfortunately, ECS BASIC wasn't powerful enough. You couldn't use it to write a game anywhere near as good as even one of the Intellivision's first cartridges, much less something as complex as home computer software.

Other ECS titles traversed familiar territory. *The Jetsons Ways With Words* was a colorful maze game that taught spelling, reading, and word recognition skills using the famous Hanna-Barbera characters. *The Flintstones Keyboard Fun* would teach typing, and *Number Jumble* was another planned math cartridge. *Astromusic* was an upcoming music version of *Astrosmash* that you would play with the 49-key music keyboard, destroying falling musical notes from the sky by pressing the right keys to form patterns of music from popular songs. *Music Conductor* aimed to teach you to play songs by following the on-screen music notation and offered pitch drills and interval recognition exercises.

Pundits were mixed as to whether the ECS would do well. "After crying wolf so many times in the past four years, Mattel unveiled a revised version of its Intellivision keyboard computer attachment at the January Consumer Electronics Show (CES)," the March 1983 issue of *Video Games* magazine said. "The new unit, expected to sell for less than $200, should be available this summer. Although [it] still features a full 60-key typewriter-style keyboard, the built-in cassette deck…has been sacrificed…"[3] A Mattel spokesperson said that testing showed consumers weren't pleased with the original's bulkiness, although the publication said that they weren't too thrilled with the price, either.

The ECS wasn't nearly as powerful as the Keyboard Component, and the Intellivision didn't dock into it. Even so, it could have been a cool setup if it wasn't so hobbled to meet a price point. Some questioned whether Mattel Electronics released the middling ECS only to stave off further legal trouble with the FTC.

Intellivision III

At the same CES in January 1983, Mattel teased Intellivision III, a system that would leapfrog even the newly released ColecoVision. The new system would still include a CP1610 CPU, but at twice the speed and with more sprites. It would feature an improved STIC chip—most probably the Super-STIC processor engineers were testing in December 1981—with up to 320-by-192-pixel resolution, the same as the new Commodore 64, plus a vast color palette. Mattel planned a new six-voice sound chip with a built-in Intellivoice speech synthesizer. The Intellivision III would also have more ROM and RAM, wireless infrared joysticks, and run all existing Intellivision games.[4]

"Discussed only in terms of total awe by those fortunate enough to have seen the prototype, [the Intellivision III] is intended to be Mattel's bid to produce the ultimate video game," wrote the editors of *Electronic Games*. "Projected to sport a $300 suggested retail price, this loaded-with-features machine sports the best graphics resolution of any video game, even more on-screen colors, a greater amount of screen RAM so that 64 objects can move simultaneously, remote joystick controls, stereo port, and much, much more. There's even a built-in voice synthesizer...Although the games previewed were described by Mattel officials as '20% complete,' they blew our socks off, anyway. Some of the multi-screen adventures, such as *Treasure of the Yucatan*, surpass anything yet seen on a home video game screen."

It turned out the prototype was only a regular Intellivision with Super-STIC installed.[5] The company also showed off a revised Intellivoice module with the same styling and color scheme as the Intellivision II. Unfortunately, it was just a block of painted wood. Mattel built two prototypes that included three additional languages in ROM, and a new version of *Space Spartans* could access those, but none of these were released.[6]

Mattel Aquarius

Confusingly, Mattel Electronics also unveiled a new computer system at the winter CES. It wasn't an Intellivision product, but it's essential to understand it in the context of the turmoil facing Mattel and how it affected our prized gaming platform.

The Aquarius home computer was designed by the Hong Kong–based Radofin, which also manufactured some Intellivision consoles. Mattel picked up the distribution rights in a fortuitous bit of good timing, as Radofin began shopping it for a distributor just as Mattel canceled the Keyboard Component. Right before the summer CES in June 1983, the company released it. Mattel billed the Aquarius as using "advanced technology to create a home computer system that's truly simple. So simple, you can write your first program minutes after you open the box." John J. Anderson, an associate editor of *Creative Computing*, was slightly less kind: "a machine so cheesy, they should have supplied rubber gloves to wear while using it."[7]

The $159.95 Aquarius featured a compact if toylike design that measured just 2 by 13 by 6 inches (HWD) and weighed 5.5 pounds. It included a Zilog Z80A processor, sharp 320-by-192-pixel graphics resolution, a palette of 16 colors, 8KB ROM with built-in Microsoft BASIC, and 4KB RAM that was expandable to 52KB. The 49-key QWERTY rubber chiclet keyboard featured stiff, bright-blue keys that were difficult to type on quickly. Inexplicably, the space bar was just a space key, the same size as the letter keys. The system connected to any television.

Mattel designed several peripherals for the machine. The Aquarius Data Recorder stored and retrieved BASIC programs on cassette. The Aquarius Printer delivered 40-column-wide thermal printouts at 80 characters per second. The 300 bps Aquarius Modem let you call online services with a direct connection. The poorly named Mini Expander (it was pretty bulky) included the Intellivision's AY-3-8914 three-voice audio chip, two detachable controllers, and two ports that could house game cartridges or a 16KB Aquarius Memory Cartridge. The Data Recorder and Printer also worked with the ECS.

For software, Mattel released Extended Microsoft BASIC, which included better editing tools, and Aquarius Logo for turtle graphics programming. The company unveiled a slew of productivity software including home records, financial planning, tax tips, a menu planner, a database for home maintenance, and This Is Today, a word-of-the-day and horoscope program that displayed information about historical events. Mattel also released Aquarius versions of many of the Intellivision's best games, such as the modestly revamped *Utopia* and *Nightstalker* (retitled as one word for some reason). You could also buy *Chess* and *Reversi* programs, and Mattel planned a full suite of educational software for math, geography, spelling, biorhythms, speed reading, Black history, and college preparation. Many seemed pulled straight out of Atari's Home Computer software lineup from a few years earlier (though the original Keyboard Component already promised Speed Reading).

Mattel also planned the Aquarius Master Expansion Module. This much larger case supported two floppy drives, the CP/M operating system, and 16KB memory expansion boards, a proposition that sounded much more like a workable personal computer. The Aquarius even got its own magazine, *Aquarius User*.

The result of all this was that no one could figure out which Mattel machine they should buy—the Aquarius, an 8-bit home computer that played some Intellivision games, or the ECS, a 16-bit computer attachment for the Intellivision game console that ran some computer-like software.[8] And like the ECS, the Aquarius was too hobbled out of the box, in this case with just one voice for sound and not enough base memory—only 1.7KB of the 4KB was available for programs, a

Figure 5.3: ...only to then also release a full-blown computer almost simultaneously: the Mattel Aquarius.

staggeringly low amount for a 1983 computer. You could barely type a document into its Fileform word processor with such little memory.[9] Mattel should have pulled an Atari and upgraded the base RAM in time for release, regardless of what the company announced; competing Atari 400s had at least 8KB on their release in late 1979 and soon came with 16KB. In the end, few customers bought either product.

The Aquarius was compact and had nice graphics for a low price, but its keyboard wasn't any fun to type on, and it wasn't even as powerful as the Texas Instruments TI-99/4A or the Commodore VIC-20, two low-end systems that predated it by two years. Those systems also came with more memory. By the time you bought the necessary expansions and peripherals needed to get any use out of the Aquarius, it ended up costing $200 or more—more than the competition, in other words. Retailers switched to selling the Aquarius bundled with the Mini Expander, although you still needed to buy the Data Recorder to store programs. Sales remained slow, and Mattel pulled the plug in October 1983, just four months after its release and nine months after its unveiling. The promised modem, expansion module, and thermal printer never appeared. One year later, you could find the Aquarius for $39 *with* the Mini Expander and four game cartridges.[10]

I once helped a friend's sister program her Aquarius in the mid 1980s. She didn't understand how it worked and asked me to try it.

She became impressed with the computer after I typed in a demo program that made Intellivision Man run across the screen. The problem was her parents didn't buy the Data Recorder with it, so we couldn't save the program to a cassette. Her dad wasn't interested in buying it, so of course, she had zero interest in writing her own programs if she couldn't save her work, which now makes me sad just thinking about it. She didn't understand it only because it wasn't fully functional.

Mattel only sold an estimated 20,000 Aquarius systems, just one-fifth of what it had projected. Six issues of *Aquarius User* were ultimately published. Seeing the writing on the wall early, designer Bob Del Principe gave the system a slogan during its development: "Aquarius: A system for the seventies."

Shark! Shark! (Mattel, January 1983)

Moving on from Mattel's mixed bag of new hardware, let's begin 1983's game releases with the excellent *Shark! Shark!*, which turns your television into a kind of giant aquarium. You're a small fish that must eat smaller fish and bite a scary black shark's tail without touching his head or fins. The more fish you eat, the larger you grow, meaning you can eat more kinds of fish. The sharks eat other fish and especially want to eat you, but they can't eat lobsters or crabs. Each time you bite a shark's tail, it becomes paralyzed briefly. Eventually, he'll turn brown and die. The game is a blast to play.

Each game starts with your yellow fish in the middle of the screen. Keep eating fish to earn points; whenever you earn another 1,000 points, you grow one size bigger (up to five). As you become larger, you can kill not just small fish but crabs, seahorses, lobsters, jellyfish, and even sharks. Soon, a size-6 jellyfish emerges, and you can't do much but avoid him. Whenever you lose a life, you start at the smallest size again.

The game displays how many fish you have remaining on the top left and your score on the right. In a two-player game, numbers for both players appear on each side. Player one controls the yellow fish, and player two has the red one; you attack each other and the rest of the fish. Because you're both the fastest fish on-screen, your human opponent is the toughest of all. You can hide in the coral reefs at the bottom, but not for long, as you'll uncover dangerous crabs and lobsters.

The direction disc moves your fish in the desired direction. Pressing a keypad key causes your fish to "dart" fast in the direction it's already heading. The side buttons stop all movement. Nibble at the shark's tail for long enough, and he'll die—which affords a respite for a few seconds, but then a new one appears. Scoring varies depending on each fish's type and size; most are worth between 100 and 350 points. Nibbling a shark's tail nets you anywhere from 150 to 350 points, depending on your size. Crabs and lobsters are worth between 500 and 750 points. As with *Asteroids*, the idea is to keep your fish near the center of the screen; otherwise, you may be surprised by the appearance of a new fish and won't be able to react in time.

Shark! Shark! was programmed and codesigned by Ji-Wen Tsao, one of the first female video game creators. It's one of the system's best titles, thanks to its addictive gameplay and challenging two-player mode. In the early 1980s, it gave players something to do besides play sports, eat dots in mazes, or shoot at things. Mattel didn't think much of the game and only commissioned 5,600 copies at launch, compared with 800,000 for *Star Strike*. Nonetheless, *Shark! Shark!* went on to earn many positive reviews in the nascent gaming press, and *Electronic Fun With Computers and Games* named *Shark! Shark!* one of the "Fifty Best Games" in its March 1984 issue.[11]

Figure 5.4: Turn your television into a giant aquarium with *Shark! Shark!*. It's a terrific game, too.

Dragonfire (Imagic, January 1983)

In the fast-paced *Dragonfire*, another striking Imagic title, dragons have driven the royal court from a treasure-filled castle. It's up to you, the Prince, to raid the castle and recover treasures for the King. To do so, you must cross bridges while dodging fireballs of dragon breath. Then you must pick up all the treasures a fearsome dragon is guarding without getting killed. Do that and exit through the door, and it's onto the next raid. After a few successful rounds, archers will begin firing arrows at you from the battlements even as you dodge flying fireballs.

The game takes place on two screens. The first depicts a bridge over a moat connecting two portions of a majestic castle rendered in beige, blue, and gray. You get seven lives; the number of lives remaining is displayed in the lower-left corner, and your score is in the lower right. You must cross the bridge from right to left, avoiding the constant barrage of fireballs. The right side of the screen acts as a hiding place; stay in there, and you won't get hit. But of course, you must enter the castle. The prince runs when you press the disc's left or right edges. You can duck the high fireballs by pressing down on the direction disc and jump over the low ones by pressing any side

Figure 5.5: The impressive *Dragonfire* complimented *Advanced Dungeons & Dragons* by offering more fantasy-themed action in an entirely different way.

button. Jumping while running gives you a little more air. Jumping from a crouching position is effective for clusters of two fireballs.

The second board is the storeroom, which contains many treasures in different shapes and colors. The entrance is once again a safe spot; you can return there for a breather whenever you need it. You must gather all the treasures to recover them for the King while avoiding the dragon's fire breath. Once you pick everything up, an exit opens at the top left of the screen; run through that to complete the level. Treasures consist of helmets, harps, lamps, chests, jugs, candelabras, and orbs and are worth anywhere from 10 to 100 points; points are also doubled beginning with the seventh dragon. Some 16 dragons are in the game, and they get tougher and tougher; one is invisible.

By itself, it's all a bit too simple to hold your attention for long, which is where the three difficulty levels come in. The Easy setting starts with the first dragon. The Medium option starts you at level 5, meaning the Archer will shoot at you on the bridge. The Hard setting begins with the ninth dragon with double scoring. *Dragonfire* is a valuable example of how the Intellivision can still handle fast action, despite its relatively sluggish CPU. *Video* awarded *Dragonfire* a certificate of merit in the fifth annual Arkie Awards for "1984 Best Videogame Audio-Visual Effects (Less Than 16K ROM)." *Electronic Games* said the game is "especially useful as an introduction to fantasy gaming for younger players — while still having enough thrills to please the rest."[12] It's a surprisingly simple game considering the scope of the graphics, but that makes it more fun to pick up and play whenever you feel like dodging fireballs (and who doesn't occasionally?).

Swords & Serpents (Imagic, February 1983)

Dragonfire is a fun title, but the excellent *Swords & Serpents* dungeon crawler delivers the deeper play experience you'd expect from a medieval fantasy setting. In some ways, it's a proto-action RPG, an action-adventure game in the vein of *Gateway to Apshai* for personal computers. Programmed by Brian P. Dougherty, the game is distinguished by its awesome two-player mode, where player one is the Warrior Prince and player two is the wizard Nilrem. Nilrem gets his own controller overlay with nine different spell keys. *Swords & Serpents* is a surprisingly long and complex game, given how little you do in it.

The story goes that you must recapture your family's ancestral castle from the Sinister Serpent. To do this, you must collect all the treasures you can find throughout the four levels of the fortress and store them in a chest on the first level while fighting off legions of Phantom Knights with your magic sword and armor. The more treasures you keep in the chest, the higher your valor score.

The game displays an overhead view of the fortress; using the direction disc, you walk with your sword held out in front, ready to fend off Phantom Knights. There's no in-game music, so you only hear your footsteps. As you walk, the screen scrolls and keeps you centered. The Phantom Knights guard the corridors and can fly through walls. You don't have to attack them with a key. Instead, you aim at an incoming knight, and it impales itself on your sword. Red Sorcerers materialize in puffs of white smoke and hurl fireballs. Sliding doors are particularly tricky, as they'll injure or kill you if you touch them.

Scrolls are scattered about. Some contain clues, and some are magic scrolls that teach the second player's wizard new spells. You can read scrolls with the helpfully named Read Scroll key and pick up treasures and other items with the not-so-helpfully-named Enter key. The middle-bottom button (0) on the keypad brings up your status, which shows each player's remaining reincarnations (lives), how many treasures you carry in hand and have stored on the first level, and your current valor points.

Each level of the fortress has a key that lets you reach the next level. You must collect the key, find the stores, and press Enter on top of the stairs to open them. Then you move the Warrior Prince onto the stairs to descend to the next level or an earlier staircase to ascend back to a previous level. There are four levels in all, and it's worth mapping them out on graph paper with a pencil. The manual contains a map of the first level already done for you.

You have a generous nine lives, which the game calls reincarnations. Each time you're hit once, you change color, and then on the second hit, you lose a reincarnation. An "X" appears in the spot where you died; this is where the next reincarnation appears a few moments later. Treasures are each worth 50 points on the first level, 100 on the second, 150 on the third, and 200 on the fourth. Each time you earn 300 valor points, either one or both of you will earn an additional reincarnation.

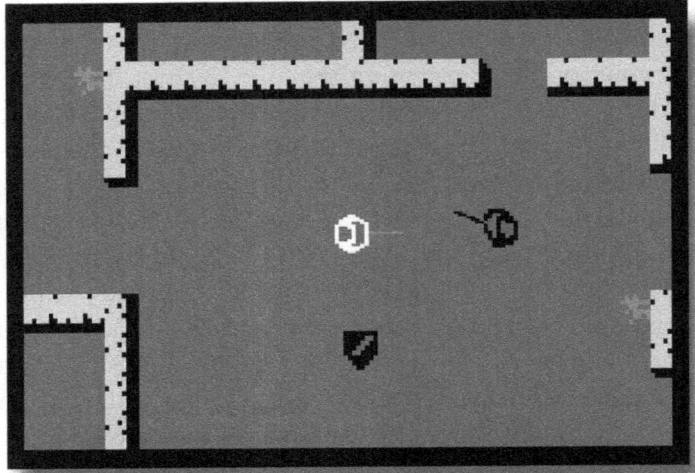

Figure 5.6: The rewarding *Swords & Serpents* offers two players a compelling, co-op dungeon crawl, and it's still fun to play even by yourself.

The Warrior Prince and Wizard Nilrem can carry a combined total of six treasures at a time. Then they must go back and store them before continuing the adventure. When you get back to the chest at the fortress's entrance, press the Enter key again to store all the treasures in hand. It can require quite a bit of walking; fortunately, transport scroll rooms can save you time. There are two on each level of the fortress. They contain scrolls that say, "Ye Read, Ye Move." Read one, and you'll reappear on the opposite side of that level in the other room.

Nilrem always starts each game with the Freeze spell, which you can cast an unlimited number of times; it immobilizes phantom knights for a short time. Nilrem can find and use eight other spells: Fireball, Heal, Fast Feet, Invincible, Destroy Walls, To Chest, Invic-Wiz, and To Knight. "To Chest" is exceptionally useful, as it does away with the need for the transport scroll rooms. Cast it, and you appear on level one next to the chest. It's also helpful to post one person as a guard while the other stores items in the chest or reads scrolls. Occasionally you'll find a golden Lantern of Life, which heals you if you're injured.

The game climaxes when you reach the lair of the Sinister Serpent—but amazingly, you don't get to kill it. There wasn't enough memory for Dougherty to program a proper ending. You can't even go past the Serpent's fire breath unless you're playing with two players; Nilrem can cast Destroy Wall to get inside the inner chamber. And when you go to pick up the final two treasures, all you see is Brian's initials: BPD.[13] It helps immensely to have a second player and wizard even to get this far.

Swords & Serpents is one of the few Intellivision games to provide different overlays for each player. The game conveyed a sense of wonder; the levels seemed huge to me as a kid, and I remember playing and playing to see how far I could get. It pulls you in; you always want to know what's around the next corner or how to reach a treasure you can see but is walled off. It's a terrific game, let down only because you need a buddy to enjoy the best experience.

Tron: Solar Sailer (Mattel, February 1983)

The Intellivoice, innovative as it was, was already floundering at retail. It coasted for some months on its three initial games, none of which became a hit despite their high quality, while the fourth remained in production. In February, six months after the Intellivoice hit the market (and after the initial pop of sales had already died down), Mattel finally released *Tron: Solar Sailer*. A new game that supported the voice module needed to be even better than the others, something that made customers on the sidelines realize they needed one. And this one wasn't.

The object is to ride along an energy beam searching for the evil Master Control Program to overload and destroy it. You battle grid bugs and tanks with cannons while listening for voice prompts that warn you of impending attacks and energy beam levels. The first screen is a zoomed-in view of a tiny portion of the computer's interior, a series of concentric rings that the Intellivision renders in two dimensions. You must find the destination sector for each stage using I/O beam access numbers. Recognizers pick you up and deposit you somewhere else to thwart your progress as you get closer. Reach the center track zero, and you'll enter the MCP, where you must collect flying numbers corresponding to the eight-digit override code. Nail it and you'll destroy the MCP.

Solar Sailer, designed by Robinson and Daglow and programmed by both Robinson and Gene Smith, rewards repeat play as you get

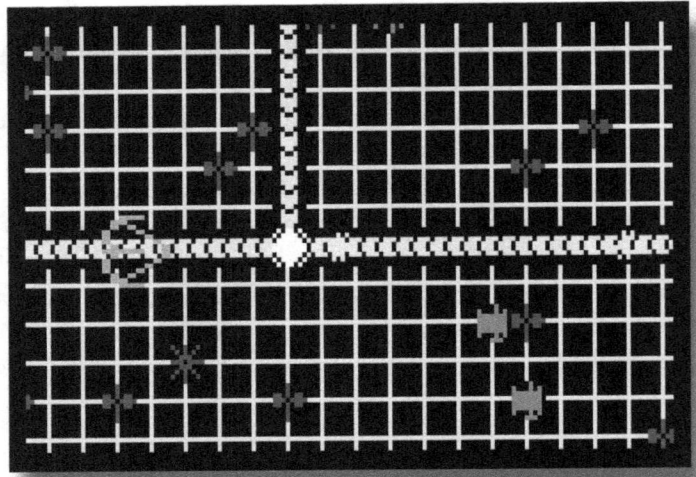

Figure 5.7: *Tron: Solar Sailer* may not have been the easiest game to pick up and play, but that type of depth and strategy marked many quality Intellivision games.

increasingly "into" the game and master its quirks. The Blue Sky Rangers have a story about this game that I am just going to quote here because I can't do it justice otherwise:

> While testing the game, Keith's boss Mike Minkoff kept getting access codes that ended in '69.' Mike accused Keith several times of skewing the random numbers for an adolescent joke. Tired of being unfairly accused, Keith put the data stream 01000101 (the binary representation of 69) in the game's opening demo screen. He then told Mike, 'Look, if I was going to put a '69' in the game, I'd put it right on the title screen!' and waited to see how long it would take Mike to notice. He never did; the game went out that way. 01000101 appeared on the demo screen, in the advertising, on the back of the box, and in the instructions. When Keith finally pointed it out, Mike said, 'But that's 45!' Mike is such a dedicated programmer; he saw the number in hexadecimal (base 16); he never made the final calculation that 45 (base 16) is 69 (base 10).

Unfortunately, *Solar Sailer*'s complex rules put off most gamers. Its cluttered screen, confusing concept, and requirement that the player take notes on paper didn't help. It was also the Intellivision's third *Tron* cartridge, which was a lot for a movie that became a box office disappointment. The film was ancient history when *Solar Sailer* finally arrived at retail, which sealed its fate. Soon, Mattel began including a coupon with the Intellivision to mail away for a free Intellivoice at the time of purchase.[14] Talking games had lost their luster.

Dracula (Imagic, March 1983)

Many horror games began to emerge in 1983 in what turned out to be a pop culture moment for the genre, thanks to the rise of slasher flicks. One of the best titles landed exclusively on the Intellivision. In this game, you don't hunt or fight Dracula—you *are* Dracula, and it is glorious.

Each night, you rise from your coffin in a graveyard, a tortured soul who must chase after townspeople to bite their necks in a desperate bid for blood. You can run in human form or turn into a bat to fly faster. You must find victims to get blood or you'll turn paler and paler. Then, when the sky lightens, you must return to the graveyard before dawn or become vaporized. Get back home to your coffin, sleep, and you'll wake up for another night of feeding.

Figure 5.8: Trade off on becoming a bat or a human in *Dracula* as you feed on victims and then return to your coffin before daylight breaks.

The game occurs on a multiscreen horizontal street. It scrolls smoothly to the right and left as you run. You use the direction disc to control Dracula. The screen doesn't scroll when you move up or down, as in what became known as beat-'em-up games later in the 1980s, such as *Double Dragon* and *Streets of Rage*. The striking graphics convey the impression of a real city street at nightfall, with brightly colored buildings. Here, only the police are fighting back; your victims just run for their lives back and forth, trying to confound you so that you don't bite them. Wolves, vultures, and constables are constant threats.

The top side buttons change your form between human and bat. As a bat, you can fly faster and search for victims more easily. But you can't bite them, you use up more blood, and you are susceptible to vultures carrying you off as food. As a human, the bottom-left side button bites victims, while the bottom right button does the same and also turns the victim into a zombie, which is perfect for sending them after constables on later levels. Victims stay zombies for 10 seconds; when this happens, grab the second controller disc to dispatch the zombie after a constable for an additional 75 points.

As you explore, sometimes you'll see eyes in darkened second-floor victims; head to the front door, knock, and see if the victim saw what you were up to. If so, they'll pretend to be out and won't answer. If they haven't seen you attack anyone, they'll answer the door, both of you will be stunned, and then you can chase after them as they run away. Biting victims nets you 50 points each and some blood; the screen displays the number of remaining victims, the current time, and your remaining blood supply.

There are three difficulty levels. In Easy mode, you start with three victims, and vultures don't appear until the second night. You can return to the graveyard without biting all the victims. Constables appear on the street on the third and fifth nights and every night after that. In Medium mode, you start with six victims, vultures appear whenever you're a bat, and constables start patrolling on the second level. Hard mode means eight victims, constables at all times, and you must bite all eight victims before you can return to the graveyard (but you still must return before daybreak). Nab all the victims and a white wolf will chase you unless you turn into a bat. When you turn white, your blood supply has been depleted. You must bite a victim fast or die.

Developed by Alan Smith, Wilfredo Aguilar, and Dave Durran, *Dracula* was a unique release for the Intellivision that Imagic didn't port to any other platforms. Alas, it probably didn't have the time to, as the company folded by the end of 1983. It's an impressive and fun game that eventually feels repetitive, but so what? It's a perfect game to play in October ahead of Halloween.

Ice Trek (Imagic, March 1983)

In an era when so many games featured Tolkien-style fantasy themes, you didn't see nearly as many that went in the direction of Norse mythology. In Imagic's inspired *Ice Trek*, programmed by Patrick Schmitz, you're the mythical Nordic warrior Vali the Avenger. You must reach the Ice Palace of Kaltkron the Terrible and melt it to save the northern lights and prevent a devastating Ice Age. It plays well and serves as a palette cleanser between nail-biting bouts in Intellivision sports games and AD&D expeditions.

The game features three screens. The first has Vali skiing across tundra from left to right while dodging a thundering herd of caribou. Touch one and it will trample you to death. If you're about to collide with one and can't avoid it with the controller disc, you can kill it with your axe by raising it with either top side button. But then you must face the wrath of the flying Wildlife Goddess and two of her deadly accurate arrows. If you successfully evade the arrows—which is not easy, to put it mildly—the next screen will be more challenging than it would have been. It's an early example of a moral imperative in a video game, where killing something penalizes you.[15]

On the second screen, you must help Vali cross an arctic river by building a bridge from drifting icebergs. Holding either bottom side button brings out Vali's grappling hook, which you throw by tapping (not holding) the disc in the direction you want it to go while still holding the side button. The longer you hold the button, the farther the hook is thrown; let it go when it's over an iceberg, and it'll break in two. You then hold the bottom edge of the disc to bring it back to the bridge. If the iceberg won't connect, tap the edge of the disc again to release the hook. You can also shoot fireballs to melt incoming icebergs that get too close before they destroy your hard work. Fall in the water or take too long, and you'll freeze to death.

Figure 5.9: The Nordic-themed *Ice Trek* puts you in charge of saving the northern lights and preventing the next Ice Age.

Finish the bridge and reach the horizon, and you'll make it to the final screen with the massive Ice Palace. You must throw fireballs at the turrets to melt them while dodging deadly black crystals hurled at you from the parapets. Pressing the left or right disc edges will let you dodge the incoming projectiles. You can raise your torch with either top side button to melt them just by touching them. Succeed in melting all the turrets, ice blocks, and flashing fiends, and you'll defeat Kaltkron the Terrible and reveal the aurora borealis once more. Then the screens repeat, but they're tougher on the next go-around.

Later levels include larger and faster caribou herds, more incoming icebergs that threaten your bridge construction, rougher waters that move the icebergs more, and at the Ice Palace, faster black crystals. *Ice Trek* is one of many games lost in the glut of new cartridges in 1983 and the ensuing market meltdown, but it's worth seeking out a copy today.

Vectron (Mattel, March 1983)

In *Vectron*, you build energy bases of different shapes and sizes. On each level, you build one base, section by section, by moving your energy block into place and then filling it with an energy blast.

Meanwhile, you must fend off "the nasties of the universe," a bunch of strange enemies that sound kind of like fake physics particles: G-spheres, red hungrees, yellow hungrees, and on later levels, splitters, diamondbacks, blue meanies, sweeps, and prizums. They nibble away at your base's sections and erase them, undoing your work. Complete an energy base, and it turns rainbow colors. You'll earn lots of bonus points and move to the next level, where you must build a base in a different shape. Get destroyed three times and the game is over.

Nothing on screen clues you in to any of this.

You're not a person, or spaceship, or anything that would make sense. Instead, you control two things. The first is your energy block, a green square cursor you move left or right by pressing the bottom action buttons—not the disc like every other Intellivision game. The disc controls the second thing: a giant V-shaped gun at the top of the screen. It aims and shoots energy blasts downward in any of seven directions, spread out like a fan. You fire the V-Gun at the energy block to fill in parts of the energy base you're supposed to build.

Yeah, about that.

You have no idea what shape the base should be. And the playfield is all black. How do you build an energy base if you don't know what it's supposed to look like? The game only lets you move the energy block to the correct places, so you must move the cursor around until you find one. Then the cursor sticks, and you can't move it again until you fire the V-Gun at it to fill it in. Now you can move it to a new space. Holding down Move Right or Move Left while using the disc completes the board faster, and you can also fire the V-Gun at annoying enemies to destroy them.

Hold on to your butt—we're *still* not done.

You also must watch your energy level! It's a bar graph at the top of the screen. Firing energy blasts drains the reserve. So does colliding with bad guys. When it falls to zero, you lose an energy block. You can re-energize it by completing a level—or by finding and shooting an E-Pak (a what?) and then catching the falling energy from it. The energy pulses inside the block in either orange (full restore), tan (partial), or brown (useless). This temporarily reinforces your energy block, making it impossible for enemies to destroy you while you build the base. Catching falling energy is impossible if your energy block is stuck, so pressing either top button calls up a "freestyle" mode that bypasses movement restrictions. Don't use it all the time, though; it's terrible for building bases because it no longer shows you where to position the energy block.

So, if you just start a game of *Vectron* and try to figure it out on your own, it's basically impossible. Once you read the manual six times, realize what you control, how to do it, and what you're supposed to do, it makes somewhat more sense. There *is* a game in there, somewhere. But it's really hard, and there are no difficulty levels to select. More enemies appear on the later screens, and after level 18, the game resets and gets harder still. (I've never made it even close to that far.)

If this all sounds insane to you, that's because it is—and it's exactly what Mattel management wanted. "Gabriel [Baum, the VP of applications software] came to me and said they really wanted an abstract game," developer Mark Urbaniec said. "I said, 'Well, you know, kind of like what?' He said, 'Well, that's just it. I want it completely abstract, totally unrelatable to anything.' So we put together *Vectron*...finally finished [and] subsequently released. Marketing came back to us and said, 'What are we going to do with this game? We can't really relate it to anything; it's too abstract.'

"So, I guess we kind of did our job—maybe a little too well," Urbaniec said. "It's kind of this game that's way out there, and now

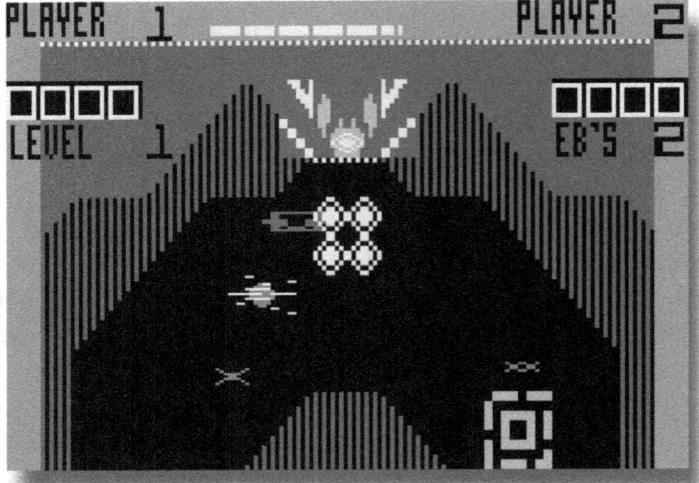

Figure 5.10: *Vectron* was exactly as abstract and unrelatable as management had wanted, and to this day maybe three people know how to play the game.

my kids look at me and say, 'What were you thinking when you did this game?'"¹⁶

Some people consider *Vectron* the best cartridge on the Intellivision. It's true! Others (most?) think it's nothing of the sort. I was glad I only spent 99 cents on it in the mid 1980s. Now that I've revisited it in depth for this book, I can probably safely put it aside and not return to it again anytime soon. But knowing what I know now, I give Urbaniec plenty of points for taking on the assignment. It's certainly worth playing just to experience the craziness.

Truckin' (Imagic, April 1983)

Ever want to drive an 18-wheeler? Hitting the open road feels sublime in Rick Levine's *Truckin'*, the world's first truck-driving simulator. In this game, you piloted a big rig across the interstates from city to city, hauling cargo to money, and steering clear of the fuzz to avoid getting expensive speeding tickets. The screen consists of two displays, one for each truck driver. In one-player games, only one side matters. Each 3D view from inside the truck cab shows mostly the road and sky. A fuel gauge sits on the bottom left, and a speedometer is on the right. On top is a rearview mirror; up there, you'll also see updated speed limit notifications. The display's center shows each driver's next location and current heading. As you drive, you'll pass by traffic and see different scenery.

Two games are available at the start. Game 1 is the "Great Interstate Race". Each driver starts in San Diego, and the object is to visit eight cities as fast as possible by choosing the best of 59 possible routes. You fill up the gas tank until the needle reaches F—this also costs money, although less than it does today—and then head off by pressing Road.

The overlay in *Truckin'* is essential, as all 12 keypad keys and four side action buttons do something. The top side buttons accelerate your truck up to a top speed of 94 mph, while the bottom-left button applies the brakes. The direction disc steers the truck, and you must keep the top edge pressed to keep the vehicle straight in its lane. You can cruise at the same speed for a long while, but anything above the speed limit will attract the attention of the fuzz. You'll see 'em creep up in your rearview mirror and need to pull over or outrun them.

The officer may eventually lose interest if you slow down to the speed limit and stay there. Slowing down in cities (below 35 mph) is also required. Crash into another truck—many swerve all over the road—and you'll lose money and time while your truck awaits repairs. You can also blow your horn to signal to another truck you want to pass; just make sure your rearview mirror clears before you return to your original lane. In two-player games, you may even pass each other; you'll know when because one truck is orange and the other is gray.

In Game 2, titled "Hauling Cargo," you still start in San Diego and must visit eight cities from a choice of 59 possible routes, but you only start with $500 and play against a set time limit (up to two hours). Each game begins on June 1 and runs as long as 60 days. You must deliver various payloads, such as corn, cattle, milk, and gravel, to earn money. The better the combinations of cargoes and destinations you choose, the more you'll make. The Local Info button shows you what loads are available in the current city and their destination requirements. Some loads can be doubled up, but others must be carried alone. You can call ahead to another city (using the appropriate keypad button) to find out in advance what loads they have. You must also occasionally park at a rest stop to reduce your exhaustion level; once it starts creeping up from zero, it reduces your maximum drive speed.

Truckin' is another Imagic game with a day-night cycle like *Atlantis* and *Dracula*. Different terrain types indicate where you are; for example, light green roadsides mean you're out in the country and must watch for deer in parks, but you can also rest for free. You'll also encounter snow and rain. I love how the game shows different cities on the horizon as you approach. For example, cities appear as skyscrapers in the distance and windmills indicate farm areas. Mountain peaks signal an upcoming park area. This, combined with the day-night cycle and the changing sky colors, makes you feel like you're driving on long routes. I also got a real kick out of teasing the cops, pegging the speedometer at 94 until one appeared, and then slowing down just in time that the cop in my rearview mirror would follow me for a while and then decide to give up.

This game effectively launched a niche genre. *Euro Truck Simulator 2* is still a top-selling and often-played title on Steam at the time of this writing, despite being launched in 2012.

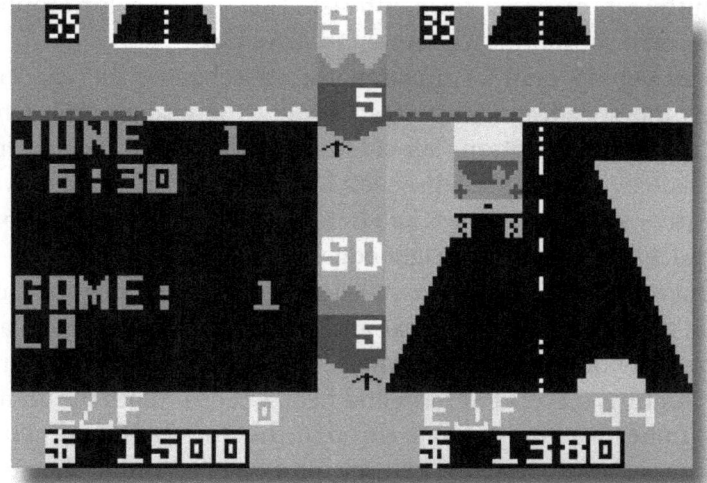

Figure 5.11: The complex, addictive *Truckin'* conveys America's vastness while making you a businessperson with your own 18-wheeler.

Safecracker (Imagic, May 1983)

In this imaginative action-strategy hybrid, you're a spy stationed in a foreign city. You must drive around and collect secret items, including cameras, keys, microfilm, gold bars, and bottles of chemicals from embassies while avoiding the secret police. You've got a blue car, safecracking skills, and a load of TNT in the trunk. Each embassy has a safe with a combination lock you must crack or blow apart before time runs out. *Safecracker* is presented from an isometric perspective depicting city streets. The cars all drive in diagonal directions. Each game starts at your hideout, a black building with a red roof. You get five chances and lose one whenever you crash or the secret police shoot you. Citizen cars are white, and secret police cars are black.

The overlay contains many essential action buttons, including for blowing up safes, entering and leaving buildings, and picking combination numbers. The top side buttons fast-dial safes and shoot forward when driving. The bottom side buttons shoot behind your car and slowly turn the safe dials. The overlay also serves as a directional aid, with four quadrants in different colors showing you the direction to the next destination: red for northwest, yellow for northeast, blue for southwest, or green for southeast. The border color around the game screen shows you which way to drive next.

Pressing up on the direction disc accelerates the car until it reaches top speed; pressing down applies the brakes, and it makes a U-turn with the bottom left side button depressed. You swerve to either side by pressing the disc's left or right edges. To turn down different streets, you must press and hold the bottom left side button and then quickly tap the left or right edge of the disc.

Once you reach an embassy—denoted by white diamond markings on the facade—stop the car and enter. The game shifts to a view of the safe with a two-digit readout. You cycle through the numbers (0–99) until you see a red flash and hear a beep—that's the combination number you want. Cycle through the dial again and approach that number more slowly. When you land on it, you enter the number. Get the door open, and you'll find a secret item—the item itself is irrelevant except for different point values, from 200 to 500—and, importantly, get a combination number for the main vault. Get back to your hideout, and you'll store the item and confirm the new number.

After you crack four safes, you must drive to the city's treasury, a tall blue building marked with dollar signs always in the same place. Enter, key in the correct numbers on the safe (no clues appear for this one, so you must know it from your embassy work), and it will open

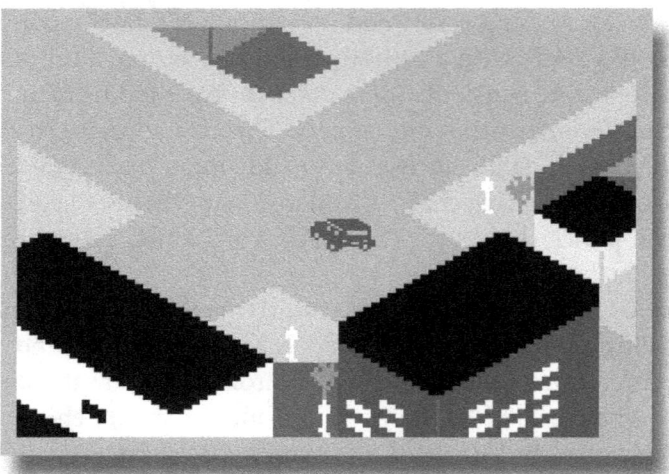

Figure 5.12: Imagic figured out the code with *Safecracker*, a code-breaking game with open-world elements in an isometric perspective.

to reveal five gold bars. Take 'em back to your hideout without getting caught by the secret police, and you'll earn 1,000 points. Now it's time for more safecracking—and stealing.

The cars have a lovely 1930s-coupe look to them. Three skill levels are available. In Easy mode, the first three raids have no street traffic, the police are pretty laid back, and one or two numbers open the safes. In Medium, there's light street traffic, the police are more aggressive, and you may need three numbers to open some safes. In Hard mode, there's plenty of street traffic, the police are very aggressive, and safes require three to five combination numbers. Shoot a white civilian car by accident and it'll bring the police after you immediately; you'll hear their sirens before you see them. Resorting to TNT to blow up a safe forgoes bonus points and will also get the police's attention. Get caught for the last time, and they'll throw you behind bars with your final score displayed.

I loved this game for the same reason I loved Synapse Software's *NYC: The Big Apple* on the Atari 800: Driving around what seemed like an open-world city felt terrific, especially when you're a 10-year-old car nut too young for a driver's license. Playing *Safecracker* again today reminded me that the controls must have taken some getting used to. It's a little weird to turn the car with the bottom-left side button and the disc simultaneously, and it's easy to crash into the sidewalks and explode. Push through that, though, and it's an innovative game.

Mattel Scrambles for a Foothold

Despite the heavy competition from Coleco, Atari, and Milton Bradley, Mattel continued to acquit itself well on the strength of the Intellivision's strong game library and bevy of innovative games you couldn't get anywhere else. The console was beginning to show its age, though. And Mattel did it no favors with a series of botched product introductions. The Intellivoice, ECS, and Aquarius all failed to move the needle at retail, and from an outsider's perspective, it was tough to understand exactly what Mattel was trying to do other than overcompensate for the failed Keyboard Component.

The Intellivision II was a lone bright spot. It gave the console an updated look and lower price to go with its continuous stream of new game releases. All told, the company's product lineup looked comprehensive but muddled in its messaging. And customers weren't biting, either. Unfortunately, things would soon get worse—and not just for Mattel.

6 | Reset

It became increasingly clear as 1983 progressed that the entire video game market was in trouble. On one hand, the Intellivision II's new lower price and simplified design helped spur adoption. "We sold about 100,000 units in 1980," Paul Rioux, former senior vice president of operations at Mattel Electronics, said. "By our third year, we did well over a million units. We progressed upward after that into 1983, which was the peak year. As I recall, we did something like 3.5 million units on a worldwide basis that year."[1] And plenty of terrific new Intellivision games were coming. But the ColecoVision overtook Mattel's system at retail, and retailers feared it was already too late for Mattel to turn it around.

On the other hand, rapidly degrading market conditions led to a management shakeup inside Mattel Electronics in mid 1983. Upper management wanted to streamline operations and refocus on software for the Intellivision, competing consoles, and home computers. Hardware was now out. Mattel laid off 660 people during the summer, phased out the ECS and Intellivoice, and scrapped plans for the Intellivision III.[2] It also cancelled a mysterious future system codenamed Decade, which was supposed to carry the company through the rest of the 1980s (hence the name). Mattel secretly appointed Dave Chandler to build a team and start working on *that* system in the middle of 1982, even before the Intellivision II was released and the III was announced.³ The new design was based on the Motorola 68000, the processor that would soon power the Apple Macintosh, the Commodore Amiga, and the Atari ST.⁴ The system would display 240-by-192-pixel bitmapped graphics, 16 colors from a palette of 4,096, antialiasing, and 32 sprites, with 16 multicolored 16-by-16 sprites per scan line.

The market had spoken, and it was oversaturated. Home computers, not consoles, were the next big thing. Consumers began to sour on the new video game and system announcements. *Electronic Games* called the transition: "If 1982 was 'The Year of the Videogame Explosion,' the one underway now may well go down in the books as 'The Year of the Affordable Home Gaming Computer.' The biggest 1983 trend is very likely to be that the video gaming and computer gaming segments of the hobby will now become even more closely tied together than they are already."⁵

Mattel didn't look good next to the competition. At the Summer 1983 CES, Coleco unveiled the Adam, a computer component for the ColecoVision that dwarfed the Keyboard Component and ECS in power. It came with 80KB of RAM, a letter-quality printer and word processor, and a next-generation cassette drive that offered faster speeds and more storage. You could get the Adam as a $400 attachment for an existing ColecoVision or as a $600 standalone computer (that essentially also contained a ColecoVision inside). Intellivision prices entered the year around $139 to $149, the same as during the prior holiday season. But by mid 1983, you could find a console for as low as $39 after the $50 rebate.⁶ Fortunately, some of the console's best games were still on the way.

BurgerTime (Mattel, June 1983)

One of the best platformers of the so-called golden age of arcades, *BurgerTime* puts you in the role of chef Peter Pepper making giant hamburgers while avoiding dangerous nasties. These include hot dogs, pickles, and eggs with legs. The Intellivision had arguably the best home version of its day, by Ray Kaestner (programming), Karen Nugent (graphics), and Bill Goodrich (audio)—even surpassing those of more powerful systems in some ways. Kaestner famously gave himself just three months to program the coin-op port to complete

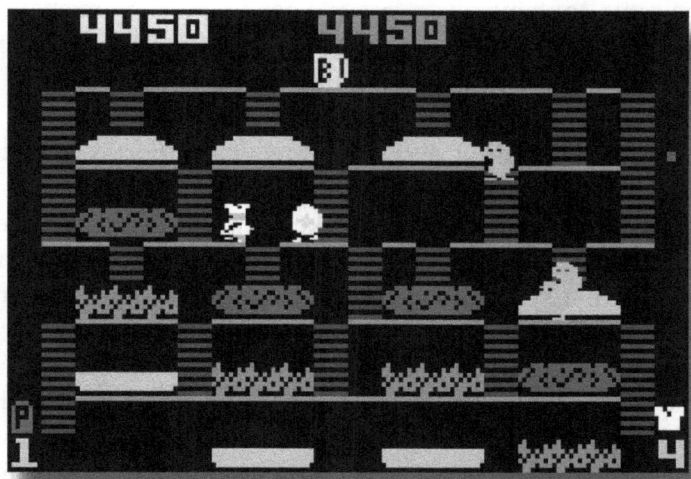

Figure 6.1: One of the Intellivision's best games, this port of *BurgerTime* delivered all the arcade's thrills and impressive graphics and sound.

it before he got married. Management got wind of this and happily made it his actual deadline. He did it in two and used the extra time to refine it and add extra animations throughout.[7]

The object is to score as many points as possible when building hamburgers consisting of buns, patties, tomatoes, and lettuce leaves. The direction disc moves the chef left and right across platforms or up and down ladders. You must run entirely over the ingredients on each part of the board to dislodge them. Once you make it to the other side, you earn 50 points, and the ingredient drops a level. If adjacent ingredients are below, those also get pushed down. You earn a higher score by squashing the nasties with an ingredient (100 points) or giving them a ride on an ingredient. If you time it right, you can do this to multiple nasties, earning you anywhere from 500 to 8,000 bonus points depending on how many fall at once (from one to five).

The side buttons spray a small red pepper cloud, temporarily paralyzing any enemies caught in it. They'll wiggle in position for a few moments, which is plenty of time for you to escape. For some reason, the manual reminds you in all caps: "YOU CAN MOVE AND SPRINKLE PEPPER AT THE SAME TIME." You start with four pinches of pepper and earn more by eating ice cream, coffee, ketchup, or French fries, worth 500 points each.

The game contains seven mazes. Each board is more challenging than the last, with different configurations of patties, buns, condiments, platforms, and ladders. Complete all seven, and the game starts over at a higher level of difficulty.

Perhaps the best thing about the Intellivision port is its high level of polish. The attract mode, colorful graphics, and distinctive background music make the game seem like a genuine coin-op, something the Atari 2600 never quite achieved across the hundreds of cartridges available for that system. The sprites are easily recognizable and are well animated. The game also shows you bonus point values whenever a meanie falls, something usually reserved for the original arcade versions. It also shows you a short cartoon at the start of each new level (although it's the same each time).

BurgerTime soon became an unofficial pack-in cartridge for the Intellivision II, in that if you bought the console, it included a coupon to get the game for free. *BurgerTime* remains one of the best Intellivision games ever released. Even today, it's the subject of many high score contests across user forums, Facebook groups, and meet-ups. The overlay also looks sharp; it mimics the whimsical box art.

Mission X (Mattel, July 1983)

Another Data East coin-op, *Mission X* (1982) is a World War II–style vertical shooter that beat Capcom's *1942* to the arcade by two years. It's an underrated game that adds an altitude mechanic, letting you climb and dive to bomb targets or engage kamikaze enemy fighters. The Intellivision version, which appeared in 1983, is a solid conversion and the only home version ever made. It's a bit of a mindless shooter and not as fast as the arcade, but I always find these games fun anyway.

You must pilot your P-38 bomber over enemy territory and target warships, aircraft carriers, trains, trucks, tanks, and anti-aircraft posts. You can shoot bullets as well as drop bombs, and depending on your altitude, you can fight enemy planes in the air as well. The terrain is a mix of water and grasslands, and the game has a nice day-and-night cycle that adds an extra challenge.

The game starts with your plane taking off from a runway; from there, press the bottom edge of the disc to climb. Over the water, you'll first encounter a fleet of warships, where enemy fighters take off and attack you in the sky. The top side buttons drop bombs, and the bottom fire bullets straight ahead. The enemy also has guided missiles that seek out your plane; you can duck these to escape them. Colorful flak is incoming from the anti-aircraft posts. Periodically, the tanks also fire at you. Flying low increases your speed but makes you more vulnerable to ground attack. Fly too low and drop a bomb, and you'll accidentally blow yourself up.

Targets are worth anywhere from 10 to 500 points, and there are 12 targets in all: roads, train tracks, anti-aircraft posts, tanks, small ships, trains, bridges, trucks, large ships, train engines, aircraft carriers, and enemy planes. You also earn 500 points for destroying both bridge sections and 80 bonus points for every second you fly low over a runway. You gain additional planes when your point total hits 10,000; 20,000; 40,000; 80,000; and so on.

Mission X isn't in 3D, but the changing altitudes and bomb drops convey an impression of depth not usually found in competing shooters. *Electronic Fun With Computers and Games* rated *Mission X* four out of four stars, saying that "Mattel's translation of this sadly neglected Data East coin-op is a delight—right down to (at last!) *intelligent* strategy tips in the back of the directions booklet."[8] (emphasis theirs). The game recalls *Xevious* and *River Raid* in some respects, but *Mission X*

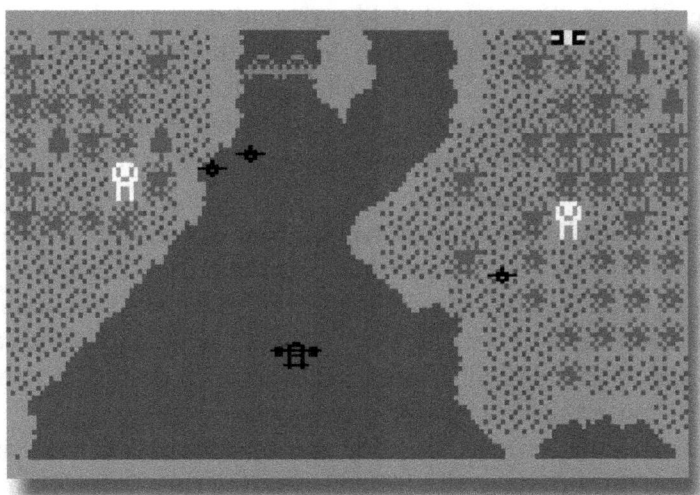

Figure 6.2: The Intellivision needed more vertical scrolling shooters, and *Mission X* was easily good enough to get your fix.

lacks the latter game's fuel mechanic, and Activision's title also has smoother animation. But neither has *Mission X*'s different altitudes, which adds plenty of strategy to the genre. It's good to have choices.

Activision

Activision became the world's first third-party software developer. It was started by four ex-Atari programmers tired of not getting bonuses, royalties, or even credit for their work on company games and other products. They banded together, launched the company in late 1979, and began releasing games for the Atari 2600 the following year. Soon, Activision became a publishing powerhouse. Its first Intellivision efforts were solid conversions of *Pitfall!* and *River Raid*. The former is the spitting image of David Crane's seminal 2600 version, while Carol Shaw's game picks up some graphical enhancements and more rounded twists in the river. Both bypass Exec for smoother 60fps gameplay. Two more Activision games started as Intellivision exclusives and showcased the system.

Beamrider (Cheshire Engineering/Activision, September 1983)

Beamrider is a futuristic space shooter with a compelling premise. You must clear a Restrictor Shield surrounding Earth above its atmosphere by sliding from beam to beam, blasting away waves of aliens divided into sectors. The game's blue wireframe graphics, overhead three-dimensional perspective, and animated shield surface recall imagery from the movie *Tron* and William Gibson's smash hit science fiction novel *Neuromancer*.

You control your ship by tapping the direction disc gently on the edges; this moves you over one beam at a time. Staying near the center of the screen affords you the most time to react. Your ship has two weapons: a laser lariat, which you can fire as many times as you want, and a limited number of torpedoes, which destroy anything on a beam. You get three torpedoes per sector.

Each sector contains 15 white enemy saucers that move in patterns; you must destroy all of them, avoiding their missiles or you'll lose a ship. The Sector Sentinel appears at the end of each sector and sends green blockers down the beam you're on, so you'll need to move over before you can shoot. Succeed in destroying it—only torpedoes work—and you'll receive bonus points for each remaining ship in your fleet. Sometimes yellow rejuvenators appear. Catch one and you'll get an extra ship, but don't shoot one, or it turns red and becomes dangerous debris you must avoid.

Whenever your ship is destroyed, or you finish a sector, you'll return to the Space Station and prepare for the next sector. Later sectors add additional dangers, such as brown space debris, yellow chirper ships, green blocker ships, and blue chargers. With 99 sectors, *Beamrider* isn't a game you get through in an afternoon. Activision later ported it to the Atari 2600, Atari 5200, Atari 8-bit computers, the ColecoVision, the Commodore 64, the ZX Spectrum, and the MSX. *Beamrider* was one of only a few games that originated on the Intellivision and were then ported to other systems.

Reaching Sector 14 and scoring at least 40,000 points was good for a patch from Activision. You had to snap a picture of the screen, get it developed, and then mail it to them in an envelope. It was a different time. *Beamrider* was another win for David Rolfe, the key APh programmer who had created Exec and *Major League Baseball*. Today, *Beamrider* remains an addictive shooter. It doesn't feel like every other space shoot-'em-up and yet still delivers the thrills the genre is known for.

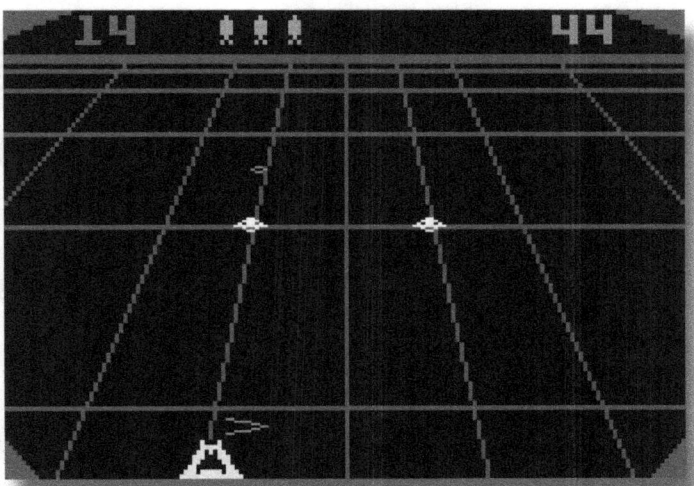

Figure 6.3: The cyberspace-inspired *Beamrider* looked like *Tempest* if you squinted, but it delivered advanced scrolling shooter action.

The Dreadnaught Factor (Cheshire/Activision, September 1983)

In this horizontal-scrolling shooter, you must pilot the Novaray Hyperfighter to take on the dreaded Zorban Dreadnaughts, tremendous and heavily armed spaceships that recall the Imperial Cruisers from *Star Wars*. The Zorban fleet threatens the unsuspecting planet Terra, ensconced behind a stargate. You must pass over each dreadnaught multiple times, taking out as many of its engines, weapons, and defenses as you can each time, and destroy it before it penetrates the stargate and destroys Terra.

Each mission begins from the stargate with the planet Terra behind you. You control the Hyperfighter with the direction disc; the right edge increases your speed, while the left reduces it. The top and bottom edges move the ship up or down on the screen. The top side buttons fire laser bolts, and the bottom ones drop strontium bombs. The game displays how many ships you have remaining, the number of dreadnaughts destroyed so far, and how far in parsecs the closest dreadnaught is from the stargate. Soon, you begin your first attack pass over the first Zorban Dreadnaught. The Hyperfighter's laser bolts can take out all blue and yellow targets, including the small and large cannons and launchers, towers, and bridges. The laser bolts can also

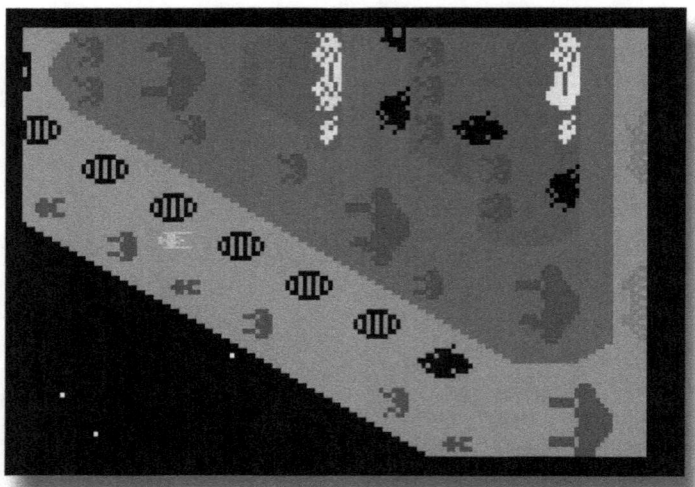

Figure 6.4: A space shoot-'em-up that conveyed battling massive alien flagships, there's still nothing like *The Dreadnaught Factor* even today.

detonate any tracking missiles before they reach you. The strontium bombs destroy the energy vents, silos, and engines. Each time you complete an attack pass, you accelerate through a galactic portal that brings you back to the stargate so you can begin another pass. During this time, the dreadnaught flies slightly closer to the stargate.

As you destroy parts of the dreadnaught, you begin to hinder its operation. Blast the bridges, for example, and it fires on you only half as often. Take out the four engines on the rear of a dreadnaught, and it will no longer propel itself forward; you can hear the dreadnaught drop in speed each time you eliminate an engine. Bomb the silos, and it will no longer be able to attack Terra—this became especially crucial as the dreadnaught got closer to your home planet. It helps to move around a lot; this is one game where you *don't* want to just stay in the center of the screen. Otherwise, you'll take on too much fire.

The most crucial task is to bomb all 16 energy vents, which will cause the entire ship to explode. Destroy the dreadnaught, and you'll move onto the next one; five different types of dreadnaught are in the game, and all present distinct challenges. You start the game with a whopping 10 Hyperfighters, and you'll need all of them. You receive two additional fighters each time you destroy a dreadnaught. Beginning on level 5, you receive four extra ships for each one. Defeat the entire fleet on level 4 or higher, and you would have qualified for a patch from Activision that certified you as a "Dreadnaught Destroyer." Seven difficulty levels are available in all, and no, I have never beaten Impossible, which features 100 dreadnaughts.

Developed by Tom Loughry for the Intellivision, *The Dreadnaught Factor* features detailed, colorful graphics and robust sound design. A review in *Joystiq*'s December 1983 issue awarded it four out of four stars, saying, "Activision's first attempt at a space-oriented game for Intellivision is a sure winner."[9] It's one of the best games for the system. Since the two later (and excellent) ports to the Atari 5200 and 8-bit computer line switched up the orientation, the Intellivision is the only way to play *The Dreadnaught Factor* as initially intended.

AD&D: Treasure of Tarmin (Mattel, October 1983)

The second and final Intellivision game to feature the TSR Dungeons & Dragons license, and possibly the most complex original Mattel game ever released, is *Treasure of Tarmin*. It's a more cerebral, turn-based dungeon crawler that shows how the Intellivision could run with more powerful computer systems of the day, such as the Atari 800 and the Commodore 64. It's also one of the first-ever first-person games for home consoles and a good use of the Intellivision's 12-key keypad. *Treasure of Tarmin* is more involved than the first AD&D game and *Swords & Serpents*, and the closest yet to a real computer role-playing game (CRPG).

In *Treasure of Tarmin*, your quest is to enter a dungeon built by an evil minotaur that stole a great treasure and other artifacts from humans. You must explore its corridors, battle his minions, and retrieve the treasures—some of which confer magical powers on you. You start the game with a bow, a quiver of arrows, some food, and a pack that can hold up to six items.

The Castle Map shows you where you are with a flashing white dot. The Tarmin Treasure is the small gold chest in the center lowest level. The map also displays ladders diagonally connecting the levels and your treasure score (the black number on the right). The top edge of the direction disc moves your character forward through the dungeon. Pressing the left or right edges changes which way you are facing. The top side buttons bring back the Castle Map view. The bottom-left side button counts food, while the bottom-right button counts arrows; both cue up a series of clicks to indicate how much you have of each.

Beneath the display is a compass, which also shows what objects are in your pack. The current level is displayed in the center, and objects in your left and right hands surround it. The three-way score on the right features six numbers. The top two are your war strength and spiritual strength; the middle two are your armor and ring defense scores, and the bottom two are your war and spiritual weapon scores. Using keys on the overlay, you can pick up or drop items, swap items between your hands or into the pack, attack monsters, rest to regain war and spiritual strength, and climb ladders. The bottom three leys let you glance left or right without turning and backing up one step.

Throughout the dungeon, eyeball murals mark the type of maze: war (green), spiritual (blue), and mixed (tan). As you explore, you must search for weapons, quivers (containing six to nine arrows), sacks of flour for food, keys, containers, treasures, and other items. The view scrolls smoothly; although the game is turn based, you move continuously by holding down the top edge of the disc. You must also find hidden doors, which you can seek by trying to open a blank wall. Gates transition you from one part of the maze to the other, and you can't go back. Ladders take you deeper into the dungeon and thus closer to the treasure. Some objects confer special abilities, such as invisibility.

Encounter a monster, and it's time to attack! The dungeons crawl with giant ants, dwarves, scorpions, snakes, alligators, dragons, skeletons (sometimes with cloaks), and giants in different colors that indicate their toughness. Get out your best weapon and watch the monster score (where the level number was in the center) and your own. You can always retreat and look for more weapons before returning to fight a monster if it's too strong. Kill the monster, and it will vanish in a puff of smoke. The worst are ghouls, wraiths, and the purple minotaur himself—these can attack with both war and spiritual weapons. Kill the minotaur on the bottom level, pick up the treasure, and you'll win the game.

Various weapons are strewn about, including knives, axes, darts, spears, and crossbows; the color indicates their strength. The same goes for armor; you'll find small and large shields, gauntlets, shirts, breastplates, and helmets. Spiritual items include fireballs, lightning

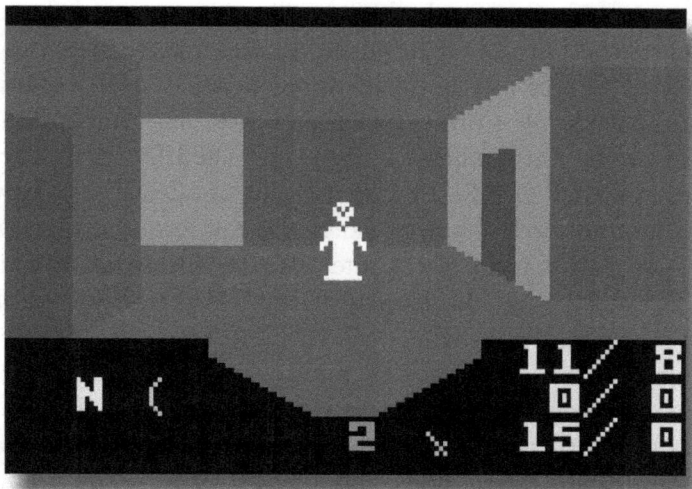

Figure 6.5: Mattel upped its RPG game with *Treasure of Tarmin*, a turn-based, 3D dungeon crawler that played as if it belonged on a computer.

bolts, rings, potions, and reusable scrolls and books. You'll also occasionally come across money belts, bags, boxes, packs, large bags, and chests—some of which are trapped. Treasures include coins, necklaces, ingots, lamps, chalices, and crowns.

Four levels of play dictate the length and difficulty of the adventure. On the more challenging levels, the mazes are larger, you take more damage in attacks, and you have less spiritual strength, food, and fewer arrows to start with. *Treasure of Tarmin* plays smoothly and has enough variety and depth to keep you busy for many hours. Everything in the game has stats, which adds depth; you'll want to keep the detailed 30-page manual handy to look everything up in the tables, so you can decide which weapons to use and when, which spells to cast, or how dangerous a foe is. When Mattel Electronics released *Treasure of Tarmin*, the company renamed its first game *Advanced Dungeons & Dragons: Cloudy Mountain*, to distinguish the two.

Masters of the Universe: The Power of He-Man (Mattel, November 1983)

One of Mattel's biggest successes was the 1981 launch of its *Masters of the Universe* toy line. The toys depicted an everlasting battle between the muscular He-Man, the alter ego of Prince Adam, and the skull-faced Skeletor on planet Eternia, where He-Man guards the secrets of the ancient Castle Grayskull. The milieu incorporated elements of both science fiction and medieval fantasy and magic. The series began with action figures and bundled minicomics. It soon expanded to children's books, DC Comics issues, and most important, Filmation's *He-Man and the Masters of the Universe* animated TV series. The series debuted in the fall of 1983 and ran for 130 episodes; it also spawned a spin-off around He-Man's sister called *She-Ra: Princess of Power*.

It was only natural for Mattel also to release an Intellivision game. Accompanying the launch of the TV series was *Masters of the Universe: The Power of He-Man*, a multiscreen game with excellent graphics, fast scrolling, and multivoice music. You must fly to Skeletor's wilderness realm, chase him on foot through mountains and forest, and then confront him in Castle Grayskull while avoiding his lightning balls, power bolts, and magic swords. Take too long, and Skeletor will finish casting a magic cyclone spell that will carry away He-Man. Catch him, and you'll fight him in a sword duel.

Figure 6.6: *Masters of the Universe* marked what could have been the start of a new generation of Intellivision games with nicer graphics and faster animation.

It's the first game Mattel sold with the "Super Graphics" logo on the box. Technically, this was sleight of hand, a marketing distinction more than some hardware upgrade. It indicated the game ran at 60fps, meaning it didn't use Exec and harnessed some other advanced programming routines. The idea was to bolster the Intellivision against the rising competition from Coleco and home computers. It was also one of the few games to credit the developers on the box—something Mattel should have been doing from the beginning.

Phase 1 has He-Man flying his Wind Raider 30 miles to reach Skeletor's realm while shooting or avoiding fireballs. You press the disc in the direction you want to move. The top side buttons fire the front-facing cannons, while the bottom side bottoms release bombs. You can hold the side buttons down for continuous fire with either weapon. Red fireballs take one hit to destroy, but white ones take six and change successive colors with every impact. Although you can fly left, you'll increase the distance you must travel by doing so, so the object is to keep flying right as fast as you can before you run out of fuel. Skeletor runs back and forth on the bottom of the screen; if you drop bombs, they'll create a crater that he'll fall into. This phase has some weird physics in that the speed and direction of the Wind Raider seem not to affect the airborne fireballs. It's still fun, even if it doesn't make much sense. You can fly low to the ground and avoid most combat, but then you'll receive a low score. Reach Skeletor's realm, and you'll land the Wind Raider in a cutscene and head off on foot.

In Phase 2, you must run across the ground from the left side of the screen to the right, where Skeletor is. He moves up and down and shoots volleys at you. Whenever a lightning ball or power bolt is about to hit you, press any side button to raise your shield and absorb the attack. Otherwise, it will push you back part of the way; red lightning sends you back to the start, while green attacks temporarily destroy your shield. The object is to catch Skeletor three times: in the forest, mountains, and Castle Grayskull. You'll also see another awesome cutscene when you chase Skeletor into the castle. You get 90 seconds on the lowest skill level and up to 120 seconds on the more challenging boards to clear these screens. Occasionally a magic sword will float across the screen; nab this for an extra five seconds or more. It's a high-scoring game; you earn an extra chance after every 100,000 points.

I remember being excited when I got this game, as it was a new release and I knew the new Super Graphics logo Mattel was pushing meant something cool. Like *Krull*, released that same year for the 2600, *He-Man* lived up to my expectations, and I played it often.

Bump 'n' Jump (Technology Consultants/Mattel, November 1983)

A vertical racing game with a big heart, *Bump 'n' Jump* puts you in control of a red race car that can bump other cars off the road or push them into the weeds. You must do that as often as possible while navigating an ever-tighter winding course and avoiding obstacles. Originally a Data East coin-op, the Intellivision conversion is a solid effort and stands up well next to the Atari 2600 and ColecoVision. (It's not to be confused with Sega's *Up'n Down*, another car combat game with cartoonish graphics, Volkswagen dune buggies, and a three-quarter perspective view on the cars.)

The origin story for *Bump 'n' Jump* is unique. "Mattel had found that there was a team on the east coast, a couple of guys who had reverse engineered the Intellivision and were programming a game on it," said David Warhol, who produced *Bump 'n' Jump* for Mattel. The two guys, Joe Jacobs and Dennis Clark, connected a PlayCable unit to a personal computer. They made their own Intellivision development system and offered their services to Mattel in a kind of right-of-first-refusal situation, presumably before going to work for a third-party publisher.[10] But Mattel accepted and gave them the *Bump 'n' Jump* port contract for $24,000. They did the game in a New Jersey basement and never stepped foot in Mattel headquarters—an extremely unusual arrangement then.[11]

"They got these guys to do the *Bump 'n' Jump* game for Mattel as an external developer, and I became the liaison for their team," Warhol said. "I met with these guys to make sure they were using the right technical parameters and tuning it correctly and interfacing with the QA guys at Mattel."[12]

The result is thrilling and addictive to play. In *Bump 'n' Jump*, you drive the car with the direction disc. Pushing on the top edge accelerates the car up to a maximum of 220 mph, as indicated by the speedometer on the top right corner of the screen. Pressing the left and right edges steers the car; the bottom edge brakes. The side buttons cause your car to leap into the air if you drive at least 100 mph. When you jump, the car gets larger as it flies higher and then smaller again as it falls back to the road. It has excellent graphics and fast, if not super-smooth, animation. The seasons even change, represented by different on-screen colors for spring, summer, fall, and winter.

A motley group of vehicles get in your way. Tractors are slow and take up space. Cycles hog the road, but you can bump them far away. The fast skull cars try to hit you. Opposing race cars are super light and fast. Dump trucks are faster than you'd expect and drop explosive debris. Yellow trucks are heavy, hard to bump, and tend to weave. Green, brown, and blue cars are light, fast, and mostly annoying because they weave everywhere. White cars also aim for you, like the skull cars, but these you can bump far away. Occasionally, the course will reach a water section with a narrow causeway you must quickly steer onto and drive over—or even an entirely water portion that you must jump over. Crashing into a railing on the side of the road or the edge of the water loses you one life. Whenever you crash, the screen displays your current score and how many cars you still have remaining before the action restarts. The farther you drive, the higher your score.

As you play, strategies for higher scores begin to come into focus. Bump opposing cars with the front of yours, and you'll slow down a

Figure 6.7: *Bump 'n' Jump* **is a silly racing game that's hard to stop playing once you start.**

lot. Doing it from the sides, however, won't affect your forward progress. Sometimes other cars bump you from behind, which speeds you up. You must always watch how your car rebounds from a bump so you don't lose control. Jumping can get you out of a tricky situation or land you on another car for bonus points—and if you're good, you can land on the island in the middle of a water section and then jump again to reach the mainland for 1,000 points. The game warns you with an alarm and an exclamation point whenever a water section is about to appear. Even then, you can easily crash into the railing. Complete a roadway, and you'll drive up to a gas pump to refuel and see your score, how many cars crashed, and your bonus. All of this makes *Bump 'n' Jump* one of the Intellivision's best cartridges.

World Series Major League Baseball (Mattel, December 1983)

Mattel promised three new games when it announced the ECS. One was *Scooby Doo's Maze Chase*, a simplified variant of the Atari 2600's *Maze Craze* involving famous cartoon characters and the ability to drop obstacles to slow the pursuit of the evil skull and crossbones. The game contains 15 screens and is a fun diversion. The other two ECS titles deserve more detailed coverage.

Let's start with *World Series Major League Baseball*, a technologically advanced baseball game by Eddie Dombrower that punches well above its weight and takes full advantage of the extra hardware. It was the first video game to show 3D television network-like camera angles of the pitcher and batter, predating even Accolade's home computer hit *Hardball!* by nearly three years. Moreover, the game harnessed the Intellivoice module for calling pitches, home runs, and other plays. Unlike the other four Intellivoice games, you didn't need the Intellivoice attached to play, and it was the last Mattel cartridge to support it.

The game requires the ECS's QWERTY keyboard only to select which league you're playing (American or National) and to scroll up and down menus. The "C" key calls up a computer demo of a game in action. The graphics are wildly different than *Major League Baseball* during play, but the control is similar. The overlay features a baseball diamond and field positions, just like in *Major League Baseball*, albeit with different icons. The top side buttons control stealing, switching fielders, and pitching, while the bottom ones are for bunting, sliding, and backing off the mound.

You have more pitch and batting options than in the earlier game. The ball's shadow helps you catch fly balls. All the players are fictional, but they are named and have their own stats that affect strategy in many ways. Nine pitchers are in each league, and each has an ERA, wins and losses, strikeouts, handedness, a durability score for how long they'll last, a control score, and speed score. All players have their positions and batting averages.

Pressing A brings up a stats page for the batter and pitcher. The V key visits the mound to see if the pitcher is still strong, okay, tiring, or bushed, meaning it's time for a reliever. As team manager, you can also change the lineup (although you can't put someone back in the game once you take them out). The game includes an option to save a game to cassette so you can load it later and continue.

When at bat, you can aim your swing with the direction disc, for example, and time it with the side button. You can steal bases, slide into base, bat in runs, and more. An inset view shows the lead runner on base. The game also distinguishes between throwing to the second baseman and throwing to whoever is on 2nd base (either him or the shortstop, if the second baseman ran to pick up a grounder).

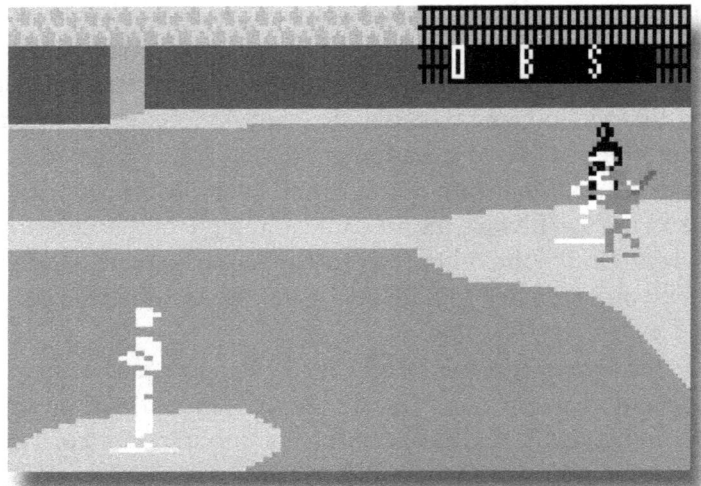

Figure 6.8: The ahead-of-its-time *World Series Major League Baseball* delivered plenty of firsts, but few people played it because it required the Intellivision, the ECS, and the Intellivoice for the best experience.

World Series Major League Baseball harnesses the two sound chips for music, the Intellivoice for speech if attached, and the ECS's extra memory for the multiple views and to calculate the ball's shadow. It's a must-play and a tour de force for the Intellivision.

Mind Strike (Mattel, December 1983)

The most polished of the cartridges released for the ECS, *Mind Strike* is a complex strategy game that harnesses the extra power of the computer attachment. It's essentially three-dimensional chess with numbers. The object is to destroy your opponent's castle while protecting your own. You move your pieces, numbered 1 through 7, toward their castle and try to capture their lower-numbered pieces whenever possible. Land a numbered piece on the opposing castle, or eliminate your opponent's pieces, and you win the game.

Mind Strike includes more than 50 different board configurations and two modes of play: Mind Strike, where you take turns and have as much time as you need, and Speed Strike, where you both move simultaneously as fast as you can. Even the title screen signals it's no ordinary Intellivision cartridge—the music sounds too rich. It uses all six voices available from the two Yamaha chips. The QWERTY keyboard selects the board, starts one or two-player games, and lets you edit board configurations. For regular play, you don't need the keyboard except to start the game—something others have figured out and released hacks that let you play it on a regular Intellivision (minus some voices of music).

The controllers let you move the cursor with the direction disc and activate and move pieces with the side buttons. You deposit pieces by pressing 1–7 on the keyboard. Each piece can move far as eight minus its capture power—for example, a 7 moves just one square, but is very powerful. You can also split pieces into two of the same total value or combine them into larger pieces. For example, you can split an 8 into a 5 and 3 and then move either of the split pieces.

"When I got to Mattel, they wanted me to train, and it was like, 'just do something for a couple of weeks,' said programmer David Warhol in a recent interview with game historian Matt Barton. "And so I was a big fan of the game Stratego growing up as a kid, and so I just had this notion of what happens if you were playing a Stratego-like game, but you could play at the same time instead of taking turns. So as I was familiarizing myself with the system, I just started programming words and pieces. It was probably after a month in my

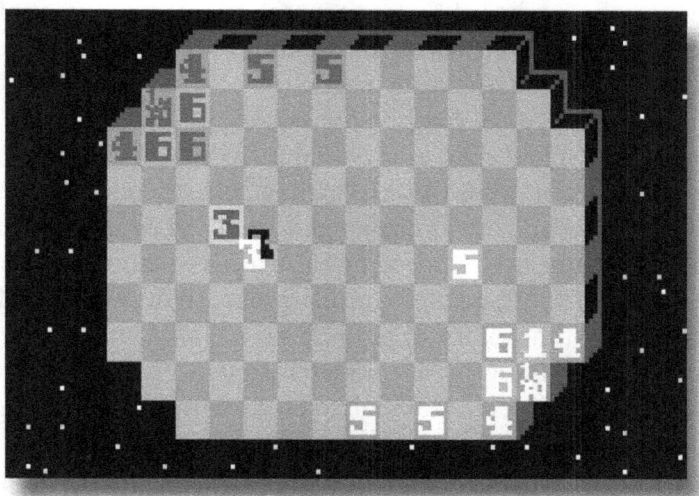

Figure 6.9: The mind-blowing *Mind Strike* turned chess upside down and inside out.

development project, they were looking at and going, 'hey, well, this could turn itself into a game.'"¹³

In describing the game, Warhol says to imagine playing checkers if you didn't have to take turns. "There are no special moves," he said, "but the more powerful pieces move slowly, and the weak pieces move quickly. You can commit to making a very powerful move that takes you eight seconds, or you can make a lot of weak moves. Better yet, you can break the pieces apart, and then move them and recombine them. So a powerful piece can become vulnerable but move farther and faster. And then you can recombine it to be a powerful piece."¹⁴

It took Warhol three months to program, design, and add all the graphics to *Mind Strike*. He intended it to be an Intellivision cartridge, but the Master Component lacked the memory necessary for a computer opponent, so he designed it for two players. The ECS had some extra RAM, and management asked Dave to change *Mind Strike* into an ECS game with a computer opponent. He suggested making the cartridge one-player for the ECS and two-player-only when inserted into an Intellivision, but marketing insisted on it being unplayable without the module to boost ECS sales.¹⁵

"We didn't have enough titles for the Keyboard Component [sic]," Warhol said. "It was a peripheral that Mattel was pushing, and so the managers decided, well, it's kind of a computery game, let's require the Keyboard Component for it. From my point of view, all the Keyboard Component did was make [Mind Strike] reach a smaller audience. It didn't really need the keyboard. But we use that to allow you to change the computer variables, if you're playing against the computer…It had eight or 10 variables in how it was assessing the board, and you can tweak those to make a custom computer player."¹⁶

The one-player game is challenging. You can adjust the computer's AI by using the keyboard, some basic math equations, and a list of strategy settings the computer considers on each of two passes before deciding its next move. It's an impressive level of depth for a console game, even if it is ostensibly a "computer game" with the ECS attached. I found *Mind Strike* cool, if difficult to play. I picked it up at a huge discount along with the ECS in the mid 1980s. One wonders what could have been possible had Mattel stuck with a single personal computer plan rather than splitting it between the Keyboard Component, the Aquarius, and the ECS, only for all three to fail in succession.

Warhol went on to become a prominent video game composer and sound designer. He opened Realtime Associates in 1986 and worked on the audio for *The Bard's Tale*, *Racing Destruction Set*, *Zak McKracken and the Alien Mindbenders*, and *Pool of Radiance*. But his time at Mattel will always hold a special place in his heart.

"My favorite moments at Mattel were walking down the corridors and hearing the sound effects of [*Mind Strike*] being played in a corner in some cube somewhere," Warhol said. "Like, 'Wow, people are actually playing this thing, this is pretty good,' and you hear them hootin' and hollerin' over the cube walls, and a couple of compliments about this is a good example of original work that came out of Mattel." Unfortunately, not everyone at Mattel agreed, Warhol said: "Then there was also the marketing comment of a guy walking out of the room going, 'Numbers? Selling a game with numbers?! What? I need characters…Give me dwarves or elves or something!'"[17]

Loco-Motion (Mattel, December 1983)

This game, a high-quality port of the lesser-known Konami arcade coin-op, puts you in the role of train engineer. And you've got quite a maze to deal with. You must rearrange the square track sections to route the train so it can pick up passengers at different stations. If the train takes too long to reach a station, the passengers will get angry and construct their own Crazy Train (cue Ozzy Osbourne), a runaway caboose. They might even start blowing up stations. Other obstacles also get in your way: Angry passengers sometimes create a Loop Sweeper to break your path if you're just going in circles, or Crazy Track pieces that randomly send you off in different directions. You start the game with three trains, and it ends when all three are lost.

The first order of business is to keep the train running so that it doesn't reach a dead end and crash. You do this with the controller disc, which lets you switch track pieces into the blank square. Once you get the hang of the disc, it's easy: You're moving the piece below the empty square, not the empty square itself. For example, pressing up on the disc moves the piece below the empty square up into it. It sounds confusing but becomes second nature. Pressing any of the side buttons accelerates the train; otherwise, it defaults to slowing down and then moving at the slowest speed. The track piece's color indicates its direction (straight, right, or left). The Panic button on the overlay acts as a "hyperspace" from *Asteroids*, except that it swaps both the train and track with another track on the screen. It also adds a pair of train stops to the board, and you can't use it if there's a Loop Sweeper or Crazy Train.

Each screen has between eight and 12 train stations along the edges. Passengers appear as face icons, either happy or not so happy. The animated yellow path light in front of your train shows your heading and changes based on the available track in your path. Switch away from a passenger's route, and you'll notice them become angry. Put the yellow path back so that it crosses their station, and they'll become happy again. Some passengers will offer a reward for bonus points if you hurry back to them. Pick up all the passengers, and you'll see a "Clear" message; if you do it without any stations exploding, you'll be awarded a "Perfect Clear."

Pressing the disc starts a regular game, while the 1, 2, or 3 keys cue up slower game speeds. You can play with one or two players, and the game includes a demo mode that you cue up by pressing any of the side buttons to start. As you clear screens, later levels have faster Crazy Trains, more train stops, and station rewards that decrease in

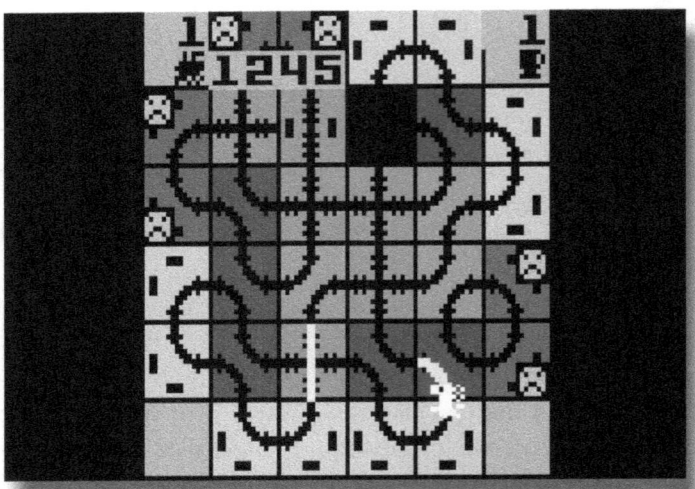

Figure 6.10: *Loco-Motion* **makes you a train engineer—possibly one on the verge of a nervous breakdown.**

value faster. The sound effects make the game. It sounds like you're operating trains and switching plastic pieces on a board.

This game could have been quite the coup for Mattel Electronics. Unfortunately for Mattel, Activision's *Happy Trails*, Carol Shaw's terrific clone of *Loco-Motion*, beat it to the punch at retail. This made Mattel executives furious, as they had properly licensed the game from Konami and had just sent it off to manufacturing, a three-month process.[18] Suddenly, another competitor released a similar game (albeit with a different backstory). *Happy Trails* garnered excellent critical reviews for its originality, possibly because so few were aware of the coin-op in the first place. In the end, Mattel decided to pull marketing support for *Loco-Motion* and cut the retail price to blow through its huge stockpile of new ROM chips. By the time the cartridge landed on shelves for the holiday, the press was less than enthused.

"The unofficial word within Mattel Electronics was that they considered suing but that Mattel and Konami couldn't agree on how to split the legal expenses," the Blue Sky Rangers wrote. "In reality, though, few if any lawsuits for design infringement were filed in the pre-crash video game industry. So many games from all of the companies borrowed features from so many other games, it seemed no one wanted to open that can of worms."[19]

Superb Games, Poor Sales

The Intellivision II was a killer buy in the 1983 holiday season, selling for as low as $69.[20] The ECS didn't fare as well. Mattel never released the Program Expander, thermal printer, or cassette tape recorder. Over half of the promised software programs never materialized; only six ECS-specific titles were released. Mattel even dropped the price of the ECS from $149 to $69 to juice sales. It didn't help. The ECS was incompatible with the Keyboard Component and not nearly powerful enough to compete with the Commodore VIC-20, much less the Commodore 64 model everyone wanted that year.

Despite the industry turmoil, many other good Intellivision games arrived in 1983. The motorcycle racer *Motocross* looked like a mashup of *Auto Racing* and *Excitebike* on the NES, and it even included a course editor. But you couldn't save your creations, and the game itself was a little choppy and difficult to control. *Buzz Bombers* offered a different take on *Centipede*; you used a can of bug spray to fend off swarms of bees in your flower garden, although a weird trapping mechanic prevents you from moving as the bees pollinate flowers that close in on you. Mattel was a bit late in releasing its own *Pinball* title, but it was worth the wait, with excellent graphics and gameplay. Pinball still wasn't far from the average player's mind in the early 1980s, as commercially available video games were just over a decade old. Pinball has continued to retain its popularity through the decades.

Third-party developers also released many titles that had been in the pipeline around this time. Atarisoft brought excellent versions of *Pac-Man*, *Defender*, and *Centipede* to the Intellivision—surprisingly, *Pac-Man* even had the intermissions, something only the Atari 5200 version could claim at the time. Parker Brothers did a nice job with its *Frogger*, *Popeye*, and especially *Q*Bert* conversions, although *Congo Bongo*, *Star Wars: The Empire Strikes Back*, and *Tutankham* all played too slowly and choppy to be effective. Coleco had more success with *Donkey Kong Junior*, *Mouse Trap*, and *Lady Bug*, three terrific ports of popular Nintendo and Universal games. None matched up to the ColecoVision version but were much more playable than its horrid *Donkey Kong* port. Coleco also released a solid port of the action-adventure coin-op *Venture* but poor *Zaxxon* and *Turbo* conversions.

Imagic released four more Intellivision exclusives: *Nova Blast*, a *Defender* clone; *Tropical Trouble*, a fun, scrolling action game that took place on an island; *Fathom*, an action game where you played as a seagull in the skies and a dolphin underwater to locate and free a trapped mermaid with your magic trident; and *White Water!*, a multiscreen rafting and exploration game with colorful graphics. Activision offered *Worm Whomper*, a wacky horizontal shooter that pit you against an insect infestation threatening your corn crops. Newcomer Interphase released two three-dimensional titles: the space shooter *Blockade Runner* and the adventure-in-the-depths *Sewer Sam*, two decent but mostly forgotten cartridges. And in the terrible *Kool-Aid Man*, you had to explore a house and locate the items necessary to make Kool-Aid, at which point the Kool-Aid Man came crashing through the wall and you controlled him to eat things.

Kool-Aid Man aside, many of the above games are well worth playing today. I'm not giving all of them entire sections for space considerations. Unfortunately, none of the above 1983 releases did anything to change the system's narrative arc.

The clouds on the horizon had finally arrived. Mattel Electronics continued to cut its staff, laying off 660 employees in the waning months of 1983, bringing its total to 1,140. Company spokespeople continued to say that "Mattel has *not* changed any of its plans, and will continue developing new software and hardware" for its video game systems despite the layoffs, but the rumor mill swirled.[21] Mattel Electronics recorded losses of $300 million in 1983. It wasn't long for this world.

7 | Forward

The video game crash was in full swing at the start of 1984, although it wasn't something the public was particularly aware of. It was more that consumers had wised up, became warier of poor-quality games, and stopped frequenting arcades. I never lost my enthusiasm for video games, and no one I knew did, either. Most of us who were around for this don't necessarily remember "experiencing the crash." I remember I got an ECS in a bargain bin purchase a year later for either $30 or $40. I forget the exact price, but it was about the same as buying a new game. It even came with *Mind Strike*, so it was a win-win. I was 12 and, without Internet access, social media, or much interest in the news, I had no idea why the ECS was so cheap. I was still a kid, though. It was messier for the adults, especially Mattel employees and investors.

Thankfully, it wasn't the end of the story for the Intellivision. A series of resurrections, tributes, and other products comprised a sustained effort to keep the console alive and well. Its fans wanted it to stay alive—starting with some of the very people who made and sold it in the first place.

The Fall of Mattel Electronics

On Feb. 4, 1984, Mattel ended its seven-year experiment with video games, computers, and electronics. It said it was quitting the home computer business and other ventures to "concentrate its resources" on its profitable toy division, which had its best year ever in 1983.[1] Mattel signed a letter of intent to sell its Intellivision game business for $20 million to a group of investors headed by Terrence E. Valeski, senior vice president for marketing and sales at Mattel Electronics.

Mattel was still doing gangbusters business in its toy division. But the situation with Mattel Electronics had gotten so precarious, an analyst said in *The New York Times*, that retailers had already begun to worry if the company would file for Chapter 11 protection. It didn't happen, but it would take some time for Mattel to regain its confidence. It was a hard fall from its peak in the video game business just 16 months prior. As many enthusiasts and gamers remember, it wasn't just Mattel. Coleco also eventually withdrew from the market. It had taken a huge hit from the disastrous Adam launch, plagued with delays, numerous insurmountable technical issues, and an extremely high return rate at retail. Milton Bradley discontinued the Vectrex and soon merged with Hasbro. Imagic, one of the best third-party software companies for the Intellivision and the 2600, closed up shop. Magnavox withdrew from computers and video games. Atari discontinued hardware sales and sold its consumer products division to former Commodore CEO Jack Tramiel.

Soon, there would be little left of the video game market in the United States as home computers took over. It would take a couple of years and a new home game console from a Japanese company to revive it.

The Rise of INTV Corporation

In buying out the rights from Mattel on February 4, Valeski told *The New York Times* the investors group planned to "absolutely" continue the business. He added that they would continue to make games, including 12 Mattel had recently announced for home computers and game consoles other than the Intellivision. Valeski said Mattel had sold 750,000 consoles in 1983 "and we have orders to ship more immediately," and that he expected the new company to make money "within 90 days."[2] Home video game sales were still up 10 percent in 1983, despite the incredible glut of product and the resulting market crash.[3] Valeski was also smart enough to secure the mailing list of registered Intellivision owners from Mattel, correctly assuming that selling new games to the existing 3 million-plus console owners would be profitable.[4] Valeski's new company, dubbed Intellivision Inc., began doing just that. It also purchased the remaining inventory from Imagic, Activision, Parker Brothers, Atari, and Interphase.

Valeski said the new Intellivision company would continue to ship machines to all the distributors that sold them and that Intellivision was planning to release new software for the Atari 2600, IBM, and Apple computers. "We're planning to introduce four new games for Intellivision as well," he said to *InfoWorld* in May, and that independent companies would code them. "We'll be producing a significant amount of software this year, at lower prices than before." He planned wholesale prices from $14.95 to $16.95 per game, instead of the previous range of $19.95 to $21.95.[5] A spokesman for the company added that it would continue to produce new games and programs for another year for the new Intellivision company and would also service the Intellivision units already sold.[6]

The newly formed Intellivision Inc. hired new programmers and continued selling stockpiled Intellivision II consoles. At the start of 1985, sales were promising enough that Valeski bought out the other investors, and Intellivision, Inc. changed its name to INTV Corporation. After running out of leftover consoles, it began to sell the $59.95 INTV System III, a duplicate of the original Master Component but with silver plates on top and a power LED. It also manufactured and sold existing Intellivision titles at reduced prices. The R&D costs for these games were long paid for, and INTV Corp. also did this by making thinner cardboard boxes and printing manuals and cartridge labels in black-and-white. It also used thinner material for the plastic overlays and left them out altogether if they weren't necessary for gameplay—something that became increasingly true as time wore on.

INTV also began selling new games. Some were titles Mattel had already completed but never released, such as *World Championship Baseball* and *Thunder Castle*. Two were from Nice Dreams, the former Mattel Electronics office in France: *World Cup Soccer* and *Championship Tennis*.[7] Mainly, though, it was by completing the development of some older titles caught out when Mattel Electronics ceased operations. For example, in 1983, Mattel had announced *Major League*

All-Star Baseball, which added a one-player mode to the Intellivision's best-selling *Major League Baseball* game from 1980. This project was never quite finished. First, Mattel killed it off when shifting all internal efforts to games for the ECS. But Mike Minkoff loved the game, and despite being promoted to the director of Intellivision, Aquarius, and M Network development, volunteered to debug the game himself after hours.[8] Eventually Minkoff ran out of time trying to sort out the very last bug when Mattel Electronics ceased operations in January 1984. The game finally resurfaced in 1986 when INTV released the completed game as *World Championship Baseball*.[9]

INTV Corporation rang up $6 million in sales in 1985 alone. With the rest of the competition out of the picture, INTV dominated until Nintendo released its new Entertainment System console nationally in 1986.[10] Even then, the Intellivision did look good next to the relaunched Atari 2600, commonly (but not officially) called the "Junior" model. A much smaller and slimmer version of the original console, the new 2600 saw next-generation games like *Solaris* push the 1977 hardware even further. But Atari Corporation's strategy was all mixed up at this point. A Toys "R" Us ad for the 1986 holiday season showed the Intellivision System III on sale for $89.97, which as game historian Steve Fulton points out, was next to Jack Tramiel's confusing three-tier strategy of selling the 2600, 5200, and 7800 game systems all between $59.97 and $99.97. As Fulton said, "the NES at $229 wiped the floor with all of them." [11]

Those who stuck with the system know INTV released a bunch of good Intellivision games over the next several years—including some that would have made a big splash, had they come out in the early 1980s while Mattel was still in control. I'll go over some of the best below.

Super Pro Sports

Let's begin with INTV's new *Super Pro* series, which further boosted the Intellivision's sports prowess. This was the Intellivision's strongest category to begin with, but the new games add one-player modes and other features the original cartridges lacked.[12] All the new games were stripped of their licenses, although it didn't affect gameplay. INTV released 11 new sports titles in total, many of which were all new, although a few were upgrades of existing cartridges.

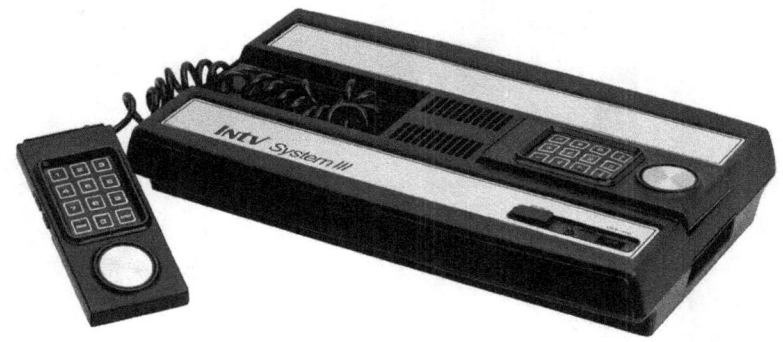

Figure 7.1: Before the Intellivision entered the post-Internet afterlife, it got a second real life thanks to Valeski's INTV Corporation. (Credit: Evan Amos)

World Championship Baseball adds the coveted one-player mode to *Major League Baseball* so you can play against the computer. It also adds fly balls, sliding into base, a scrolling feature for the far end of the field, and some minor tweaks to the sprites. *Super Pro Football* is a reworked version of *NFL Football* with a one-player mode and a new play system that lets you select from on-screen stats and formations. It has some minor graphical enhancements, like a shadow under the ball when it's in flight. *Slam Dunk Super Pro Basketball* lets you manage the team while playing the game. You can choose from 70 players with stats roughly based on real people in the NBA, and you have a budget, so you can't just add all the highest-paid players. You can put players in the game and take them out. The game now includes 3-pointers, fouls, free throws, time-outs, and a one-player mode.

The all-new *World Cup Soccer* offers a one-player mode, updated graphics, and a three-dimensional view of the net and goalie when making shots. You can tackle, head the ball, get called for a penalty, and switch players mid-game. *Championship Tennis* features a vertical court orientation, single and doubles play, and several venues including Flushing Meadows and Wimbledon. *Chip Shot Super Pro Golf* includes 10 courses based on famous ones worldwide. It has more clubs to choose from, it supports hooks and slices, and the wind affects your shot. *Slap Shot Super Pro Hockey* is almost the same as the original game; it just looks nicer and adds the one-player mode. *Mountain Madness Super Pro Skiing* packs far more courses, including

Figure 7.2: As good as the Intellivision's original sports games were, it got another round of even better titles with the *Super Pro* series.

randomly generated ones. A new course editor lets you design your own. The game adds ice and ground patches and 15 difficulty levels.

Body Slam! Super Pro Wrestling puts you ringside in a packed arena during the WWF heyday of the sport (albeit without the license). The game includes 12 wrestlers, 26 different moves, six skill levels, and one-player, one-on-one, and tag-team modes. *Super Pro Decathlon* is essentially a "me too" copy of *The Activision Decathlon* for Atari systems, except five years late. It contains 10 events (as does its namesake), plus support for three difficulty levels and up to four human players. Finally, the excellent *Spiker! Super Pro Volleyball* by Steve Ettinger almost didn't make it out the door before INTV closed. The game features six-person teams, one- and two-player modes, a full assortment of volleyball moves, six difficulty levels, and a two-against-the-computer mode.

No one would say the Intellivision was deficient in sports titles in its heyday—it was one of the console's greatest strengths. But these later versions were all improvements, and it's a shame many people didn't get to try them unless they hung on to the platform past its shelf life. We can enjoy them now, though. It's a simple hack when playing the Intellivision today: Play these versions instead of the original Mattel cartridges, and you can play by yourself or with a friend—not to mention enjoying some additional enhancements in the bargain.

Thunder Castle (Mattel/INTV Corporation, October 1985)

INTV released plenty of other good titles as well. *Thunder Castle* is a medieval fantasy-themed maze game with excellent graphics. You're a valiant knight in shining armor who must slay the monsters of Thunder Castle, including dragons, sorcerers, and demons. There are three mazes: the enchanted forest, the castle proper, and the dungeon below. You must kill three dragons in the forest maze to advance to the castle: green, yellow, and then red. Six sorcerers guard the faster castle maze in three pairs, and nine demons guard the fastest dungeon maze in groups of three.

The direction disc moves your knight in four directions, and the side action buttons let you use objects. The mazes contain gates that block and open up paths. Magic items give you extra points, or sometimes extra abilities. Bats, mice, and red skulls energize you, letting you kill monsters in the three mazes. It helps to think of the game as *Pac-Man* without the dots. The wandering special creatures are like power pellets; even the same strategy works, where you wait until a monster is very close before "eating" a special creature and getting energized. And just like in *Pac-Man*, you're only energized for a few moments, and the monsters immediately begin to run away from you. The opening and closing gates let you briefly trap monsters, and if you're as good as I am, they're also great for trapping yourself by accident.

Magic objects appear throughout the game. You can only carry one at a time and each one can only be used once; if you pick up another object while carrying one, you'll lose the first one. The grail energizes the knight, the same as the special creatures do. The crown freezes the monsters, the necklace speeds you up, the lantern doubles your energy, and the key lets you move through a gate or wall. The ring acts as a medieval hyperspace, transporting you to a random location in the maze that may or may not be helpful. You start each game with four knights, and earn additional lives at 5,000, 10,000, 20,000, 50,000, and 100,000 points. Candlesticks also give you an extra life, and coins are worth 500 points. The comb is cursed—pick it up by accident, and it cuts your score in half.

Thunder Castle was programmed by Connie Goldman and David Warhol in 1982 and 1983 before Mattel Electronics shut down. Goldman's animation skills were her biggest strength, according to the Blue Sky Rangers, and you can really see it in this title.[13] Each level begins with an interstitial screen depicting a well-drawn giant dragon, wizard, or demon. The maze, castle, and dungeon graphics look sharp. The knight's colorful multicolor sprite is a step above what was seen in earlier Intellivision titles, with his prominent shield, helmet, and sword. The same goes for the dragon and its fire breath. Goldman's work made *Thunder Castle* a real showcase for the Intellivision. The dungeon is particularly fun, with its talking skull graphics and torture devices. "I collaborated with Connie Goldman on that, who was a just a brilliant graphics artist who I've worked with for decades after that," Warhol said.[14]

The audio was equally top notch. In the background, the game plays a multivoice version of Schubert's Symphony No. 8 (aka the "Unfinished Symphony"), which is one of my favorite pieces of music ever. It also plays a triumphant fanfare when your knight is energized.

"I think it's one of the first games that had wall-to-wall music, where instead of just the beginning of the level and the end of the level, or when you power up or something like that, it had [music] as soon as you powered it on to when you yanked the cartridge out," Warhol said. He added that the game also played Mussorgsky and Beethoven. "Because these cartridges are so small, I wrote an audio driver that specifically would compress the music down to its bare essentials, so that I could get as much music in there as I did with the cartridge."[15]

To my eye, *Thunder Castle* deserves the Super Graphics label along with *Masters of the Universe*, even though it didn't get it. Also, don't miss the *Mystic Castle* version, a homebrew hack that speeds up gameplay, adds new mazes, and features four difficulty levels. It gets its name from what *Thunder Castle* was supposed to be called. Even the regular game is fantastic—and plenty difficult. "I remember [the game] was tuned pretty hard," Warhol said. "It wasn't one of these games [like] *Astrosmash*, [where you could] level up a play for an hour. [*Thunder Castle* was more like] a hockey stick, just kind of went boom. I remember sitting down at a trade show recently, and picking it up and going, crap, I can't even get through the third level of it."[16] I'll add that it's easy to get stuck in a rut on level 2, avoiding

Figure 7.3: *Thunder Castle* **is a beautiful action-adventure game with a fantasy theme.**

the wizards, catching the mouse, and chasing the wizards to no avail. Making better use of the magic items helps.

Thin Ice (Mattel/INTV Corporation, August 1986)

A whimsical and kid-friendly maze game with echoes in *Amidar*, *Pepper II*, and *Qix*, *Thin Ice* is a blast to play and should have gotten more attention than it did in the late 1980s. In this charming game with catchy background music, you must help Duncan the penguin skate around on (you guessed it) thin ice, dunking other penguins in the water as well as seals and polar bears. You cut the ice as you skate, which shows up as a white line; draw a square around an animal, connect it, and the animal will fall in the water. But if a penguin or polar bear crosses the line, they erase part of it. Shrimp cocktails give you extra speed. Dunk all the penguins and the Zamboni will come out to clean up the ice for the next round—which, naturally, is tougher than the last.

The seal chases you by following the white line and turning it red. You can also erase part of the line and confuse the seal briefly or draw a quick square and dunk the seal for 1,000 points. But if the seal catches you, you lose a life. The polar bears move fast, but you can freeze them momentarily with the side buttons on the controller. You get five freezes to start and can earn more by catching lobsters. If a polar bear touches Duncan, you lose a life. The later levels are tougher and faster; you get a free life for every 10,000 points you earn. My seven-year-old daughter took to this one immediately, happily unaware of the company turmoil that led to the game's release decades ago.

According to the Blue Sky Rangers, *Thin Ice* started out as a sexist game called *Disco No. 1* from Data East; Robinson drew up a plan in May 1982 to remake it around penguins on a frozen lake, complete with the Zamboni, and programmed a demo. Mattel engineer Julie Hoshizaki completed the game in May 1983 with new graphics from Monique Lukan-Bakerlink. Marketing suggested a mascot, which is how they arrived at *Duncan's Thin Ice* (as the title screen reads).[17]

By this point, Mattel Electronics was already in trouble, so management brought in a consultant to re-evaluate their project portfolio. The consultant suggested canning a bunch of games and keeping *Thin Ice*, but it needed a fisherman instead of a penguin. This upset everyone. Eventually, the consultant was let go, and the team pivoted and started bringing back Duncan in the code. But then—then!—marketing said they should now make it a game for the Olympics because Mattel had just spent millions of dollars on a 1984 Winter Olympics license, and they needed a game.[18] The

Figure 7.4: *Thin Ice* **is lots of fun and, amazingly, nothing like** *Pengo***.**

team switched directions again and started remaking the game as an ice-skating competition, but with *Duncan's Thin Ice* still hidden in the code in a larger (16KB) cartridge. Then just when this was about to go into production, Mattel Electronics shut down. Seeing the perfect opportunity, INTV revived the game and released it as an 8KB game with just the original code intact.[19]

Fun fact: The game's musical theme, "Carnival of the Penguins," was George "The Fat Man" Sanger's first video game soundtrack. He went on to score more than 200 games, including *Wing Commander*, *Loom*, *The 7th Guest*, and others. At the 2002 Classic Gaming Expo in Las Vegas, his Team Fat band played "Carnival of the Penguins" live in a surf-rock arrangement, dubbed "Surfin' on Thin Ice." The event served as a CD release party for the band, back when CD release parties were still a thing.[20]

Tower of Doom (Realtime Associates/INTV, March 1987)

As a certified CRPG nut, I automatically gravitate to any game resembling *Tower of Doom*. And this one is downright brilliant, with its blend of arcade and roguelike elements. Some find it even better than *Treasure of Tarmin*, and I agree, as it takes better advantage of the Intellivision's strengths while minimizing its weaknesses. Designer Dan Bass originally intended *Tower of Doom* as a third game to use the Advanced Dungeons & Dragons license, but the game was canned as part of the Mattel Electronics wind-down. A few years later, INTV hired several people to finish the game and didn't see any reason to secure an expensive new license from TSR.

Even without the official AD&D branding, *Tower of Doom* is an interesting action-strategy hybrid that pulls in elements of both previous Intellivision games and makes something new. You must explore the Tower of Doom, collect treasure, and decipher how to use the artifacts that lie within while fighting off an array of monsters. You start at the top of the tower and work your way down through the various mazes. As with the classic Atari 2600 game *Adventure*, in some variations the mazes are the same each time, and in others they change each time you play. But this is a much deeper game.

You begin by selecting one of 10 adventures, which determines the size and length of the quest. Then you choose one of 10 characters

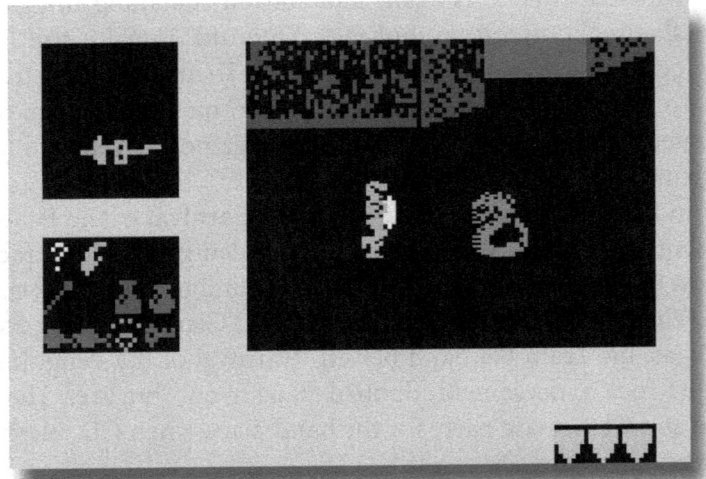

Figure 7.5: The suspenseful *Tower of Doom* marked the closest the Intellivision ever got to a proper CRPG during its original time on the market.

to play, such as the Warlord, Archer, and Friar. Each has different abilities and something of a difficulty curve (some characters have poorer stats, for example). The top-right portion of the interface shows an overhead view of your surroundings. The left side holds the level map—amazingly, the game auto-maps for you—and three rows of icons for checking your status or what's in your inventory, as well as buttons to use items, open doors, and descend stairs. Your hit points are indicated below the overhead view as a meter containing yellow shields against your maximum hit points. Sometimes the game shows you messages; these appear at the bottom of the screen.

The direction disc moves your character through the maze. The top side buttons use items; the bottom-right button toggles your pack, while the bottom-left one drops an object. As you explore, the fog of war clears. Various items are strewn about. The sparse but dramatic audio effects sound otherworldly. Come across a monster, and the game switches to a close-up view of the battle, with gorgeous two-color sprites showing the knight and foe. The whole game takes place in real time, and it takes some practice to navigate your pack, equip the correct item, and use it. *Tower of Doom* came out more than seven years after the Intellivision itself and was proof that the system—incredibly—still had plenty of life left.

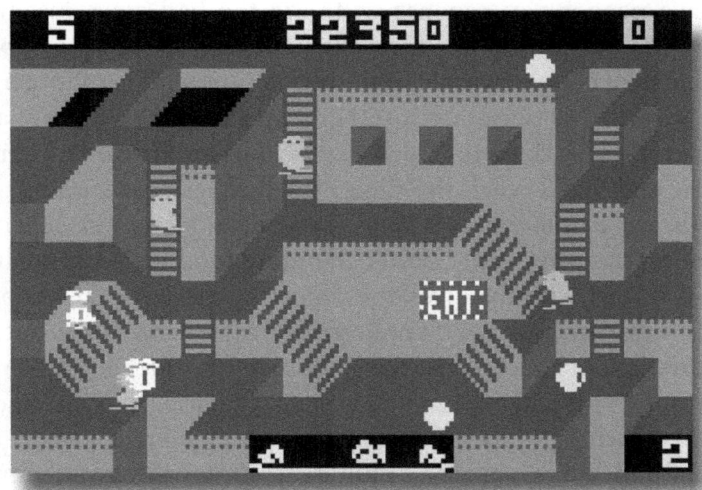

Figure 7.6: *Diner* **was one of the console's best games and unfortunately arrived too late for most people to notice it.**

Diner (Realtime Associates/INTV Corporation, April 1987)

Ray Kaestner's *Diner* amounts to an unofficial sequel to *BurgerTime*, and it's a riot. Peter Pepper is back and is now a short-order cook at a diner, where rotten food threatens to spoil his efforts by throwing the good food all over the place. Using the controller, you must run around the diner kicking food balls—red meatballs, green lettuce heads, white rice, tan mashed potatoes, and yellow macaroni—down ramps to the plate at the bottom of the screen. You must do this while avoiding the five rotten bananas, cherries, hot dogs from the first game, and the worst of them all, Mugsy the Mug o' Root Beer on each level. Work with me here.

The board is more death trap than diner, with ladders, holes, moving floor pieces, and other obstacles. It adds quasi-3D elements to what is still a 2D platformer in the way it draws the staircases and platforms. (If you've played the zombie game *Realm of Impossibility* on an Atari 8-bit or Commodore 64, it's the same idea.)

Each time you kick a food ball, you get 50 points. Squash a piece of rotten food with it, and you get 500 points, and the point total multiplies if you nab several pieces of food at once. Each squashed piece gets up after a few moments, so there's never any respite. Fortunately, you have pepper you can use to freeze the bad guys, just like in *BurgerTime*. As you fill up plates of food, side orders also appear—bonus cups of coffee, sundaes, malts, soda cans, and hamburger buns that are worth 250 points each and give you an extra pepper shake.

Four levels each contain different layouts and hazards. Complete them all and you'll reach the Blue Plate Special bonus round. Here, you must eat as many food balls as you can, and the more side orders you got on the prior four boards, the more food balls appear in this stage. You start with five lives and an extra one every 20,000 points. The collision detection is a bit unforgiving, as in *BurgerTime*, but I find this game easier to play—possibly because it was never an arcade game first, trying to get you to pump quarter after quarter into the machine.

The colorful graphics include little nifty details such as the flashing "Eat" and "Ray's" signs and multicolor sprites. After you complete each level, it scrolls smoothly over to the next. The charming background music and brief interstitial screens keep things lively. But the gameplay keeps you coming back to this one. With some sharper graphics, it's easy to envision *Diner* as a compelling arcade coin-op next to a *Mappy* or *Bubble Bobble* cabinet. It's an Intellivision exclusive. I never had this one back in the day and now I'm addicted, which doesn't bode well for my to-do list. Few people bought this game originally thanks to its late release, but it's certainly worth having now.

Sunset on the Intellivision

By 1987, the NES had rejuvenated the American video game industry, and the Sega Master System, the Atari 2600, and the Atari 7800 competed for a distant second place. In this climate, the INTV was still doing well. The small company ran low on inventory as it struggled to produce enough games to meet demand.[21] At the 1987 Winter CES, INTV Corporation demonstrated nine new games and showed off the System IV, a new iteration of the console with detachable controllers. It never made it to market, though. The next year, INTV put the kibosh on selling at retail entirely and returned to mail order as its primary sales channel. In its new fall catalog, INTV listed the again-renamed Intellivision Master System for $69.95, with most newer games selling for between $14.95 and $18.95 a pop. The hardware was nearing 10 years old. Some new cartridges were ill-advised—*Pole Position* and

Commando were beyond the system's capabilities, and the poor conversions only made it look even older.

Mostly, though, INTV-era releases were solid. The best were of particularly high quality but arrived far too late to be competitive. *Dig Dug* was a colorful, smooth port of the popular 1982 coin-op with slick animation and an excellent rendition of the catchy background music. In *Hover Force*, you pilot a combat helicopter to fight terrorists who have taken over a city, shooting them in their helicopters and putting out fires with water cannons. The fun racing game *Stadium Mud Buggies*, the last title INTV released, stretched the Intellivision's 10-year-old hardware with a three-quarter isometric perspective but couldn't hold a candle to NES games.

Eventually, though, INTV had to renew licensing agreements with Nintendo and Sega, and it became clear it was time to sunset the Intellivision platform. In 1990, the company ceased production of the Intellivision after a remarkable 11-year run. INTV signed with Nintendo to make NES games but didn't find success fast enough and wound down its operations the following year. It did release one Nintendo cartridge—a mediocre port of *Stadium Mud Buggies*.

INTV's contribution to the Intellivision platform was surprisingly solid given the circumstances of the time. It released 23 new

Figure 7.7: INTV signed off after releasing *Stadium Mud Buggies*, the Intellivision's last title before the company succumbed to Nintendo and Sega.

cartridges during its tenure. It's estimated INTV was responsible for selling another 500,000 consoles on top of the original 3 million estimate that were sold during Mattel Electronics' reign.[22] Atari also soon ended production of its slim 2600, which it had last redesigned in 1986. Between the Nintendo Entertainment System, the 16-bit Sega Genesis unveiled in 1989, and everything happening on the home computer front, there was no longer room in the market for the two systems that fought the first console war. The games were great, but it was time to move on.

The final breakdown of Intellivision game releases was 118 game cartridges, one compilation cartridge, and six games for the ECS. Add eight cassettes for the original Keyboard Component if you want to be generous. Fortunately for us, much more was in store for the Intellivision platform in the decades to follow—starting with a dot-com-era resurgence of the original Blue Sky Rangers.

8 | New Beginnings

Intellivision fans have much to celebrate. This is true for many vintage platforms, of course. The rise of the Internet meant fans of old game consoles and computer systems would always have a community—a place where people chatted, bought and sold hardware, emulated old games on modern computers of the day, and even developed new games and mods. All that wonderful stuff is the subject of the rest of this chapter. Let's start with a brief overview of the developments following INTV's shutdown in 1990 and leading up to the Intellivision scene, which will help inform how we got to where we are today and what's available now.

Emulators for old platforms became viable in the mid 1990s, in some cases before the bodies (of the consoles, at least) were even cold. Robinson launched BlueSkyRangers.com, a new website at the dawn of the dot-com era that held archived documents, screenshots, images, manuals, and more: "In 1995, I started a website that introduced people to the first time the behind the scenes what was it like to program back then."[1] Around the same time, Carl Mueller Jr. created the first Intellivision emulator with the help of William Moeller, Scott Nudds, and Sean Kelly. Robinson also got to work on new product. He and another former Mattel programmer Stephen Roney formed Intellivision Productions in 1997 and released the free *Intellivision for PC Volumes 1 and 2*, which included the previously unreleased *Deep*

Pockets Super Pro Pool & Billiards. They also made available *Your Friend the EXEC*, a programmer's guide for the Intellivision's Exec OS. Within a few years, enthusiasts assembled an SDK for programming homebrew games.[2] In 1999, Activision released its own *A Collection of Intellivision Classic Games* for the PlayStation. The compilation contained 30 games licensed from Intellivision Productions and video interviews with the programmers.[3]

That one did well, but the first popular compilation most fans remember now is *Intellivision Lives!*. Introduced in December 1998 for Microsoft Windows and Macintosh computers on a hybrid CD-ROM, *Intellivision Lives!* featured 60 games from Mattel Electronics and INTV Corporation, including several unreleased titles. "Back then, we didn't have all the graphics and sound we could do today, so the work went into making the game fun," Robinson said in a San Diego News 8 news segment promoting the launch of the CD-ROM. "They're simple games, they're very addictive, they're very fun—they're not a game where you have to learn a bunch of rules and it takes three to four days to complete one game."[4] A follow-up compilation called *Intellivision Rocks!* came out in 2001 and added ECS, Intellivoice, Activision, and Imagic games. Both compilations harnessed Carl Mueller Jr.'s PC emulator, the first to run Intellivision games on then-modern computers. Steve Roney contributed a Mac version of the emulator. A few unreleased games made it onto the collection: *King of the Mountain*, *Brickout*, and the Risk-like *Takeover*.[5]

You played the games using a combination of USB and keyboard controllers, and the CD-ROM included overlay graphics and plenty of background material. None of the original licensing agreements remained in force, so the compilations dropped the sports league and AD&D licenses from the titles. Also missing were *Masters of the Universe*, *BurgerTime*, *Lock 'N' Chase*, the *Tron* titles, and Atarisoft games. Later ports of *Intellivision Lives!* included versions from Crave Entertainment for the original Xbox, the PlayStation 2, and the GameCube. Virtual Play Games released it for the Nintendo DS some years later. It rocked to be able to play these games, and later versions of the collections included on-screen materials about the Intellivision and its history, which was wonderful.

A running issue across the board for Intellivision emulation is approximating the original controllers. Thanks to their distinct design

Figure 8.1: *Intellivision Lives!* made it to a variety of platforms in the early 2000s, such as this Windows CD-ROM version.

and need for overlays, it's much tougher with this console than it is when emulating many other game consoles.

One way not to do it is with a gamepad. In 2003, Techno Source unveiled the Intellivision 15 and Intellivision 25. These direct-to-TV systems contain the hardware inside a gamepad controller that plugs into your television. These aren't as accurate because they're rewrites for NES-class hardware instead of running in emulation, and the controllers are utterly wrong. Still, the idea had merit enough that, by the end of 2006, the company sold some 4 million, a number I wouldn't have believed had I not come across it in my research for this book.[6] Several online services released ways to play Intellivision games in the aughts, including the VH1 Online Arcade, GameTap, THQ Wireless, and Microsoft's Game Room service for Xbox Live and Games for Windows Live. A version even appeared for Windows Phone.

Intellivision Flashback

Most products mentioned above disappeared as the consoles went out of production, the online services were discontinued, and people stopped buying the not-so-accurate direct-to-TV gaming devices. But Intellivision emulation received another big jolt in 2014 when AtGames released the Intellivision Flashback, a console like its already successful Atari 2600 Flashback system, with 60 built-in games you choose from an on-screen menu. It was sold through retailers such as Toys "R" Us, Walgreens, Family Dollar, and Dollar General, and you could also find it on Amazon.

The Intellivision Flashback is a miniature replica of an Intellivision Master Component that instantly reset the market for emulating the console. AtGames had already learned from some mistakes with its earlier 2600 and ColecoVision releases, so the Intellivision model came closer than those two did in modeling the console—especially when it came to the controllers, which are dead ringers for the originals. They're improvements, with a lighter weight and much softer side buttons that are easy to press. It was accompanied by the release of a "We Were There" promotional video showing scenes from life in the early 1980s and life today (as in 2014), and promising to bring back family game night with something that "doesn't drive their parents crazy," with "no download this, update that—just real, fun video games the way it was meant to be."[7]

Unfortunately, the console has some of the same omissions as the *Intellivision Lives!* collection, lacking *BurgerTime*, *Masters of the Universe*, *Lock 'N' Chase*, and all the Imagic, Activision, and Atarisoft games. The two AD&D games are present, renamed *Crown of Kings* and *Minotaur* without the TSR licenses (now owned by Wizards of the Coast). The Flashback does include the Intellivoice games, though. AtGames got the emulation mostly right, and the system includes a small set of overlays that work with a few of the games. It should have included all of them, but AtGames made a full set available for an extra $14.99. Limited edition "Blue Sky Rangers" box sleeves are also available, each with different autographs from the developers.

Emulation and Controllers

Usually, emulation is an easy and fun process. Maybe it has some quirks, but it's otherwise attainable by most people and a wonderful option. This is…less true for the Intellivision. Numerous emulators exist for the console, although the selection isn't as robust as for some other vintage consoles. Your options are the terrific jzIntv (Windows, Mac, Linux), Bliss (Windows), MAME, Nostalgia, and Pantheon. Some add ECS and additional hardware emulation. Most are accurate but already quite old and were designed to run on earlier versions of Windows, not Windows 10 or 11.

To emulate the Intellivision, you'll also need to locate the BIOS files and ROM images of the games. The usual disclaimers about legal gray areas apply here, so I can't provide locations where to download these. (And hey, as prices remain reasonable, picking up copies of the original cartridges isn't much of a hardship.) On the Mac side, OpenEmu does the work for you; it includes the Bliss core and wraps it in a beautiful, collector-style interface that shows you the game boxes and a full graphic of the Intellivision controller you can use to map the keys and buttons for each player. RetroPie offers an inexpensive way to put up Intellivision games on your living room TV, although you'll want a controller option with a longer cord.

Three significant obstacles remain, though: the controllers, the overlays, and the two-player requirements of some games. The biggest challenge is the first, the lack of readily available controllers that mimic Mattel's unique design. Not only are there no USB versions of the controllers available, but the controllers that come with the Master Component are hardwired into the console.

You do have some options. The one I had the most success with is the Vision-daptor (www.2600-daptor.com/Vision-daptor.htm). It's a similar design to the 2600-daptor many people use to connect 9-pin Atari-style joysticks to USB. The Vision-daptor is a three-inch-long, 0.75-inch-high adapter that has a pair of dip switches to let you configure Intellivision, ColecoVision, and Sega Genesis compatibility. All three use a 9-pin connector that looks the same as Atari's and Commodore's but has additional pins to account for the direction disc and the extra keys and buttons. On one end is a 9-pin male port; the other contains the box-style USB Type-A port that I still associate with 20-year-old printers and MIDI keyboard controllers. Either way, USB-A cables are readily available from any retailer.

The trick here is to obtain either a Sears Tele-Games Super Video Arcade or an Intellivision II, both of which have detachable controllers, or an Intellivision Flashback system, which also has the same 9-pin connectors. The Sears models are the most like the original Master Component; the II-style light gray controllers are attractive, with black keypads and keys outlined in red. But the Intellivision keypads are flatter and not as satisfying to press, unlike the bubbled membrane style of the original design. Some also say the Intellivision II controllers are less reliable, but we're talking four decades no matter what, and a little maintenance here and there will always be called for.

Anyway, this is how I do it: I connect a Sears Super Video Arcade controller to a Vision-daptor. Out the other side, I run a USB Type-A cable to my PC running Windows 11 and jzIntv. For macOS, I use a Type-A–to–Type-C adapter to connect the Vision-dapter to my MacBook Pro running OpenEmu. It looks a little ridiculous, and I used cable ties to make it look slightly less so.

You'll also want a pile of overlays, which I got by ordering the extra Intellivision Flashback pack and the reprints from the Blue Sky Rangers website, in addition to the ones I've re-accumulated over the years by buying and trading original Intellivision cartridges. Fortunately, they're still quite easy to come by new or used.

The controllers that come with the Intellivision Flashback are excellent replicas, believe it or not. It feels different from an original Intellivision controller, but it's better—I know it's blasphemy to say such a thing, but even if you're a fan of the Intellivision's controllers, it's *probably* true it doesn't extend to how stiff the side buttons are. Intellivisionaries.com lists two different kinds of adapters for various Intellivision consoles. Buy the adapter that turns it into an

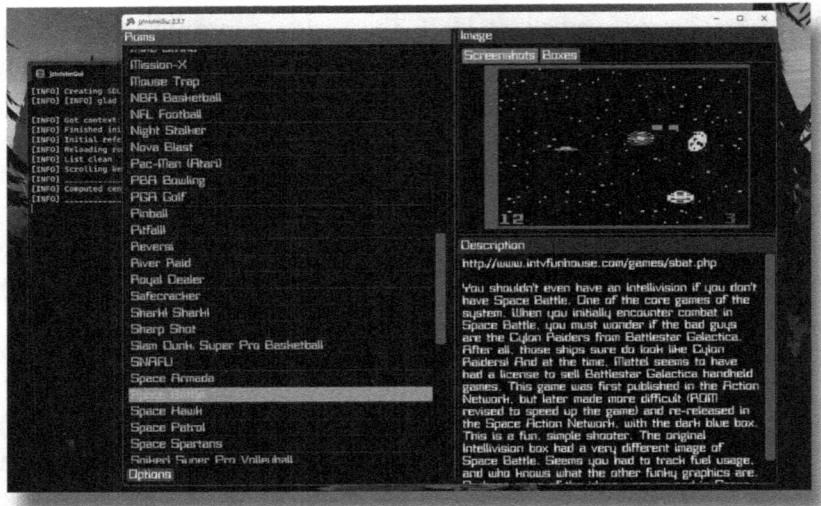

Figure 8.2: Emulators such as Joe Zbiciak's jzIntv (above) deliver an excellent Intellivision experience; you just need a controller.

Intellivision II controller, and you can then use the Vision-daptor to connect it to your PC or Mac. Note: There are two different versions of the Flashback controller, each with a different pinout, because nothing is easy.

Another option is to purchase a boutique or custom controller. The RetroGameBoyz' Arcade Stick ($149.99) is a beautiful tank of a unit that comes with a stick, keypad, and arcade-style buttons. You can select options for Sanwa parts and whether you want a frame over the keypad so you can insert overlays. I haven't tested this unit, but it looks fantastic. It works with the Intellivision, Intellivision II, and the Sears Super Video Arcade. If you go with the Vision-daptor, you'll need to activate the controller—another step that's different from other console emulators. When plugging in the USB cable for the Vision-daptor, you need to hold down the "0" key on the controller for a few seconds. It will signal to the adapter that you have an Intellivision controller and not one for a different system. You still need to do this even if you've set the DIP switches correctly. Once you do that, you'll find that you need to properly map all the keys to your emulator—a simple task in OpenEmu but not in some other emulators.

If you want to get close to the original Intellivision experience in emulation, there *are* ways to get it to work. But as many people will tell you, having the original hardware is easiest—and best. That's the subject of our next section.

Collecting

As you may have noticed, collecting for our favorite systems has become trickier. As the decades wear on, systems get old or unreliable, boxes get crushed, and soon there are fewer and fewer examples available, which drives up prices. It seems like the values have rocketed up in recent years, though. The good news is that the Intellivision has largely escaped the higher levels of speculation around rare Apple computers, first-edition boxed copies of NES games, and the like. It's also not as subject to the high valuations of rare games for the Atari 2600, its arch-nemesis. And nearly all the rarest 2600 games aren't very good to play; they're entirely collector's items.

As part of working on this book, I spent several years re-amassing a collection of Intellivision gear, including three consoles, 50 cartridges, and more than 20 complete-in-box games. Still, I'm not the collecting type—I had sold off everything in the late 1990s because I had no room for it all in tiny New York City apartments, and even with a house and a family, I still don't really have the room for it now. But of course, I wanted it all again so I could double-check all the games on real hardware, and just experience it all the way it was originally.

As is often the case, I found that buying in lots was the most economical way to build a collection. I did resort to individual game purchases to fill out the collection the way I wanted. I'm not a fan of shrink-wrapped games, but that's fine if you are! I prefer to play everything, and my view has always been that we don't put shrink-wrapped items in museums, either, so there's no need to keep them as such in our homes. Put it in a protective case if you must, but at least it will be preserved and enjoyed.

Hopefully, you can use this book as a guide to what you want to collect, or what you think is missing from your collection. I did my best to provide an overview of the best and most *significant* games available for the system, but there's nothing wrong with collecting all the originals. Many of them are worth firing up anyway just to see what they were like, and who knows—maybe you'll find you like one of them much more than I did.

One of the best things about the Intellivision is the beautiful game packaging. The earliest games have album-style foldout boxes, cartridges, white plastic cartridge trays, glossy color manuals, overlays, and sometimes catalogs and warranty cards. Occasionally a game comes with a second manual, such as the playbook included with *NFL Football*. Things get trickier when you try and track the different versions of each cartridge. Several box color changes—for example, from blue to red—occurred, as well as later INTV games that came with less expensive-to-produce materials, such as black and white manuals, thinner overlays, and cheaper boxes that only opened from the top like games on other platforms. An incredible number of resources are out there now to help you collect, thanks to the diligent work of Intellivision enthusiasts the world over.

You'll also want a CRT television of some kind to plug the system into. I'll get to flat-panel TVs in a moment, but of course a CRT provides the best original experience and does a lot to soften and layer the Intellivision's blocky graphics. The more wood paneling the television

Figure 8.3: It's a lot of fun to collect for the Intellivision—not only are the games great and the hardware mostly reliable, but it's all still inexpensive. Let's hope that doesn't change! (Credit: Jamie Lendino)

set has, the better. (Bring a hand truck.) If you'd rather skip the CRT, any $3 RF-to-coax adapter will let you connect a stock Intellivision to an LCD television with a built-in tuner.

If you're really daring, the occasional Keyboard Component surfaces. A 2014 eBay auction featured one that sold for $2,568.

Mods and Add-Ons

The great thing about collecting for retro and vintage systems these days is the wide range of mods and add-ons that can enhance your experience of using them. These products harness technology that was either prohibitively expensive or unavailable in the 1980s. The Intellivision doesn't lend itself to pure modding as easily as some other platforms. But there are still things you can do to improve yours. None of these mods or add-ons are required to enjoy your Intellivision system, but they can solve specific issues you may have encountered.

The first is the quality of its video output. Several mods exist that let you add RGB, composite video, and even HDMI support for modern TVs, including amplifiers from Fred Kano, Yannick, Crayon King, and Unstablewarpfield. You can buy them from online stores such as

RetroRGB (www.retrorgb.com) and RetroFixes (store.retrofixes.com), though availability is uneven. You may need to track the product you want and see if another batch will be made soon.

Flash storage is possibly the single most crucial mod or add-on available for the Intellivision. One of my favorites is the brilliant LTO Flash!, a cartridge with a microSD card slot that lets you play any ROM you want just by selecting it from an on-screen menu. The convenience of this is amazing. The LTO Flash! lets you save your collection of actual cartridges from wear and tear, it means you don't have to get up to change what you're playing, and it loads instantaneously just like a real cartridge.

Other add-ons let you power up the Intellivision without needing to use the original cartridges. The Intellicart! Intellivision Cartridge Emulator (Chad Schell) consists of a cartridge with a DB9 connector you plug into your computer's 9-pin serial port and companion Windows software that you use to transfer and load ROMs. You plug the cartridge into the Intellivision and turn on the system, which brings up the Intellicart title screen. Then you run the software on the PC, select a ROM, and transfer it. With a successful download, the Intellivision reboots and runs the ROM image as if the real cartridge is loaded. When you turn off the Intellivision, the ROM is erased from the Intellicart and you can load another one. Schell's Cuttle Cart 3 is

Figure 8.4: The brilliant LTO Flash! cart lets you load every Intellivision game ROM, plus homebrews, onto a single cartridge. (Credit: Jamie Lendino)

an improved version of the Intellicart. These are generally no longer available, although you may find one for sale on the used market.

The Ultimate PC Interface for the Intellivision, by Hafner Enterprises, is like Intellicart but with a more modern USB connector. It also supports the ECS keyboard and Music Synthesizer, and it doubles as a ColecoVision interface for fans of that system, with support for the console, driving wheel, Super Action controller, and more. It also works with Intellivision Flashback controllers.

Finally, a big pain point for many Intellivision players is the controllers, specifically the stiff side buttons that are tiresome to press repeatedly and can lead to cramps. Several enterprising modders improved the feel of the buttons and have detailed their procedures in AtariAge forum threads and in YouTube videos. There's even talk of changing the disc to a D-pad, which is heresy as far as I'm concerned, but I certainly get the impulse. IntellivisionDude made an excellent YouTube video showing it with a Sega Genesis D-Pad if you're curious.

Homebrews

As we've seen, many games made in the 1980s weren't released until later, so that alone has provided new gaming opportunities. But starting in the late 1990s, a full homebrew scene sprouted out of the corners of the Internet. One of the best things about the Intellivision today is how just about anyone can make games now. All kinds of resources are available for free online that didn't exist in the 1980s—never mind not having the resources necessary to burn our games to cartridges.

More than 100 completed homebrew games are out there, and several hundred more are either abandoned or still in progress, with new ones coming online all the time. I'm highlighting just a few games that offer a good cross-section of the best of what's available, but there are *many* more worth playing. Some of them are free, some are low-cost downloads, and some cost as much as a full retail game ($60 to $70). Even at the higher prices, these games are high-quality labors of love that do not see many sales at all, and it's expensive to produce cartridges, color boxes, manuals, and other materials in low quantities.

Finally, many homebrew games were produced in limited quantities as complete-in-box products, some of which are no longer available. Some have digital ROMs available, for free or for pay, but others are impossible to get now. I'll make note of what I know now to the best of my ability, but acquiring some of these games today may take more than a little persistence. It's worth the effort, though, as programmers are getting more out of the Intellivision than we ever thought possible in its heyday. Think of them as collector's items that you also get to play and enjoy. With that, let's step through a small sampling of the best homebrews available.

A Tale of Dragons and Swords (Elektronite, 2020): An amazing adventure game that combines real-time, smoothly animated dungeon exploration with a full soundtrack and lovely textured graphics. The game features an introductory sequence with beautiful graphics, and NPCs give you tips throughout. An 8-bit action RPG in the vein of *The Legend of Zelda*, but on 1979 hardware. ($69.99, available from Blue Sky Rangers)

Christmas Carol vs. the Ghost of Christmas Presents (Left Turn Only, 2012) A maze game in the vein of *Pac-Man*, but with excellent graphics, a lovely holiday theme, and eight different boards with intermissions. As one of Santa's most trusted elves, you must confront an evil snowman that broke into Santa's Workshop and stole presents. A companion children's book is now available as well. (*Free ROM download from www.carolvsghost.com/*)

D2K Arcade (Elektronite, 2012) This lovely port of *Donkey Kong* is, yes, much more faithful to the arcade. All four boards appear, including the pie factory, plus there are digital sampled effects, two game variations, and the ability to play as three characters (Mario, Bruno, and Toni) with their own strengths and weaknesses. It's so satisfying that this exists just to right the wrong of the original Coleco port. ($20 PayPal donation, available at carlmuellerjr.blogspot.com)

Defender of the Crown (Elektronite, 2021) A cinematic strategy game set in the Middle Ages, *Defender of the Crown* defied convention on 16-bit computers with its mix of action sequences and tabletop-style play. In this lovingly crafted Intellivision port, the music sounds almost identical to the Atari ST version's, which makes sense, as the ST's three-voice Yamaha sound chip is very similar to the GI. ($69.99, available from Blue Sky Rangers)

The Gooninuff (CollectorVision, 2021) A wonderful platformer in the same vein as the MSX version of the classic adventure game

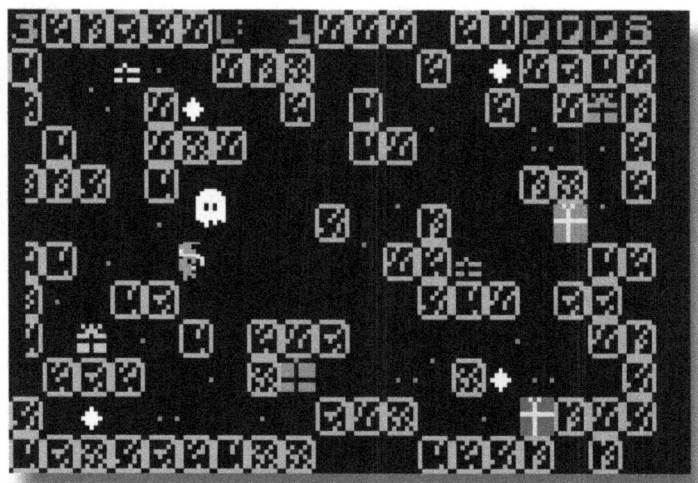

Figure 8.5: A screenshot of the lovely *Christmas Carol vs. the Ghost of Christmas Presents*.

The Goonies, based on the 1985 blockbuster of the same name with its ragtag group of misfits on a grand adventure. This one is a more straightforward play, as you control only one character unlike in the 8-bit computer ports. *The Gooninuff* features excellent graphics, music, and animation. (*Free ROM download, available from forums. atariage.com/topic/342629-gooninuff-now-free/*)

    Intellivania (Matthew Kiehl, 2021) A terrific port of the famous NES game *Castlevania*, *Intellivania* looks and sounds stunning. It also plays just as fast and smoothly as the original. It contains multiple levels with the appropriate soundtrack for each, all the power-ups, and more. I need some kind of magazine award to give out: The Must Be Seen to Be Believed Award. ($15.99 digital ROM from IntellivisionCollector.com; $70 packaged version from Intellivision Revolution)

    Ms Night Stalker (IntelligentVision, 2014)*:* A superior take on the original, in *Ms Night Stalker* you play as the missus, out to rescue her man trapped in the maze. The game adds nine mazes, faster play, and changes up the AI so that you don't know what robot is next. The robots and bats also get smarter as the game progresses. ($5.00 digital ROM from Intellivision.us; a packaged version comes and goes in availability)

The Sorrow of Gadhlan' Thur (Kai Magazine Software, 2021) This incredible Metroidvania-style game is a spitting image of the kind of side-scrolling, open-world adventure game you'd find in the 1990s, typically a hybrid of *Metroid* and *Castlevania: Symphony of the Night*. *The Sorrow of Gadhlan' Thur* has a lengthy introduction and plenty of different kinds of levels, objects to collect, equipment, enemies, towns, dungeons, and temples, with intricate music and sound effects playing the entire time. (€17.00 for ROM download; €59.00 for a physical copy)

Stonix (Arnauld Chevallier, 2004) A stellar take on *Arkanoid*, *Stonix* comes with 100 board layouts, colorful graphics, punchy sound effects, and the same falling capsule power-ups that define this amped-up *Breakout* clone.

Many excellent conversions and clones of coin-ops and cartridges for other systems that the Intellivision didn't get during its heyday are now available as well. These include *Choplifter*, *Cosmic Avenger*, *Death Race*, *Galaxian*, *Gorf*, *Jungle Hunt*, *Klax*, *Moon Patrol* (as *Space Patrol*), *Moonsweeper*, *Ms. Pac-Man*, *Omega Race*, *Space Invaders*, *Wizard of Wor*, and more. The Blue Sky Rangers also released some titles from the vault, including *Brickout!* (a *Breakout* clone also available in the Intellivision Flashback), *Deep Pockets Super Pro Pool & Billiards*, *Number Jumble*, and *Takeover*, a Risk-like strategy game Mattel never released. If you're interested in diving into Intellivision programming yourself, Óscar Toledo G. has written two absolutely essential guides that are well worth your time: *Programming Games for Intellivision* and *Advanced Game Programming for Intellivision*. He also created the IntyBASIC language to ease the development of Intellivision games.

Just want to browse? Here are some more of the best places to shop for Intellivision homebrew ROMs and physical cartridge releases:

CollectorVision Games (collectorvision.com) An independent game developer, publisher, and manufacturer of homebrew games for the Intellivision and ColecoVision. It's also the home of the Phoenix, the FPGA-based ColecoVision project, and a members-only CollectorVision club is also available.

Good Deal Games (gooddealgames.com) A retro-gaming store jam-packed with physical copies of Intellivision homebrews (among other platforms).

Intellivision Collector (intellivisioncollector.com) A Canadian site that sells a variety of packaged and digital download homebrews, plus a few choice hardware accessories like cartridge housings and coax adapters.

Community

The Intellivision community is more vibrant than ever these days, with dozens of sites, podcasts, YouTubers, Facebook groups, and more. Strap in, as there are so many wonderful resources out there that this chapter is going to be one fast ride. Many of these sites have been around for more than two decades, with roots that go back to the mid 1990s when the Web was first surging. Here is just a small cross-section of what's worth checking out today:

The Blue Sky Rangers (blueskyrangers.com): In addition to being an incredible resource from the original Mattel game developers and one of the first fan sites (MakingIt) to appear in the early days of the Web, the site also links to a special eBay store that sells reprint editions of some classic Intellivision games, plus a variety of homebrews and new and used original titles.

Figure 8.6: Keith Robinson made sure the Intellivision lived on, from 1995 until his death in 2017. The website still thrives.

Intv Prime (intvprime.com): The current keeper of the updated FAQ, Intv Prime hosts Papa Intellivision's collection of scanned internal documents from his days at Mattel Electronics. Intv Prime also hosts an annual Intellivision day on December 3 to celebrate the console's birthday (the start of the Fresno test launch in 1979). It even streamed an Intellivision tournament from the 2022 Portland Retro Gaming Expo.

AtariAge (atariage.com) Despite the name of The Other Console Brand™ in the title (which I love dearly), this is arguably the best Intellivision forum on the planet and is now part of Atari. You can also buy physical copies of homebrew games from the AtariAge store.

Intv Funhouse (intvfunhouse.com): A long-running, comprehensive storehouse of Intellivision history and its games, along with personalized thoughts and reviews. For collectors, it also has a useful browser of game variants.

The Intellivisionaries Podcast (intellivisionaries.com): The venerable in-depth podcast that covers the Intellivision console and games hosted by Paul Nurminen, Rick Reynolds, and Chris Martin.

IntelligentVision (intellivision.us) An older site that holds a vast compilation of Intellivision technical details, including programming tutorials, utilities, libraries, and engines (via wiki.intellivision.us), plus information on several dozen homebrew games.

Intellivision Invasion (facebook.com/groups/intellivisioninvasion/) An informal gathering of awesome Intellivision fans, where you can talk shop, post eBay auctions and videos, and more.

Reddit (reddit.com/r/intellivision/) A quieter channel (believe it or not) for Intellivision fans, quiet only because there are so many other places to gather.

Plenty more resources are available, including Facebook groups, Discord channels, Twitter accounts, and more. As the expression goes, I'm only scratching the surface here. Although the Intellivision was sold from 1979 through 1990, it's more alive than ever.

Intellivision Entertainment

One of the biggest sagas of the past few years for Intellivision fans has concerned the Amico, a modern-day hardware interpretation of

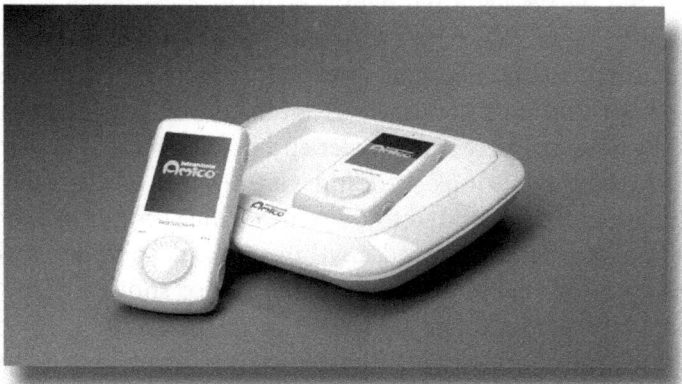

Figure 8.7: The troubled Intellivision Amico is still vaporware at the time of this writing; here's hoping that changes one day.

the console spearheaded by veteran video game music composer and *Video Games Live* owner Tommy Tallarico. A lifelong Intellivision fan, Tallarico bought a stake in Intellivision Productions after the untimely death of Keith Robinson in 2017 and launched a new company, Intellivision Entertainment to manufacture and release the Amico. The idea is like what the new Atari did with the VCS reboot: Design and release an all-new console and controllers that run enhanced versions of the original games plus new titles, and in the process reintroduce the idea of a family console to the non-gaming public.

"Our target is the non-gamer, the family," he said in a May 2018 interview. "We want simplicity. There is no system where young and old and non-gamers can play together in the home. People play on mobile, but it is still a very solitary experience."[8] Regarding the original Intellivision, he said, "I'd play it with mom and dad and brother… We could all understand it. We didn't have to read a manual or play 50 hours to finish a game."[9] Which is true! And all models of the Amico look awesome, from the base model to the limited-edition woodgrain and gold version. The controllers are a gobsmackingly obvious upgrade. Instead of translucent plastic overlays, build in color touch-enabled LCDs where the numeric keypads are supposed to go. We've had the technology for this for more than a decade, and it's only become cheaper and easier.

Alas, just like with the new Atari VCS, Intellivision Entertainment ran into issues and had to delay the console's release several times.

Most of the delays were pandemic-related; the original launch was supposed to be October 10, 2020, and we all know how that turned out. But Intellivision also had some self-inflicted errors in addition to the delays. A leaked document from the developer forums showed the hardware specs were more lower end than expected. Teaser videos that made the console look stunning were few and far between. When they did appear, they tended to reuse the same seconds of footage for each game and barely showed anything new, despite being released months apart. In one infamous case, the videos showed demos using stolen art assets from other games.

At the time of this writing, the Amico is still nowhere to be found. Speculation has run rampant that it will never be released. It would be wonderful to play a modern interpretation of the Intellivision, but I also don't want to see customers lose their Kickstarter deposits or engineers who worked on the console to lose their jobs. Atari eventually delivered on the VCS in 2021 and has since gone on to release some incredible new products such as *Atari 50: The Anniversary Celebration* and the streamlined 2600+ console. I have no stake in the Amico situation other than wishing everyone well and hoping for the best outcome.

9 | Forever

Mattel remains one of the largest companies headquartered in Los Angeles, with 33,900 employees and $5.43 billion in sales in 2022. After relocating its headquarters to El Segundo in 1991, it made increasingly large acquisitions over the years, such as Fisher Price (including Little People and View-Master, 1993), International Games (the makers of UNO, 1996), Tyco Toys (the company behind many toy race tracks, Matchbox cars, and the Magic 8 Ball), and Pleasant Company (the American Girl brand, 1998). But Mattel hasn't had any connection to the Intellivision for 40 years (hey, the compilations were named that for a reason).

From my personal research, it's not clear the Mattel of today even remembers this period. A small display of Mattel history resides in the company's Handler Team Center, where toys are designed. Exhibits move in and out on occasion, and sometimes Intellivision memorabilia shows up in addition to the electronic handhelds. Some employees over the years have made efforts to get the rights back, but nothing has come of them; it doesn't appear the brand carries enough weight to make it viable for Mattel.

The console, however, continues to bind a community of players, programmers, and other enthusiasts looking to discover either what they had missed in the 1980s or weren't around yet to experience. The most dedicated fans today play in tournaments, top off their collections, introduce new players, run fan sites, own YouTube channels, or even develop new games. It's fun to just talk about the Intellivision with people, as Robinson said when demonstrating the machine in an early 2000s TV segment. "Isn't this a wonderful machine?" he asked the host while showing off the controller. "There's a plastic membrane inside, there are actually no moving parts inside of this, a nice plastic membrane that has that nice squishy feel. The computer inside of this was a 16-bit processor. With the games in the late 80s the Nintendo when it first came out was 8-bit. So we were about 10 years ahead of our time."[1]

In the end, several factors did in the Intellivision. The biggest reason was the market shift, of course, the glut of game systems and poor quality cartridges that sank the home video market in 1983. Consumers had had enough of video games. They may have still played them, but they weren't buying as many, or they were instead buying home computers, which were a stunning value in comparison.

Robinson cited changing tastes in pop culture, specifically the rise of music videos, which are a footnote today but first became huge in the early 1980s. "MTV came out, which initially just showed videos 24 hours a day, with very few commercials," he said. "Kids stopped using their TVs to play video games and started watching videos all day long. Atari got out of the business, Coleco got out of the business, Mattel got out of the business. And the only person who stayed in was the former marketing director at Mattel. He's the one who kept Intellivision going through the 80s. In 1985 and 1986, Intellivision was the only game system still being sold in the United States."[2]

The Intellivision itself also had some issues. Many people disliked the controller, especially the disc. I've never had a problem with it, even in directional games. It's ideal for some titles, and I always thought it worked fine for the rest. I owned an Intellivision from the beginning, so I guess I got used to it. One of my closest friends disagrees. He thinks it's the worst game controller ever designed on the face of the Earth. (What does he know, anyway?) The thing that I always disliked and still do today is how stiff the side action buttons are. Although there was some variation in build quality throughout the Intellivision's life cycle, all systems I've played with have had stiff side buttons, which makes it difficult and tiring to play shooters. Accidentally crunching up or losing the overlays wasn't great, either.

The lack of a signature game didn't help. Several came close: *Major League Baseball*, *Astrosmash*, and possibly *Advanced Dungeons & Dragons*. Of course, countless others were excellent, such as *BurgerTime*, *Utopia*, and *Night Stalker*—I've detailed dozens of them in this book. But a system seller is vital to kick off a platform, and Intellivision didn't really have one, unlike the Atari 2600 (*Space Invaders*), the ColecoVision (*Donkey Kong*), or the Atari 400/800 computers (*Star Raiders*) early on or the Nintendo Entertainment System (*Super Mario Bros.* to start), the Sega Genesis (*Sonic the Hedgehog*), and the Super Nintendo (*Super Mario World*) later. Even systems considered market failures often had one, such as the Atari Jaguar (*Tempest 2000*) and the Sega Dreamcast (*Soulcalibur*). *Major League Baseball* was terrific, but not everyone likes baseball, and it was only a two-player game. I'll throw in my pet issue about how most of the first batch of games were two-player-only, though being an only child was the exception rather than the norm in the late 1970s. And what Mattel gained in professional sports licenses, it lost in arcade conversions. Without its own coin-op IP or licensing deals with major arcade machine vendors, the Intellivision could claim few cartridges that "played just like the arcade," as ColecoVision games advertised on their boxes, until it was too late.

The Keyboard Component also played a part. From the beginning, Mattel conceived of the Intellivision not as a game console but as a hybrid console and computer. Although it was a reasonable strategy to take in the late 1970s, the result was that it blurred the company's focus and diluted its resources irrevocably. Fielding the two separate components in a staggered release muddled the marketing, the distribution, and all the early press coverage. In a market where fast execution was suddenly paramount, persistent GI chip shortages and manufacturing issues hindered Mattel every step of the way.

The Blue Sky Rangers maintain to this day that the Keyboard Component was "hopelessly impractical" and impossible to produce for a reasonable selling price and that "if it hadn't been for Dave 'Papa Intellivision' Chandler's reputation, the project probably would have been killed off early on. Instead, his group was allowed to continue tinkering, trying to bring the cost down."[3] It hobbled the company by keeping its key players busy with that instead of potentially much more lucrative games for the Intellivision. "By 1983, the Intellivoice,

Entertainment Computer Module, Aquarius, Intellivision III and other hardware were all either marketed or in development at Mattel," said Robinson in 2015.[4] "But they couldn't sell enough games to cover the expenses. Had they concentrated on the original Intellivision console and games, then maybe they could have survived, essentially what INTV Corp. did."[5]

One thing about the Intellivision is certain: It really was intelligent television. It would be years before another console matched the depth of strategy in *Utopia* or the sophisticated sports plays possible in its games. Back then, you needed to upgrade to a home computer to enjoy similarly involved gaming experiences. Even Prince was a fan, as a recent article in the U.K. music magazine *Long Live Vinyl* said: "Prince was big on Mattel Intellivision, which was infinitely better than Atari but not marketed so well," stated Dez Dickerson, Prince's long-time guitarist, in an interview as part of the article. "Prince and I got locked in battles on *Super Pro Football*. We'd have running tournaments, getting to the point where we almost couldn't wait to be done with the show, so we could get back on the bus and resume playing. Prince hated to lose, but it took him two tours to finally beat me. He got crazy about it."[6]

Ultimately, and to its benefit, Mattel focused on video games as family entertainment. "The idea was these games would be played by moms, dads, children all together. It was really intended as family entertainment," said Robinson in an early 2000s Fox News profile that contrasted the innocence of Intellivision gaming with the violence in video games such as *Grand Theft Auto* and *Mortal Kombat*. "Looking [back at them] today, people say these games are family friendly."[7]

A Different Time

The dawn of the video game era lends itself to wearing rose-tinted glasses, as we all wax nostalgic for our childhoods, or if we weren't around then, romanticize a time when things were simpler. But from the perspective of game developers, it was true. "It was the dawn of the environment, the dawn of the era, and I mean we were in a cube farm," Warhol said. "If you see the scene in the first *Tron* movie, whether you're looking out at a cube, all these cubes, that's kind of that's kind of what it was."

Warhol said that Mattel didn't have enough hardware for everybody to develop games. "You'd end up working at your own workstation for a couple of hours working on a routine, and then you'd have to go to a communal area to render code and debug it, and go back and forth," he said. "Eventually, they had more development systems. It was very collaborative."[8]

"[As to] a lot of crazy stuff going on," he continued, "the Mattel managers hired a bunch of creative people as opposed to a bunch of technology-driven people, because they wanted the creativity in the product. I gotta hand it to them for making that decision. There were a lot of really wacky things happening on the floor at least in our group."[9]

Warhol also believed the way you made games back then also contributed to how much fun they were to play. Specifically, that there were so few assets to connect, he said. It meant that game design was really all about the gameplay. "There was so little memory, we're making games that were 4KB or 8KB," he said. "You couldn't have a lot of graphics. You ended up playing the game, and then tuning it, playing it some more, tuning it, playing it some more…As storage became more available, [now] people are throwing in more and more assets… geez, I wouldn't know if it's 50% or 75% asset production, and at most, 20 or 25% tuning. And it was really the other way around at Mattel, because when you bought one of those games, you had to be able to play it for hour after hour after hour after hour. They were all very primitive mechanics, maybe the first-time interpretation of some of these things in the home environment."[10]

Robinson agreed that working at Mattel was fantastic. "It was like working in a college dorm," he said. "I wasn't sure that this video game thing was really going to last, so they just kind of hired people right out of college. They got 'em cheap, no experience, threw them into whatever spare rooms they had around Mattel, and said, well, do something. And within a year, people were investing around the world based on what a bunch of crazy 20-year-olds were doing at Mattel."[11]

The result was that you could sense it in the product. It came through in the originality and quality of the console design and especially the games. It's why we play them today. It's why I wrote this book. "The group of people who worked on the Intellivision were creative, smart and funny," said Robinson, "and I think that is why so many of the games are still so fun."[12]

Acknowledgements

This book was made possible thanks to some incredible people. Matthew Murray, a phenomenal editor who helps keep me sane. My boss, Wendy Sheehan Donnell, for teaching me so much about writing and editing. Mom and Dad, for starting me on the path with video games back when few others had them. My wife Allison, for her tireless emotional support. My daughter Siena, for being a wonderful inspiration and for playing all these blocky old games with me.

I'd also like to thank some old friends I grew up with playing Intellivision games: Carlo Bonavita, David Passantino, Javier Rivera, and Michael Scondotto. Special thanks to Bill Lange for his stellar proofreading skills, and to Steve Fulton for uncovering some incredible early 1980s game ads and articles. I'd like to thank Jeff Fulton and Óscar Toledo G. for their kind support. Next, I'd also like to thank some of the bright lights that made the Intellivision what it was: Dave Akers, Gabriel Baum, Wendell Brown, Don Daglow, Eddie Dombrower, Steve Ettinger, Bill Fisher, Julie Hoshizaki, Ray Kaestner, Gary Kato, Joe King, Rick Levine, Tom Loughry, Kevin Miller, Mike Minkoff, Karen Nugent, Pat Ransil, David Rolfe, Stephen Roney, Carol B. Shaw, Alan Smith, Ken Smith, John Sohl, John Tomlinson, Ji Wen Tsao, and David Warhol.

Finally, in the same spirit, I'd like to acknowledge three people key to the Intellivision experience who are no longer with us: David

"Papa Intellivision" Chandler, who passed away in 2011 at the age of 87. Hal Finney, the programmer behind *Space Battle* and co-creator of *Star Strike*, died in 2014 at the age of 58. And the effervescent Keith Robinson, who died in 2017 at 61. May they rest in power.

Bibliography

1977 Data Catalog, General Instrument Corporation, Microelectronics, Section 4B, 4B-1 through 4B-55.

"4 Ex-Officers of Mattel Among 5 Indicted on Conspiracy Charges." *The New York Times*, Feb. 17, 1978, D3.

Abin, Len. "The Best Video Games of 1982." *Time*, Dec. 4, 1982, 52.

"Advanced Dungeons & Dragons Cartridge." Blue Sky Rangers website. history.blueskyrangers.com/mattelelectronics/games/addcloudy.html

Ahl, David H. "The World's Worst Computers," *Creative Computing*, September 1985, 88–89.

"Ask the Blue Sky Rangers!" Intellivision newsletter, September/October 2003. intellivisionbrasil.com.br/doc/informativo/2003_IntellivisionNewsletter_Set-Out.pdf

"Astrosmash." Blue Sky Rangers website. history.blueskyrangers.com/mattelelectronics/games/astrosmash.html

"Atari-Intellivision TV Battle." *The New York Times*, Dec. 14, 1981, D4.

Aycock, John. *Retrogame Archaeology: Exploring Old Computer Games*. Switzerland: Springer, 2016.

Baer, Ralph H. *Videogames: In the Beginning.* Springfield, NJ: Rolenta Press, 2005.

Belair Jr., Felix. "Mattel Consents to Abide by Stern S.E.C. Rulings." *The New York Times*, Aug. 6, 1974, 41.

Berlin, Leslie. *Troublemakers: Silicon Valley's Coming of Age.* New York: Simon & Schuster, 2017.

Bloom, Steve. *Video Invaders.* New York: Arco Publishing, 1982.

Blumenthal, Howard. "Mattel's Intellivision," *Video*, August 1980, 29.

Bright, Walter, in a posted response to "First Electronic Games Used Calculator Chips." news.ycombinator.com/item?id=34272079

Brown, William Michael. "Mission X Marks the Spot," *Electronic Fun With Computers and Games*, September 1983, 48.

"Bump 'n' Jump." Blue Sky Rangers website. history.blueskyrangers.com/mattelelectronics/games/bumpnjump.html

Burnham, Van, ed. *Supercade: A Visual History of the Videogame Age 1971-1984.* Cambridge, MA: The MIT Press, 2001.

Caruso, Denise. "Software for Defunct Machines." *InfoWorld*, May 14, 1984, 35.

Chandler, David. "Intellivision History and Philosophy." Mattel internal document, 1982.

Chandler, David P. Switch Apparatus, U.S. Patent US4246452A, filed 5 January 1979, and issued 20 January 1981. patents.google.com/patent/US4246452A

"Classic Gaming Expo 2000: Keynote Addresses: Intellivision." Classic Gaming Expo 2000, via GameSpy. web.archive.org/web/20111108143531/http://classic-gaming.gamespy.com/View.php?view=Articles.Detail&id=389

"Consumer Electronics Personals." *Weekly Television Digest With Consumer Electronics*, Oct. 2, 1978, 14.

Consumer Guide's How To Win At Video Games. New York: Pocket Books, 1982.

"Corporations: All's Swell at Mattel," *Time*, Oct. 26, 1962. content.time.com/time/magazine/0,9263,7601621026,00.html

Bibliography | 255

"Donkey Kong." Blue Sky Rangers website. history.blueskyrangers.com/coleco/donkeykong.html

Donovan, Tristan. *Replay: The History of Video Games*. Sussex, UK: Yellow Ant, 2010.

Dunn, Jeff. "Chasing Phantoms - The History of Failed Consoles." GamesRadar, July 15, 2013. www.gamesradar.com/chasing-phantoms-history-failed-consoles/

Earls, John. "Like It's 1999…" *Long Live Vinyl*, November 2019, 58.

"Early Intellivision Promotional Video." BlueSkyRangers YouTube Channel, posted Dec. 3, 2019. www.youtube.com/watch?v=Am1ECAbRDy4

"EF's Fifty Best Games." *Electronic Fun With Computer Games*, March 1984, 21–28.

"The Electric Company Math Fun." Blue Sky Rangers website. history.blueskyrangers.com/mattelelectronics/games/mathfun.html

Fisher, Bill. "Intellivision: Programmer Interviews." BlueSkyRangers YouTube channel, posted Jan. 10, 2007. www.youtube.com/watch?v=bewzUlJEjcA

Forman, Tracie. "Videogames Meet Cable TV." *Electronic Games*, April 1983, 76.

Gimini TV Game Circuits. General Instrument Corporation, 1978 Microelectronics catalog, 60–68.

"Happy Trails." Blue Sky Rangers website. history.blueskyrangers.com/activision/happytrails.html

Hayes, Thomas C. "Mattel Is Counting on Its Toys." *The New York Times*, Feb. 4, 1984, 35.

Herman, Leonard. *Phoenix IV: The History of the Videogame Industry*. Springfield, NJ: Rolenta Press, 2016.

Hillkirk, John. "Vidgame Inventory Worrisome." *USA Today*, Nov. 14, 1982, via Steve Fulton tweet on Nov. 14, 2022.

Hunter, William. "New Kid on the Blocks." The Dot Eaters. thedoteaters.com/?bitstory=console%2Fintellivision&all=1

"Intellivision Console Demonstration Cartridge." BlueSkyRangers YouTube channel, posted June 3, 2007. www.youtube.com/watch?v=We8lQgv_GOY

"Intellivision: Fox News Magazine Profile." BlueSkyRangers YouTube Channel, posted Jan. 19, 2007. www.youtube.com/watch?v=ipe5AJTpe8I

"Intellivision history." IntellivisionLives archive. web.archive.org/web/20170623040513/http://www.intellivisionlives.com/history.php

"Intellivision IV Master Component [Unreleased]," Blue Sky Rangers website. history.blueskyrangers.com/hardware/intellivision4.html

"Intellivision: Mike Minkoff on Snafu." BlueSkyRangers YouTube channel, posted May 30, 2008. www.youtube.com/watch?v=kTSOVKwMIjQ

"Intellivision on PlayStation." IntellivisionLives archive. web.archive.org/web/20170727212643/http://www.intellivisionlives.com/retrotopia/psx.shtml

"Intellivision: Ray Kaestner on BurgerTime." BlueSkyRangers YouTube channel, posted June 26, 2008. www.youtube.com/watch?v=91fmS1l6xII

"Intellivision®: San Diego News 8 Profile." BlueSkyRangers YouTube channel, posted Feb. 1, 2007. www.youtube.com/watch?v=0kQCbv_C-Z4

"Intellivision Super-STIC test video." BlueSkyRangers YouTube channel, dated Dec. 17, 1981, posted Oct. 26, 2019. www.youtube.com/watch?v=hgiVI_jCo24

"Intellivision® TV Commercial: PlayCable Comparison." BlueSkyRangers YouTube channel, posted Oct. 10, 2007. www.youtube.com/watch?v=Q-oMtXSVKyU

"Interview: David Rolfe." Good Deal Games, 2003. www.gooddealgames.com/interviews/int_rolfe.html

"INTV Corporation." Blue Sky Rangers website. history.blueskyrangers.com/intvcorp/

JCPenney Christmas 1979 catalog. 463.

Johnson, Ethan. Interview with David Rolfe. *Candid Conversations in Code: Interviews With the First Generation of Video Game Programmers* (Self-published, 2020).

Katz, Arnie; Kunkel, Bill; and the editors of *Electronic Games*. "Video's Guide to Electronic Games." *Video*, November 1982, 46-56, 120.

Kent, Steven L. *The Ultimate History of Video Games: From Pong to Pokémon and*

Beyond—*The Story Behind the Craze That Touched Our Lives and Changed the World*. New York: Three Rivers Press, 2001.

"Keyboard Component #1149." Blue Sky Rangers website. history.blueskyrangers.com/hardware/keyboardcomponent.html

"Keyboard Component." IntellivisionLives archive. web.archive.org/web/20170629111841/http://www.intellivisionlives.com/bluesky/hardware/keyboard_tech.html

"Keyboard Overview." Mattel Electronics internal document dated Feb. 8, 1982 via the Internet Archive. archive.org/details/19820602KeyboardComponentPlans/mode/2up?view=theater

K*mart ad from A Dec. 14, 1983 via Steve Fulton tweet on March 19, 2022.

Klooster, Eric. "Mattel Aquarius – Home computer with the shortest career." History of Home and Game Computers, computermuseum.50megs.com/brands/aquarius.htm

Kubey, Craig. *The Winners' Book of Video Games*. New York: Warner Books, 1982.

Kunkel, Bill, and Laney Jr., Frank. "Arcade Alley: Armchair Athletes: Sports, Mattel-Style." *Video*, August 1980, 92.

Kunkel, Bill, and Laney Jr., Frank. "The Third Annual Arcade Awards." *Video*, January 1982, 76.

Kunkel, Bill, and Katz, Arnie. "Arcade Alley: Mixed Reviews for Intellivision." *Video*, March 1982, 40–42.

Kunkel, Bill, and Katz, Arnie. "Arcade Alley: The Arcade Awards, Part 1." *Video*, January 1984, 40–42.

Kunkel, Bill, and Katz, Arnie. "The Videogames: How They Rate." *The New York Times*, Nov. 21, 1981, Section 1, 12.

Kunkel, Bill, and Katz, Arnie. "Video's Guide to Electronic Games." *Video*, 47–56, 108.

"Largest Publicly-Owned Companies Headquartered in Los Angeles County: Ranked by Sales Revenue, 2021." *Los Angeles Almanac*. www.laalmanac.com/economy/ec03.php

Leibson, Steven. "A History of Early Microcontrollers, Part 9: The General Instrument PIC1650," *Electronic Engineering Journal*, Jan. 2, 2023. www.eejournal.com/article/a-history-of-early-microcontrollers-part-9-the-general-instruments-pic1650/

Levine, Richard S. "'PBA Bowling' Among 100 Greatest." Rick S. Levine, July 7, 2017. web.archive.org/web/20170917224553/http://www.rickslevine.com/blog/pba-bowling-among-100-greatest/

Lindsey, Robert. "Mattel Settles 5 Class Lawsuits." *The New York Times*, Nov. 4, 1975, 47.

"Lock 'N' Chase." Blue Sky Rangers website. history.blueskyrangers.com/mattelelectronics/games/locknchase.html

"Loco-Motion." Blue Sky Rangers website.

Loguidice, Bill. "A History of Gaming Platforms: Mattel Intellivision." Gamasutra (now *Game Developer*), May 8, 2008. www.gamedeveloper.com/console/a-history-of-gaming-platforms-mattel-intellivision

Loguidice, Bill, and Barton, Matt. *Vintage Game Consoles: The Greatest Gaming Platforms of All Time*. Burlington, MA: Focal Press, 2014.

Mace, Scott. "Electronic Christmas, Zappy New Year," *InfoWorld*, Dec. 20, 1982, 33.

"Magnavox's Signing." *Weekly Television Digest With Consumer Electronics*, Jan. 28. 1974, 12.

Mason, Graeme. "40 years on, celebrating the Mattel Intellivision." Eurogamer, May 27, 2019. www.eurogamer.net/40-years-on-celebrating-the-mattel-intellivision

"Matt Chat 157: David Warhol and Mattel's Intellivision (fixed)." Matt Barton's YouTube channel, posted Jul. 15, 2012. www.youtube.com/watch?v=WeMseLpbREQ

"Mattel Cuts Staff Again." *Electronic Games*, December 1983, 12.

"Mattel Delay." *Weekly Television Digest With Consumer Electronics*, Nov. 12, 1979, 11.

Mattel Electronics 1980 Intellivision catalog, 3.

Mattel Electronics 1981 Intellivision catalog. PDF scan with business card stapled to the back cover. archive.org/details/1981IntellivisionCatalog

"Mattel Electronics Games." Blue Sky Rangers website, history.blueskyrangers.com/game-list.html

"Mattel Electronics Intellivision." Old Computers. www.old-computers.com/museum/doc.asp?c=1205

"Mattel Hiked Prices." *Weekly Television Digest With Consumer Electronics*, Oct. 15, 1979, 10.

"Mattel's Video Game." *Weekly Television Digest With Consumer Electronics*, May 15, 1978, 10.

"Master Component #2609." IntellivisionLives archive. web.archive.org/web/20170630220531/http://www.intellivisionlives.com/bluesky/hardware/intelli_tech.html

Mastrapa, Gus. Mott, Tony, ed. *1001 Video Games You Must Play Before You Die*. New York: Universe, 2010.

"Mind Strike." Blue Sky Rangers. history.blueskyrangers.com/mattelelectronics/games/mindstrike.html

Moss, Richard. "Build, gather, brawl, repeat: The history of real-time strategy games." Ars Technica, Sept. 15, 2017. arstechnica.com/gaming/2017/09/build-gather-brawl-repeat-the-history-of-real-time-strategy-games/

Mott, Tony, ed. *1001 Games You Must Play Before You Die*. New York: Universe, 2011.

Newman, Michael Z. *Atari Age: The Emergence of Video Games in America*. Cambridge, MA: The MIT Press, 2017.

Odd Lot advertisement in October 1984, via Steve Fulton tweet on Nov. 5, 2022.

Orth, Steven A. "Ice Trek," INTV Funhouse. intvfunhouse.com/games/ice.php

"The Player's Guide to Fantasy Games." *Electronic Games*, June 1983, 47.

"Playing Hardware to Get." *Video Games*, March 1983, 20.

Pollack, Andrew. "The Video Game Sales War." *The New York Times*, June 9, 1982, D1.

Polskin, Howard. "Behind the Scenes With the Blue Sky Rangers Who Dream Up Mattel's Video Games." *TV Guide*, June 19, 1982, 39–44.

"Remembering Keith Robinson and Intellivision - Electric Playground Classic." Electric Playground Network YouTube channel, posted June 19, 2017. www.youtube.com/watch?v=wJJT1ZI6yl4

Roode, Michael. "Memories of PlayCable." *Classic Gamer Magazine*, April 2004, 15.

Rovin, Jeff. *The Complete Guide to Conquering Video Games: How to Win Every Game in the Galaxy*. New York: Collier Books, 1982.

"Royal Dealer." Blue Sky Rangers website. history.blueskyrangers.com/mattelelectronics/games/royaldealer.html

Salen, Katie, and Zimmerman, Eric. *The Game Design Reader: A Rules of Play Anthology*. Cambridge, MA: The MIT Press, 2005.

Schamus, Marty. "The Home Front." *Joystiq*, December 1983, 54.

Schley, Stewart. "Look ma, no cartridge!" *CED*, Dec. 31, 2005, via the Wayback Machine. web.archive.org/web/20131129023025/https://www.cedmagazine.com/articles/2005/12/look-ma,-no-cartridge!

Sears advertisement, *Time*, Dec. 4, 1982, 6.

Smith, Alexander. *They Create Worlds: The Story of the People and Companies That Shaped the Video Game Industry, Vol. I: 1971-1982*. Abingdon, UK: Routledge, 2020.

"Software Developers Kit for the Intellivision Video Game System." SDK-1600, last updated Nov. 20, 2002. sdk-1600.spatula-city.org/old-index.html

"Space Armada." blueskyrangers.com. history.blueskyrangers.com/mattelelectronics/games/spacearmada.html

"Space Battle." Blue Sky Rangers website. history.blueskyrangers.com/mattelelectronics/games/spacebattle.html

Stilphen, Scott. "DP Interviews…David Rolfe," *Digital Press*, www.digit-press.com/library/interviews/interview_david_rolfe.html

Store ad in a June 16, 1983, newspaper, via Steve Fulton tweet on Dec. 10, 2021.

Sullivan, George. "Screen Magic." *Blip*, July 1983, 3–6.

Sullivan, George. *Screen Play: The Story of Video Games*. New York: Frederick Warne, 1983.

Takahashi, Dean. "Intellivision lives: Tommy Tallarico Will Relaunch 1980s Console." VentureBeat, May 29, 2018. venturebeat.com/games/intellivsion-lives-tommy-tallarico-will-relaunch-1980s-console/

Tam, Jeffrey. "Intellivision: Its Legacy and the Evolution of Baseball Games," Case History, STS 145, March 2002.

"Thin Ice." Blue Sky Rangers website. history.blueskyrangers.com/intvcorp/thinice.html

"Thunder Castle." Blue Sky Rangers website. history.blueskyrangers.com/intvcorp/thundercastle.html

"Top 25 Video Game Consoles." IGN (no date listed). www.ign.com/lists/top-25-consoles/14

Toys 'R' Us ad from Nov. 19, 1986, via a Steve Fulton tweet on Nov. 6, 2022.

"Triple Action." Blue Sky Rangers website. history.blueskyrangers.com/mattelelectronics/games/tripleaction.html

"Tron: Deadly Discs," Blue Sky Rangers website, history.blueskyrangers.com/mattelelectronics/games/deadlydiscs.html

Tsiokos, Costa. "TV PIXXX: Remote Gaming, 80's Style." *Population Statistic*, June 15, 2021. www.populationstatistic.com/archives/2008/06/15/tv-pixxx-remote-gaming-80s-style/

"Utopia." Blue Sky Rangers website. history.blueskyrangers.com/mattelelectronics/games/utopia.html

"U.S. Ski Team Skiing." Blue Sky Rangers website. history.blueskyrangers.com/mattelelectronics/games/skiing.html

Uston, Ken. *Ken Uston's Guide to Buying and Beating the Home Video Games*. New York: Signet, 1982.

"Vectrex." *Retro Gamer*, Jan. 24, 2014. www.retrogamer.net/profiles/hardware/vectrex/

"Video Game Preview '83." *Electronic Games*, May 1983, 22.

"Video Games Are Blitzing the World." *Time*, Jan. 18, 1982.

"Video Screen." *Computer & Video Games*, February 1982, 19.

Weiss, Brett. *The 100 Greatest Console Video Games 1977-1987*. Atglen, PA: Schiffer Publishing, 2014.

Weinstein, Stephen B., *Getting the Picture: A Guide to CATV and the New Electronic Media*, 1986, 92.

"We Were There" Intellivision Flashback Promo Video. BlueSkyRangers YouTube channel, posted Sep. 25, 2014. www.youtube.com/watch?v=sbw2AjGtCiM

Wolf, Mark J. P., ed. *Before the Crash: Early Video Game History*. Detroit: Wayne State University Press, 2012.

Wolf, Mark J. P., ed. *The Encyclopedia of Video Games: The Culture, Technology, and Art of Gaming* (2 volumes). Westport, CT: Greenwood Press, 2012.

"World Championship Baseball." Blue Sky Rangers website. history.blueskyrangers.com/intvcorp/wcbaseball.html

Yates, Jean. "Mattel Unveils Game Plan." *InfoWorld*, March 2, 1981, 1, 28.

Zito, Tom. "Playing a Calculated Game." *The Washington Post*, Oct. 20, 1977. www.washingtonpost.com/archive/lifestyle/1977/10/20/playing-a-calculated-game/37e7d080-087a-4811-84e9-8d40647e3d5c/

| Notes

Introduction

1. "Magnavox's Signing," *Weekly Television Digest With Consumer Electronics*, Jan. 28. 1974, 12.
2. Tam, Jeffrey, "Intellivision: Its Legacy and the Evolution of Baseball Games," Case History, STS 145, March 2002.

Chapter 1

1. "Corporations: All's Swell at Mattel," *Time*, Oct. 26, 1962. https://content.time.com/time/magazine/0,9263,7601621026,00.html
2. Ibid.
3. Belair Jr., Felix, "Mattel Consents to Abide by Stern S.E.C. Rulings," *The New York Times*, Aug. 6, 1974, 41.
4. Lindsey, Robert, "Mattel Settles 5 Class Lawsuits," *The New York Times*, Nov. 4, 1975, 47.
5. "4 Ex-Officers of Mattel Among 5 Indicted on Conspiracy Charges," *The New York Times*, Feb. 17, 1978, D3.
6. Donovan, Tristan, *Replay: The History of Video Games* (Sussex, UK: Yellow Ant, 2010), 69.
7. Zito, Tom, "Playing a Calculated Game," *The Washington Post*, Oct. 20, 1977. www.washingtonpost.com/archive/lifestyle/1977/10/20/playing-a-calculated-game/37e7d080-087a-4811-84e9-8d40647e3d5c/
8. Donovan, 69.

9   Bright, Walter, in a posted response to "First Electronic Games Used Calculator Chips," news.ycombinator.com/item?id=34272079
10 Herman, Leonard, *Phoenix IV: The History of the Videogame Industry* (Springfield, NJ: Rolenta Press, 2016), 47.
11 Smith, Alexander, *They Create Worlds: The Story of the People and Companies That Shaped the Video Game Industry, Vol. I: 1971-1982* (Abingdon, UK: Routledge, 2020), 469.
12 Chandler, David, "Intellivision History and Philosophy," Mattel internal document, 1982.
13 *1977 Data Catalog*, General Instrument Corporation, Microelectronics, Section 4B, 4B-1 through 4B-55.
14 Chandler, "Intellivision History and Philosophy."
15 "Master Component #2609," IntellivisionLives archive. web.archive.org/web/20170630220531/http://www.intellivisionlives.com/bluesky/hardware/intelli_tech.html
16 Zito, Tom, "Playing a Calculated Game," *The Washington Post*, Oct. 20, 1977
17 *Gimini TV Game Circuits*, General Instrument Corporation, 1978 Microelectronics catalog, 60-68.
18 Johnson, Ethan, interview with David Rolfe, *Candid Conversations in Code: Interviews With the First Generation of Video Game Programmers* (Self-published ebook, 2020, no page number).
19 Johnson, *Candid Conversations in Code* (no page number).
20 "Interview: David Rolfe," Good Deal Games, 2003. www.gooddealgames.com/interviews/int_rolfe.html
21 Ibid.
22 Johnson, *Candid Conversations in Code* (no page number).
23 Stilphen, Scott. "DP Interviews…David Rolfe," *Digital Press*, www.digitpress.com/library/interviews/interview_david_rolfe.html
24 Ibid.
25 "Classic Gaming Expo 2000: Keynote Addresses: Intellivision," Classic Gaming Expo 2000, via GameSpy. web.archive.org/web/20111108143531/http://classicgaming.gamespy.com/View.php?view=Articles.Detail&id=389
26 Stilphen, David Rolfe interview.
27 Interoffice memo from Dave Chandler to Yale Harrison and Glen Hightower, May 18, 1978.
28 Letter from Osco Drug, Inc. to Mattel Sales, Feb. 27, 1978.
29 Stilphen, David Rolfe interview.
30 "Mattel's Video Game," *Weekly Television Digest With Consumer Electronics*, May 15, 1978, 10.
31 Chandler, "Intellivision History and Philosophy."
32 Ibid.

33 "Consumer Electronics Personals," *Weekly Television Digest With Consumer Electronics,* Oct. 2, 1978, 14.
34 Chandler, "Intellivision History and Philosophy."
35 Ibid.
36 Ibid.
37 Chandler, "Intellivision History and Philosophy."
38 Hunter, William, "New Kid on the Blocks," The Dot Eaters. thedoteaters.com/?bitstory=console%2Fintellivision&all=1
39 Leibson, Steven, "A History of Early Microcontrollers, Part 9: The General Instruments PIC1650," *Electronic Engineering Journal,* Jan. 2, 2023. www.eejournal.com/article/a-history-of-early-microcontrollers-part-9-the-general-instruments-pic1650/
40 "Master Component #2609," IntellivisionLives archive. web.archive.org/web/20170630220531/http://www.intellivisionlives.com/bluesky/hardware/intelli_tech.html
41 "STIC," IntelliWiki. wiki.intellivision.us/index.php/STIC
42 Loguidice and Barton, 72.
43 "Master Component #2609," IntellivisionLives archive.
44 Ibid.
45 Chandler, David P. Switch Apparatus. U.S. Patent US4246452A, filed 5 January 1979, and issued 20 January 1981. patents.google.com/patent/US4246452A
46 "Mattel Hiked Prices," *Weekly Television Digest With Consumer Electronics,* Oct. 15, 1979, 10.
47 Ibid.
48 "Mattel Delay," *Weekly Television Digest With Consumer Electronics,* Nov. 12, 1979, 11.
49 Chandler, "Intellivision History and Philosophy."
50 Ed Krakauer interview with Alexander Smith, Oct. 7, 2016, in *They Create Worlds,* 472.
51 Chandler, "Intellivision History and Philosophy."
52 JCPenney Christmas 1979 catalog, 463.
53 Gottschalk's ad, as shown by Hunter, "New Kid on the Blocks," The Dot Eaters.
54 Intellivision keynote, Classic Gaming Expo 2000.
55 "The Electric Company Math Fun," Blue Sky Rangers website. history.blueskyrangers.com/mattelelectronics/games/mathfun.html
56 "Keyboard Component #1149," Blue Sky Rangers website. history.blueskyrangers.com/hardware/keyboardcomponent.html
57 "Intellivision Console Demonstration Cartridge," BlueSkyRangers YouTube channel, posted June 3, 2007. www.youtube.com/watch?v=We8lQgv_GOY
58 "Early Intellivision Promotional Video," BlueSkyRangers YouTube Chan-

nel, posted Dec. 3, 2019. www.youtube.com/watch?v=Am1ECAbRDy4
59   Mattel Electronics 1980 Intellivision catalog, 3.

Chapter 2

1   Herman, 63.
2   Dunn, Jeff, "Chasing Phantoms - The History of Failed Consoles," GamesRadar, July 15, 2013. www.gamesradar.com/chasing-phantoms-history-failed-consoles/
3   Donovan, 79.
4   Chandler, "Intellivision History and Philosophy."
5   Hayes, Thomas C., "Mattel Is Counting on Its Toys," *The New York Times*, Feb. 4, 1984, 35.
6   Blumenthal, Howard, "Mattel's Intellivision," *Video*, August 1980, 29.
7   "Mattel Electronics Games," Blue Sky Rangers website, history.blueskyrangers.com/game-list.html
8   Kunkel, Bill, and Laney, Frank, "Arcade Alley: Armchair Athletes: Sports, Mattel-Style," *Video*, August 1980, 92.
9   Kunkel, Bill, and Katz, Arnie, "Video's Guide to Electronic Games," *Video*, 47–56, 108.
10   "Top 25 Video Game Consoles," IGN, www.ign.com/lists/top-25-consoles/14
11   "Space Battle," Blue Sky Rangers website. history.blueskyrangers.com/mattelelectronics/games/spacebattle.html
12   Katz, Arnie; Kunkel, Bill; and the editors of *Electronic Games*, "Video's Guide to Electronic Games," *Video*, November 1982, 53.
13   "U.S. Ski Team® Skiing," Blue Sky Rangers website. history.blueskyrangers.com/mattelelectronics/games/skiing.html
14   Smith, 474.
15   Ibid.
16   Chandler, "Intellivision History and Philosophy."
17   Ibid.
18   "Intellivision®: Fox News Magazine Profile," BlueSkyRangers YouTube Channel, posted Jan. 19, 2007. www.youtube.com/watch?v=ipe5AJTpe8I
19   Kent, 195.
20   Chandler, "Intellivision History and Philosophy."
21   Herman, 75.
22   Donovan, 79.

Chapter 3

1   Yates, Jean, "Mattel Unveils Game Plan," *InfoWorld*, March 2, 1981, 1, 28.
2   "Astrosmash," Blue Sky Rangers website. history.blueskyrangers.com/mat-

telelectronics/games/astrosmash.html
3   Ibid.
4   Ibid.
5   "Snafu," Blue Sky Rangers website. history.blueskyrangers.com/mattelelectronics/games/snafu.html
6   "Intellivision®: Mike Minkoff on Snafu." BlueSkyRangers YouTube channel, posted May 30, 2008. www.youtube.com/watch?v=kTSOVKwMIjQ
7   Levine, Richard S. "'PBA Bowling' Among 100 Greatest," Rick S. Levine, July 7, 2017. web.archive.org/web/20170917224553/http://www.rickslevine.com/blog/pba-bowling-among-100-greatest/
8   Kunkel, Bill, and Katz, Arnie, "Arcade Alley: Mixed Reviews for Intellivision," *Video*, March 1982, 40–42.
9   "Space Armada," blueskyrangers.com. history.blueskyrangers.com/mattelelectronics/games/spacearmada.html
10 "Triple Action," Blue Sky Rangers website. history.blueskyrangers.com/mattelelectronics/games/tripleaction.html
11 Ibid.
12 "Video Screen," *Computer & Video Games*, February 1982, 19.
13 Kunkel and Katz, "Arcade Alley: Mixed Reviews for Intellivision," *Video*, March 1982, 40–42.
14 Blumenthal, "Mattel's Intellivision," *Video*, August 1980, 29.
15 Roode, Michael, "Memories of PlayCable," *Classic Gamer Magazine*, April 2004, 15.
16 Weinstein, Stephen B., *Getting the Picture: A Guide to CATV and the New Electronic Media*, 1986, 92.
17 Forman, Tracie, "Videogames Meet Cable TV," *Electronic Games*, April 1983, 76.
18 Roode, "Memories of PlayCable," *Classic Gamer Magazine*, April 2004, 15.
19 "Intellivision® TV Commercial: PlayCable Comparison," BlueSkyRangers YouTube channel. www.youtube.com/watch?v=Q-oMtXSVKyU
20 Schley, Stewart, "Look ma, no cartridge!" *CED*, Dec. 31, 2005, via the Wayback Machine. web.archive.org/web/20131129023025/https://www.cedmagazine.com/articles/2005/12/look-ma,-no-cartridge!
21 Tsiokos, Costa, "TV PIXXX: Remote Gaming, 80's Style," Population Statistic, June 15, 2021. www.populationstatistic.com/archives/2008/06/15/tv-pixxx-remote-gaming-80s-style/
22 Herman, 89.
23 "Atari-Intellivision TV Battle," *The New York Times*, Dec. 14, 1981, D4.
24 Herman, 87.
25 Smith, 522.
26 "Keyboard Component," IntellivisionLives archive. web.archive.org/web/20170629111841/http://www.intellivisionlives.com/bluesky/hardware/keyboard_tech.html

27 Mattel Electronics 1981 Catalog, PDF with scan of business card stapled to the back cover. archive.org/details/1981IntellivisionCatalog
28 "Keyboard Component," Blue Sky Rangers website. history.blueskyrangers.com/hardware/keyboardcomponent.html
29 "Mattel Electronics Intellivision," Old Computers. www.old-computers.com/museum/doc.asp?c=1205
30 "Keyboard Component," Blue Sky Rangers website. history.blueskyrangers.com/hardware/keyboardcomponent.html
31 Ibid.
32 "Keyboard Overview," Feb. 8, 1982, scanned to file CCF10232011_00020.pdf, via Intv Prime site. www.intvprime.com/papa-intellivision-searchable-content/
33 Kunkel, Bill, and Katz, Arnie, "The Videogames: How They Rate," *The New York Times*, Nov. 21, 1981, Section 1, 12.
34 Kunkel, Bill, and Laney Jr., Frank, "The Third Annual Arcade Awards," *Video*, January 1982, 76.
35 "Intellivision Super-STIC test video," BlueSkyRangers YouTube channel, dated Dec. 17, 1981, posted Oct. 26, 2019. www.youtube.com/watch?v=h-giVI_jCo24
36 Moss, Richard, "Build, gather, brawl, repeat: The history of real-time strategy games," Ars Technica, Sept. 15, 2017. arstechnica.com/gaming/2017/09/build-gather-brawl-repeat-the-history-of-real-time-strategy-games/
37 "Utopia," Blue Sky Rangers website. history.blueskyrangers.com/mattelelectronics/games/utopia.html
38 Abin, Len, "The Best Video Games of 1982," *Time*, Dec. 4, 1982, 52.
39 "50 Greatest Game Design Innovations," *Edge*, Nov. 1, 2007. web.archive.org/web/20100924064303/http://www.next-gen.biz/features/50-greatest-game-design-innovations?page=0%2C3
40 "Lock 'N' Chase," Blue Sky Rangers website. history.blueskyrangers.com/mattelelectronics/games/locknchase.html
41 Ibid.
42 "Intellivision® TV Commercial: Henry Thomas," BlueSkyRangers YouTube channel, posted Jan. 15, 2007. www.youtube.com/watch?v=KsmIma0ZQtQ
43 Sourced from scanned "I'm waiting to sign a $2.50 check with your name on it" mailer, and a separate scan of letterhead and the check that said, "Glad to have you on the Intellivision Team!" with Plimpton's signature.

Chapter 4

1 Uston, Ken, *Ken Uston's Guide to Buying and Beating the Home Video Games* (New York: Signet, 1982), 6–8.

2   Rovin, Jeff. *The Complete Guide to Conquering Video Games: How to Win Every Game in the Galaxy*. New York: Collier Books, 1982, 7–8.
3   Ibid.
4   Pollack, Andrew, "The Video Game Sales War," *The New York Times*, June 9, 1982, D1.
5   Herman, 109.
6   "The Player's Guide to Fantasy Games," *Electronic Games*, June 1983, 47.
7   Kunkel, Bill, and Katz, Arnie, "Arcade Alley: The Arcade Awards, Part 1," *Video*, January 1984, 40–42.
8   "Advanced Dungeons & Dragons Cartridge," Blue Sky Rangers website. history.blueskyrangers.com/mattelelectronics/games/addcloudy.html
9   Fisher, Bill, "Intellivision: Programmer Interviews," BlueSkyRangers YouTube channel, posted Jan. 10, 2007. www.youtube.com/watch?v=bew-zUlJEjcA
10 Ibid.
11 Polskin, Howard, "Behind the Scenes With the Blue Sky Rangers Who Dream Up Mattel's Video Games," *TV Guide*, June 19, 1982, 39–44.
12 Ibid.
13 "Classic Gaming Expo 2000: Keynote Addresses: Intellivision," Classic Gaming Expo 2000, via GameSpy. web.archive.org/web/20111108143531/http://classicgaming.gamespy.com/View.php?view=Articles.Detail&id=389
14 "Tron: Deadly Discs," Blue Sky Rangers website, history.blueskyrangers.com/mattelelectronics/games/deadlydiscs.html
15 Sullivan, George, "Screen Magic," *Blip #6*, July 1983, 5.
16 Sullivan, George, *Screen Play: The Story of Video Games*, 55.
17 Sullivan, *Screen Play*, 56.
18 "Vectrex," *Retro Gamer*, Jan. 24, 2014. www.retrogamer.net/profiles/hardware/vectrex/
19 "Donkey Kong," Blue Sky Rangers website. history.blueskyrangers.com/coleco/donkeykong.html
20 Ibid.
21 "Royal Dealer," Blue Sky Rangers website. history.blueskyrangers.com/mattelelectronics/games/royaldealer.html
22 Loguidice and Barton, 79.
23 "Master Component #2609," IntellivisionLives archive. web.archive.org/web/20170630220531/http://www.intellivisionlives.com/bluesky/hardware/intelli_tech.html
24 Hillkirk, John, "Vidgame Inventory Worrisome," *USA Today*, Nov. 14, 1982, via Steve Fulton tweet on Nov. 14, 2022.
25 "Mattel Electronics Intellivision," Old Computers. www.old-computers.com/museum/doc.asp?c=1205
26 Ibid.

27 Ibid.
28 Herman, 113.
29 Untitled newspaper ad via Steve Fulton tweet on Oct. 22, 2022.
30 Mace, Scott, "Electronic Christmas, Zappy New Year," *InfoWorld*, Dec. 20, 1982, 33.
31 Sears advertisement, *Time*, Dec. 4, 1982, 6.
32 "Playing Hardware to Get," *Video Games*, March 1983, 20.
33 Mace, "Electronic Christmas, Zappy New Year," *InfoWorld*, Dec. 20, 1982, 33.
34 Katz, Arnie; Kunkel, Bill; and the editors of *Electronic Games*, "Video's Guide to Electronic Games," *Video*, November 1982, 50.
35 Ibid.
36 Ibid.
37 "Top 25 Video Game Consoles," IGN, www.ign.com/lists/top-25-consoles/14

Chapter 5

1 "Mattel Electronics Intellivision," Old Computers. www.old-computers.com/museum/doc.asp?c=1205
2 "Intellivision: Intelligent Television," GameSpy archive. web.archive.org/web/20080623232114/http://classicgaming.gamespy.com/View.php?view=ConsoleMuseum.Detail&id=17&game=9
3 "Playing Hardware to Get," *Video Games*, March 1983, 19.
4 "Mattel Electronics Intellivision," Old Computers. www.old-computers.com/museum/doc.asp?c=1205
5 Herman, 119.
6 Ibid.
7 Ahl, David H. quoting John J. Anderson, "The World's Worst Computers," *Creative Computing*, September 1985, 88–89.
8 Herman, 120.
9 Klooster, Eric, "Mattel Aquarius – Home computer with the shortest career," History of Home and Game Computers, computermuseum.50megs.com/brands/aquarius.htm
10 Odd Lot advertisement in October 1984, via Steve Fulton tweet on Nov. 5, 2022.
11 "EF's Fifty Best Games," *Electronic Fun With Computer Games*, March 1984, 27.
12 "The Players Guide to Fantasy Games," *Electronic Games*, June 1983, 47.
13 "Ask the Blue Sky Rangers!," Intellivision newsletter, September/October 2003. intellivisionbrasil.com.br/doc/informativo/2003_IntellivisionNewsletter_Set-Out.pdf
14 Mattel had begun advertising in television commercials that customers

who purchased a Master Component between Feb. 12 and May 31, 1983, would receive a free Intellivoice by mail.
15   Orth, Steven A. "Ice Trek," INTV Funhouse. intvfunhouse.com/games/ice.php
16   Urbaniec, Mark, "Intellivision: Programmer Interviews," BlueSkyRangers YouTube channel, posted Jan. 10, 2007. www.youtube.com/watch?v=bewzUlJEjcA

Chapter 6

1   Kent, 196.
2   Hayes, Thomas C. "Mattel Is Counting On Its Toys," *The New York Times*, Feb. 4, 1984, Section 1, 35.
3   "Intellivision IV Master Component [Unreleased]," Blue Sky Rangers website. history.blueskyrangers.com/hardware/intellivision4.html
4   Ibid.
5   "Video Game Preview '83," *Electronic Games*, May 1983, 22.
6   Store ad in a June 16, 1983 newspaper, via Steve Fulton tweet on Dec. 10, 2021.
7   "Intellivision: Ray Kaestner on BurgerTime," BlueSkyRangers YouTube channel, posted June 26, 2008. www.youtube.com/watch?v=91fmS1l6xII
8   Brown, William Michael, "Mission X Marks the Spot," *Electronic Fun With Computers and Games*, September 1983, 48.
9   Schamus, Marty, "The Home Front," *Joystiq*, December 1983, 54.
10   "Bump 'n' Jump," Blue Sky Rangers website. history.blueskyrangers.com/mattelelectronics/games/bumpnjump.html
11   Ibid.
12   "Matt Chat 157: David Warhol and Mattel's Intellivision (fixed)," Matt Barton's YouTube channel, posted Jul. 15, 2012. www.youtube.com/watch?v=WeMseLpbREQ
13   Ibid.
14   Ibid.
15   "Mind Strike," Blue Sky Rangers. history.blueskyrangers.com/mattelelectronics/games/mindstrike.html
16   "Matt Chat 157: David Warhol and Mattel's Intellivision (fixed)," Matt Barton's YouTube channel, posted Jul. 15, 2012. www.youtube.com/watch?v=WeMseLpbREQ
17   "Intellivision: Programmer Interviews," BlueSkyRangers YouTube channel, posted Jan. 10, 2007. www.youtube.com/watch?v=bewzUlJEjcA
18   "Loco-Motion," Blue Sky Rangers website. history.blueskyrangers.com/mattelelectronics/games/loco-m
19   "Happy Trails," Blue Sky Rangers website. history.blueskyrangers.com/activision/happytrails.html

20 K*mart ad from A Dec. 14, 1983 via Steve Fulton tweet on March 19, 2022.
21 "Mattel Cuts Staff Again," *Electronic Games*, December 1983, 12.

Chapter 7

1   Hayes, Thomas C. "Mattel Is Counting On Its Toys," *The New York Times*, Feb. 4, 1984, Section 1, 35.
2   Ibid.
3   "INTV Corporation," Blue Sky Rangers website. history.blueskyrangers.com/intvcorp/
4   Ibid.
5   Caruso, Denise, "Software for Defunct Machines," *InfoWorld*, May 14, 1984, 35.
6   Hayes, Thomas C. "Mattel Is Counting on Its Toys," *The New York Times*, Feb. 4, 1984, 35.
7   "INTV Corporation," Blue Sky Rangers website. history.blueskyrangers.com/intvcorp/
8   "World Championship Baseball," Blue Sky Rangers website. history.blueskyrangers.com/intvcorp/wcbaseball.html
9   Ibid.
10 "Intellivision history." IntellivisionLives archive. web.archive.org/web/20170623040513/http://www.intellivisionlives.com/history.php
11 Toys 'R' Us ad from Nov. 19, 1986, via a Steve Fulton tweet on Nov. 6, 2022.
12 Loguidice, Bill, "A History of Gaming Platforms: Mattel Intellivision," Gamasutra (now *Game Developer*), May 8, 2008. www.gamedeveloper.com/console/a-history-of-gaming-platforms-mattel-intellivision
13 "Thunder Castle," Blue Sky Rangers website. history.blueskyrangers.com/intvcorp/thundercastle.html
14 "Matt Chat 157: David Warhol and Mattel's Intellivision (fixed)," Matt Barton's YouTube channel, posted Jul. 15, 2012. www.youtube.com/watch?v=WeMseLpbREQ
15 Ibid.
16 Ibid.
17 "Thin Ice," Blue Sky Rangers website. history.blueskyrangers.com/intvcorp/thinice.html
18 Ibid.
19 Ibid.
20 Ibid.
21 Herman, 170.
22 Loguidice and Barton, 82.

Chapter 8

1. "Intellivision®: Fox News Magazine Profile," BlueSkyRangers YouTube Channel, posted Jan. 19, 2007. www.youtube.com/watch?v=ipe5AJTpe8I
2. "Software Developers Kit for the Intellivision Video Game System," SDK-1600, last updated Nov. 20, 2002. sdk-1600.spatula-city.org/old-index.html
3. "Intellivision on PlayStation," IntellivisionLives archive. web.archive.org/web/20170727212643/http://www.intellivisionlives.com/retrotopia/psx.shtml
4. "Intellivision®: San Diego News 8 Profile," BlueSkyRangers YouTube channel, posted Feb. 1, 2007. www.youtube.com/watch?v=0kQCbv_C-Z4
5. "Intellivision on PlayStation," IntellivisionLives archive. web.archive.org/web/20170727212643/http://www.intellivisionlives.com/retrotopia/psx.shtml
6. "Intellivision history." IntellivisionLives archive. web.archive.org/web/20170623040513/http://www.intellivisionlives.com/history.php
7. "We Were There" Intellivision Flashback Promo Video, BlueSkyRangers YouTube channel, posted Sep. 25, 2014. www.youtube.com/watch?v=sb-w2AjGtCiM
8. Takahashi, Dean, "Intellivision lives: Tommy Tallarico Will Relaunch 1980s Console," VentureBeat, May 29, 2018. venturebeat.com/games/intellivsion-lives-tommy-tallarico-will-relaunch-1980s-console/
9. Ibid.

Chapter 9

1. "Remembering Keith Robinson and Intellivision - Electric Playground Classic," Electric Playground Network YouTube channel, posted June 19, 2017. www.youtube.com/watch?v=wJJT1ZI6yl4
2. Ibid.
3. "Keyboard Component," Blue Sky Rangers website. history.blueskyrangers.com/hardware/keyboardcomponent.html
4. Mason, Graeme, "40 years on, celebrating the Mattel Intellivision," Eurogamer, May 27, 2019. www.eurogamer.net/40-years-on-celebrating-the-mattel-intellivision
5. Ibid.
6. Earls, John, "Like It's 1999…," *Long Live Vinyl*, November 2019, 58.
7. "Intellivision®: Fox News Magazine Profile," BlueSkyRangers YouTube Channel, posted Jan. 19, 2007. www.youtube.com/watch?v=ipe5AJTpe8I
8. "Matt Chat 157: David Warhol and Mattel's Intellivision (fixed)," Matt Barton's YouTube channel, posted Jul. 15, 2012. www.youtube.com/watch?v=WeMseLpbREQ
9. Ibid.

10 Ibid.
11 "Remembering Keith Robinson and Intellivision - Electric Playground Classic," Electric Playground Network YouTube channel, posted June 19, 2017. www.youtube.com/watch?v=wJJT1ZI6yl4
12 Ibid.

Index

A

ABPA Backgammon 40–42
Action Network 44
Activision 190, 207, 228
Advanced Dungeons & Dragons: Cloudy Mountain 118–121, 196
Advanced Dungeons & Dragons: Treasure of Tarmin 193–196
Aguilar, Wilfredo 175
Alcorn, Al 17, 20
Altair 8800 20
Amico 242–244
APh Technological Consulting 18, 21, 23, 27–28, 151
Apple II 20, 46
Apple Macintosh 186
Aquarius 161–165
   Data Recorder 163–164
   Master Expansion Module 163
   Memory Cartridge 163
   Modem 163
   Printer 163
Aquarius User (magazine) 163, 165
"Arcade Alley" (*Video*) 79, 100
Arcadia 2001 50
Armor Battle 39–40
Astromusic 160
Astrosmash 82–84
Atari 17, 20, 98, 102, 212
   400 and 800 home computers 46, 59
   2600 20–23, 31, 142
   5200 SuperSystem 142
   ST 186
AtariAge 88
Atari Corporation 214
Atarisoft 208
AtGames 229–230
Atlantis 135–137
attract mode 26
Audio Cassette 159
Auto Race (handheld) 18
Auto Racing 61–63
Avalanche 83

AY-3-8910 (GI chip) 31, 49
AY-3-8914 (GI chip) 31

B

B-17 Bomber 126–128
Baer, Ralph 16, 19
Bally Midway 133
Bally Professional Arcade 21
Bandai 49–50
Barbie (Mattel) 15
Baseball (handheld) 18
BASIC programming 99, 159, 163
Basketball (handheld) 18
Bass, Dan 221
Battlestar Galactica
   handheld 18
   TV series 59
Baum, Gabriel 130, 178
Beamrider 190–191
Beauty & the Beast 146–147
Becker, Mike 135
Bishop, Scott 71
Bliss (emulator) 230
Blockade Runner 208
Blue Sky Rangers 130–132, 172, 241, 247
Body Slam! Super Pro Wrestling 216
Boxing 214
Brickout! 228, 240
Brooks, John 88
Bump 'n' Jump 198–200
BurgerTime 186–188
Bushnell, Nolan 16
Buzz Bombers 207

C

Caltech 23, 27
Carnival 151
cassette deck 46
Centipede 208
CES (*see* Consumer Electronics Show)
Championship Tennis 213, 215

Chandler, David 21–23, 28, 33, 75, 185, 247
Chang, Richard 21
Channel F 22
Channing, Richard 18
Chatty Cathy (Mattel) 15
Chess (Aquarius) 163
Chevallier, Arnauld 240
Children's Learning 45
Chip Shot Super Pro Golf 215
Christmas Carol vs. the Ghost of Christmas Presents 238–239
Cinematronics 143
Clark, Dennis 198
Cloudy Mountain 196 (*also see Advanced Dungeons & Dragons*)
Coleco 17, 19, 144, 146, 186, 208, 212
   Adam 186
   Telstar 17, 20, 144
ColecoVision 144–146, 185–186, 208
collecting 233–235
CollectorVision 238, 240
Colored Squares mode 30
Color Stack mode 30
Commando 225
Commodore 212
   64 207
   Amiga 186
   PET 2001 20, 46
   VIC-20 207
community 241–242
Compro Electronics 115, 153
Computer & Video Games (magazine) 92, 101
Computer Adapter (ECS) 159
Computer Keyboard (ECS) 159
Computer Space (Syzygy Engineering) 16, 100
Concept 2000 59
Congo Bongo 208
Consumer Electronics Show 23, 27–29, 81, 157, 161, 224
Control Disc 33

Index | 277

controllers (Intellivision) 32–34, 231–233
Conversational French 78, 99
CP1610 (GI chip) 30, 122, 157, 161
Creative Computing Video and Arcade Games (magazine) 123
Crown of Kings 230
Cuttle Cart 3 236

D

D2K Arcade 238
Dabney, Ted 16
Daglow, Don 80, 110, 130, 171
Data East 113, 198
Data Recorder (Aquarius) 164
Decade 185
DEC PDP-11 30, 95
Decuir, Joe 20
Deep Pockets Super Pro Pool & Billiards 227
Defender 208
Defender of the Crown 238
Del Principe, Bob 165
Demon Attack 137–139
Denham, Joshua 75–76
Denker, John 18
Dig Dug 225
Diner 223–224
Disney 132–133
Disney's Tron 132
Dombrower, Eddie 201
Donkey Kong 144–146, 208
Donkey Kong Junior 208
Dracula 173–175
Dragonfire 167–168
Dreadnaught Factor, The 192–193
Duncan's Thin Ice 219–221
Dungeons & Dragons (TSR license) 118, 193
Durran, David 136, 175

E

ECS 159–161, 185, 201, 207

ECS BASIC programming 160
Electric Company, The 42
Electronic Fun With Computers & Games (magazine) 121, 166, 189
Electronic Games (magazine) 101, 121, 154, 168, 186
electronic handhelds 18–19
Electronics Magazine 152
Elektronite 238
Emerson 50
emulation 230–233
Entertainment Computer System (ECS) 159–161
Ettinger, Steve 216
Exec (operating system) 23–24, 27, 31, 157, 197
Exidy 23, 58–59
Extended Microsoft BASIC 163

F

Fairchild Channel F 20, 25
Fathom 208
Federal Trade Commission (FTC) 99, 161
Filmation 196
Fisher, Bill 125, 128
Flintstones Keyboard Fun 160
Football (handheld) 18
Foreground/Background mode 30
Fresno, California (Intellivision test market) 34
Frog Bog 106–108
Frogger 208
Fulop, Rob 137
Fulton, Steve 214

G

Game Maker 159
Game Networks 44
Gaming Network 45
Gemini 144
General Consumer Electronics

(GCE) 142
General Instrument (GI) 21, 27, 29–30, 94–95, 122
George Plimpton 75–77, 79, 98, 114–115, 152
Gimini 8900 Programmable Game Set 23
Gimini TV Games (chipset) 21
Goldman, Connie 218
Good Deal Games 240
Gooninuff, The 238–239
Gottschalk's 35–36, 78
GTE/Sylvania 50
Guitar Lessons & Music Composition 99
Gun Fight (Midway) 20

H

Hafner Enterprises 237
handheld games 18
Handler, Elliot 15
Handler, Ruth 15–16
Hanimex 50
Happy Trails 207
Hasbro 212
Hawley, Chris 88
"Heavy Sixer" (Atari 2600) 31
Hightower, Glen 18, 23
homebrew games 237–241
Home Pong (Atari) 17, 20
Horse Racing 65–67
Hoshizaki, Julie 114, 220
Hot Wheels (Mattel) 16
Hover Force 225
Huber, Tim 75

I

Ice Trek 175–176
Imagic 134–137, 139, 208, 212
Intel CPUs 20
Intellicart! Intellivision Cartridge Emulator 236–237
IntelligentVision 239, 242

Intellivania 239
Intellivision (Master Component) design 31-32, 36, 50, 142
national launch 51
Intellivision II 157–158, 162, 183, 185, 207, 232–233
Intellivision III 161, 185
Intellivision Collector 241
Intellivision Computer Adapter (ECS) 159
Intellivision Entertainment 242–243
Intellivision Flashback 229–232
Intellivision for PC Volumes 1 and 2 227
"Intellivision Galactic News Update" (commercial) 117
Intellivision Inc. 213
Intellivision Invasion 242
Intellivision Lives! 228
Intellivision Productions 227, 243
Intellivision Rocks! 228
Intellivision System III 214
Intellivisionaries Podcast 242
Intellivoice 121–123, 129, 162, 185
Intermission Code 25
Interphase 213
INTV Corporation 212, 213, 214, 215, 224–225
Intv Funhouse 242
Intv Prime 241
INTV System III 213

J

Jack LaLanne's Physical Conditioning 99
Jacobs, Joe 198
James, Dave 25
JCPenney 34, 36–37, 77–78, 151
JCPenney Christmas Book 37, 78
Jeane Dixon's Astrology 99
Jerrold 94–95
Jetsons Ways With Words 160
Joystiq (magazine) 193

Index | **279**

jzIntv (emulator) 230

K

Kaestner, Ray 223
Kai Magazine Software 240
Kano, Fred 235
Kassar, Ray 98
Kato, Gary 138
Katz, Arnie 56, 69, 79, 88, 100
Katz, Michael 18, 50
Keyboard Component 29, 45–48, 78, 98–99, 152–154
Kiehl, Matthew 239
King of the Mountain 228
Kingsley, Chris 40
Knight Rider (TV series) 122
Kool-Aid Man 208
Krakauer, Ed 21, 28, 36, 75, 142
Kuhn, Malcolm 75
Kunkel, Bill 56, 69, 79, 88, 100

L

Lady Bug 208
Las Vegas Poker & Blackjack 37–39
Las Vegas Roulette 39
Lavine, Rick 142
Lawson, Jerry 20
LEDs 18
Left Turn Only (LTO) 238
Leno, Jay 99
Levine, Rick 130
Lock 'n' Chase 113–114
Loco-Motion 205–207
Loughry, Tom 193
LTO Flash! 236
Lucasfilm 59
Lukan-Bakerlink, Monique 220

M

Macy's 45
Magnavox 16–17, 20, 212
   Odyssey 100, 143

Odyssey² 21, 123
Maine, Stephen 30
Major League Baseball 51–53, 78
MAME (emulator) 230
Mantle, Mickey 95
Master Component 28–29, 31, 45–46, 50–51
Masters of the Universe: The Power of He-Man 196–198
Math Fun 42–44
Matson, Harold "Matt" 15
Mattel 15, 18, 22, 24, 37, 94, 186, 213, 245, 247
Mattel Electronics 18, 21, 28, 50, 75, 98, 185, 209, 211–212
Maurer, Rick 134
Melody Blaster 159
Meteor! 83, 102
microprocessors 20–21
Microsoft BASIC 162
Microsurgeon 139–142
Midway 20
Miller, Kevin 42
Milton Bradley 19, 27, 143, 212
Mind Strike 202–205
Miner, Jay 20
Minkoff, Mike 85, 130, 172
Minotaur 230
Mission X 188–190
MIT 16
M Network 102, 106, 154
mods and add-ons 235–237
MOS Technology 20–21, 27
   6502 20, 46
   6507 20
Motocross 207
Motorola 20
   6800 20
   68000 186
Mountain Madness Super Pro Skiing 215
Mouse Trap 208
Mr. BASIC Meets Bits 'N' Bytes 159

Ms Night Stalker 239
Music Conductor 160
Music Synthesizer (ECS) 159

N

NASL Soccer 68–69
national launch (Intellivision) 51
National Semiconductor 21–22, 27
NBA Basketball 53–55
NEC D780C 49
NFL Football 29, 55–57
NHL Hockey 63–65
Nice Dreams 213
Night Stalker 104–106
Nilsen, Al 77
Nintendo 208, 214, 225
Nostalgia (emulator) 230
Nova Blast 208
Number Jumble 160

O

O'Connell, Frank 75–76, 81
OpenEmu (emulator) 231–233
overlays 33–35

P

Pac-Man 208
Pantheon (emulator) 230
Papa Intellivision 21, 247 (*also see* Chandler, David)
Parker Brothers 208
pause (Intellivision feature) 25
PBA Bowling 86–88
PGA Golf 69–71, 76
Physical Conditioning 78
Pinball 208
Pitfall! 190
PlayCable 94–96, 198
Plimpton, George 75–77, 79, 98, 114–115, 152
Pole Position 224
Pong (Atari) 17, 100

Popeye 208
Printer 40 (Keyboard Component) 47
Program Expander (Aquarius) 159

Q

*Q*Bert* 208

R

Radio Shack 154
  TRS-80 20
Ransil, Pat 135, 137
RCA 20
Realtime Associates 223
RetroFixes 235
RetroGameBoyz 233
RetroPie 231
RetroRGB 235
Reversi 163
Reynolds, Scott 71
Rioux, Paul 185
River Raid 190
Robinson, Keith 76, 131, 171, 220, 227–228, 243, 246, 249
Rochlis, Jeff 18, 22, 27–28, 75
Roklan Corporation 145–146
Rolfe, David 23–24, 27, 37, 39, 51, 59, 191
Roney, Stephen 125, 128, 227
Rovin, Jeff 117–118
Royal Dealer 151
running man (sprite) 24–25

S

Safecracker 181, 182, 183
Sanger, George "The Fat Man" 221
Schell, Chad 236
Scooby Doo's Maze Chase 200
Sea Battle 59–61
Sears 17, 50, 151
  Tele-Games Super Video Arcade 231

Sega 225
Sewer Sam 208
Shark! Shark! 165–166
Sharp Shot 151
Shaw, Carol 207
Simon (Milton Bradley) 19
Skiing 71–73
Slam Dunk Super Pro Basketball 215
Slap Shot Super Pro Hockey 215
Smith, Alan 175
Smith, Gene 171
Smithsonian (museum) 142, 151
Snafu 84–85
Sohl, John 130
Sorrow of Gadhlan' Thur, The 240
Space Armada 88–90
Space Battle 57–59
Space Hawk 102–104
Space Spartans 123–126
Spacewar! (MIT) 16
Speak & Spell 19
Speed Reading 99
Spelling Challenge 99
Spielberg, Steven 114
Spiker! Super Pro Volleyball 216
Sports Network 44
Sprinter 40 (Keyboard Component) 47
Stadium Mud Buggies 225
Stampede 151
Standard Television Interface Chip (STIC) 30–31, 161
Star Fire 23, 24, 58
Star Raiders 59, 126
Star Strike 92, 93, 94
Star Trek (TV series) 58
Star Wars (movie) 59, 84
Star Wars: The Empire Strikes Back 208
Stewart, Brad 134
STIC (chip) 30–31, 161
STIC 1B (chip) 102
Stock Analysis 78

Stonix 240
Strategy Network 45
Studio II (RCA) 20
Sub Hunt 108–110
Super Graphics 197–198
Super Pro Decathlon 216
Super Pro Football 215
Super Pro series 214–216
Super-STIC (chip) 102, 161–162
Super Video Arcade (Sears) 154
Super Vision 8000 (Bandai) 49–50
Swords & Serpents 168–171
Sylvania 29, 35–36, 78
System IV 224

T

Takeover 228
Tale of Dragons and Swords, A 238
Tandy 20, 153
Tandyvision One 153
Technology Consultants 198
Tedelex 50
Tele-Games Super Video Arcade 50
Telstar (Coleco) 17, 20, 144
Tennis 73–74
test markets (Intellivision) 34
Texas Instruments 19, 27
thermal printer (Keyboard Component) 47
Thin Ice 219–221
Thunder Castle 217–218
Toledo G., Óscar 240
Tower of Doom 221–222
Toys "R" Us 151, 214
Tramiel, Jack 214
Treasure of Tarmin 193–196
Triple Action 90–92
Tron: Deadly Discs 132–134
Tron: Maze-a-Tron 148–151
Tron: Solar Sailer 171–173
Tropical Trouble 208
Truckin' 179–181
TSR (Tactical Studies Rules) 118,

121, 193, 230
Turbo 208
Tutankham 208
TV Guide (magazine) 112, 130
TV Powww 97

U

Ultimate PC Interface 237
Universal 208
Urbaniec, Mark 178–179
USCF Chess 151
Uston, Ken 117–118
Utopia 110–113

V

Valeski, Terrence E. 212, 215
Vectrex 142–143, 212
Vectron 176–179
Venture 208
Video (magazine) 51, 56, 69, 79, 92, 154, 168
Video Games (magazine) 161
Videoplexer 115
Vision-daptor 231–233

W

Wagner, Ray 23
Warhol, David 131, 198–199, 203–205, 218, 249
Warner Communications Inc. 98
White Water! 208
Winans, Mike 114
Wizards of the Coast 230
World Championship Baseball 213–215
World Cup Soccer 213, 215
World Series Major League Baseball 200–202
Worm Whomper 208
WPIX channel 11 97

Y

Yannick 235
Your Friend the EXEC (book) 227

Z

Zaxxon 208
Zilog 20, 162
Z80 20
Z80A 162

| About the Author

Jamie Lendino is an author, editor, mix engineer, and technology enthusiast. In addition to his books about vintage computers and video games, Jamie has written for PCMag, ExtremeTech, *Popular Science*, *Electronic Musician*, *Consumer Reports*, *Sound and Vision*, and CNET. He has also appeared on CNBC, NPR's *All Things Considered*, and numerous television and radio programs across the United States. He lives with his wife, daughter, and two bonkers cats in Collingswood, New Jersey.

Printed in the USA
CPSIA information can be obtained
at www.ICGtesting.com
CBHW031205251124
17649CB00061B/204/J